Self-Help and Mutual Aid Groups: International and Multicultural Perspectives

Self-Help and Mutual Aid Groups: International and Multicultural Perspectives

Francine Lavoie
Thomasina Borkman
Benjamin Gidron
Editors

Routledge
Taylor & Francis Group
LONDON AND NEW YORK

Self-Help and Mutual Aid Groups: International and Multicultural Perspectives has also been published as *Prevention in Human Services*, Volume 11, Numbers 1/2 1994.

First published in 1994 by Routledge
The Haworth Press, Inc., 10 Alice Street, Binghamton, NY 13904-1580 USA

This edition published 2013 by Routledge

Routledge
Taylor & Francis Group
711 Third Avenue
New York, NY 10017

Routledge
Taylor & Francis Group
2 Park Square, Milton Park, Abingdon,
Oxfordshire OX14 4RN

First issued in paperback 2016

Routledge is an imprint of the Taylor and Francis Group, an informa business

Library of Congress Cataloging-in-Publication Data

Self-help and mutual aid groups : international and multicultural perspectives / Francine Lavoie, Thomasina Borkman, Benjamin Gidron, editors.

p. cm.

"Has also been published as Prevention in human services, volume 11, numbers 1/2, 1994."

Includes bibliographical references and index.

ISBN 1-56024-716-9 (acid free paper)

1. Self-help groups–Cross-cultural studies. 2. I. Lavoie, Francine, 1951- . II. Borkman, Thomasina. III. Gidron, Benjamin.

HV547.S427 1995

361.4–dc20 94-44762

CIP

ISBN 13: 978-1-13899-603-8 (pbk)
ISBN 13: 978-1-56024-716-6 (hbk)

Self-Help and Mutual Aid Groups: International and Multicultural Perspectives

CONTENTS

ABOUT THE EDITORS

Francine Lavoie, PhD, is Professor of Community Psychology at Université Laval in Québec, Canada. She is also a member of the Research Committee of Self-Help Canada, a national organization devoted to the development of mutual aid groups in Canada. Dr. Lavoie has served as a consultant on federal and provincial boards on matters relating to alternative resources in mental health, and was Director of the research group *Groupe de recherche sur l'appropriation psychosociale.* She has written on mutual aid groups and her present project is on ethical issues in the collaboration between professionals and self-help groups.

Thomasina J. Borkman, PhD, is Professor of Sociology in the Department of Sociology and Anthropology at George Mason University in Fairfax, Virginia. Dr. Borkman has conducted research on self-help groups in the health and human service arena and self-help agencies in the field of alcoholism and mental health for the past 24 years. She has written many journal articles, book chapters, and monographs on self-help groups and is known for her contributions on "experiential knowledge," the distinctive wisdom from lived experience that self-help groups develop. Dr. Borkman has received a Fulbright to York University in Toronto to study self-help groups in relation to the health care system.

Benjamin Gidron, DSW, is David Schwartzman Chair in Community Development in the Spitzer Department of Social Work at Ben-Gurion University of the Negev in Beer-Sheva, Israel. He has also taught at Hebrew University School of Social Work and UCLA School of Social Welfare. His major research interests are the nonprofit sector, self-help groups, and voluntary organizations, and he has conducted cross-cultural empirical research on the benefits of self-help participation in parents groups. Dr. Gidron is Founder and President of the International Society of Third Sector Research.

Preface

Mutual aid self-help groups such as Alcoholics Anonymous, the National Alliance for the Mentally Ill, parents of murdered children, or Mended Hearts are the focus of this volume. These groups and organizations have been variously termed self-help groups, mutual help groups, support groups and mutual aid self-help groups by researchers and practitioners working with them. Some attention needs to be paid to terminology so that the readers have a common understanding of what social units are being discussed in this volume.

Self-help has been variously defined as individuals using self-help books by themselves for self-improvement, in a political context or in relation to self-help mutual aid groups. As Frank Riessman pointed out in his address at the International Conference on Self-Help/Mutual Aid in Ottawa, September 1992, the "self" in self-help can have several referents. Often the "self" refers to an individual whether engaging in a do-it-yourself project following instructions in a self-help book or participating in a social context with experiential peers. But self-help is also used in political circles to refer the idea that lower levels of government or communities need to finance their own projects or develop projects through their own efforts. On the national level, you will hear calls for states or local communities to develop and finance their own housing, welfare, medical or social services.

In this book the "self" refers to individuals participating in mutual aid or self-help groups. There is a growing consensus among researchers and professional observers of these groups that

[Haworth indexing entry note]: "Preface." Lavoie, Francine, Thomasina Borkman, Benjamin Gidron. Published in *Self-Help and Mutual Aid Groups: International and Multicultural Perspectives* (ed: Francine Lavoie, Thomasina Borkman, and Benjamin Gidron). The Haworth Press, Inc., 1994, pp. xiii-xxi. Multiple copies of this article/chapter may be purchased from The Haworth Document Delivery Center [1-800-3-HAWORTH; 9:00 a.m. - 5:00 p.m. (EST)].

they should be differentiated from similar groups owned and controlled by professionals, although the terminology of what to call them has not been settled. This issue is compounded by the fact that professionals are involved in a variety of ways with many member-owned groups.

The public tends to use "support group" as a generic term to refer to experiential peer led groups or professionally controlled groups or any and all varieties. Increasingly, researchers in the area use "support group" to refer primarily to professionally owned groups and to use self-help group, mutual help group or mutual aid self-help group to those that are primarily owned by consumers. In this volume, Gidron and Chesler in a major theoretical article that conceptualizes a framework for studying groups internationally and inter-culturally, use the term self-help group. Other contributors to this volume also use the term "self-help groups" including Stewart, Bank, Crossman and Poel. They are discussing the same types of groups or social units as Humphreys and colleagues or Kennedy and Humphreys who use the term "mutual help groups" in their papers in this volume. The term mutual aid group is also used, particularly in Canada.

Another terminological issue is the boundaries of problem areas that are usually included or included here as part of individual self-help in the context of mutual aid. There is an evolving researcher's network that originated in the United States with the Surgeon General's Workshop on Self-Help and Public Health convened by then-Surgeon General C. Everett Koop in 1987. This researcher's network has shown primary interest in groups dealing with health, human, and social service issues pertaining to individuals. Economic and material self-help such as food banks and cooperatives, housing, and economic development have usually not been studied. Neither have crime related community self-help activities such as neighborhood watch patrols (see Milofsky (1988) Community Self-Help Organizations). There is ambiguity here because researchers do not usually include them, but Katz and Bender (1990, p. 30) recently included economic self-help in a revised and updated typology categorizing self-help groups by type of problem. A related aspect of these boundaries are that these economic and crime prevention issues tend to be developed at the level of the neighborhood, city or state, where the "self" is the community, not the individual.

To date there are about 200 researchers interested in studying self-help groups as defined here that are part of a network maintained by a multidisciplinary interest group of the Society for Community Research and Action of the American Psychological Association. Psychologists, social workers, and sociologists tend to join the network as well as nurses and educational psychologists. This division reflects the professional division of the authors in this volume.

Gidron and Chesler whose paper presents the first theoretical framework for studying self-help mutual aid cross-culturally and interculturally define self-help broadly as the "recruitment and mobilization of peers in an informal and non-hierarchical setting and sharing of their common experiences are basic building blocks for almost all forms of self-help, in all nations and cultures" (this volume). Self-help groups, as they employ the term, refer to specialized "communities of interest and belief" that transcend geographical boundaries.

For the International Conference on Self-Help/Mutual Aid from which the papers of this volume were selected, the research track organizers defined self-help/mutual aid in terms of the kinds of health and social issues dealt with in specialized groups found in urban industrialized societies. This relatively narrow definition of self-help/mutual aid was done primarily because of the research traditions of the organizers. However, with our experience from this first international conference, it seems appropriate to consider expanding our definitions of self-help/mutual aid for the international study of them. Several aspects of this come to mind immediately. For example, within a society like the United States there are intercultural variations in where and how support is given. In the African-American community the church has historically and currently played a central role in spawning groups and social units that had support or social advocacy functions. An example is of a prayer group for men at a black church in Illinois. After 10 minutes of prayer, the members shared their experiences about common social and personal problems they faced. Is this a self-help group? Although it is not named a self-help group, it has the functions and dynamics of one. In societies with differing forms of economic development, support structures are likely to be quite varied. In developing countries where traditional kith and kin relationships in geographical areas and tribal or village bonds still occur, are the support structures found in them the functional equivalent of self-help groups or not? Furthermore, their local groups are probably more likely to be oriented toward material aid such as food, economic development, and housing than the chronic diseases that characterize so many self-help groups in industrialized countries. The varying orientations in different countries to the roles and authority of professionals, the complementary or alternative status of self-help groups in the social service system and consequently, professionals' differing involvement in self-help endeavors complicate the comparison of self-help across nations.

The narrowness or inclusiveness of the definition of self-help/mutual aid that is used has a lot of research implications. One obvious example is that your definition of what is included and excluded affects what you use as a sampling frame. Do you look in black churches for groups that are not called "self-help groups" but perform the functions of them? Do you include in your sample community self-help organizations that might have informal groups dealing with specialized issues dealt with by other self-help groups? These issues need to be addressed as a first priority in order to further the development of international research in self-help/mutual aid. The editors of this book are in favor of opening a dialogue among researchers that hopefully will lead to broadening our definitions of self-help/mutual aid to be more inclusive of local support and empowering structures in developing countries along with the better recognized self-help groups seen in this volume.

To date, literature on cross-cultural and intercultural self-help is very meager. This should not come as a surprise as the field is relatively new, the research on this phenomenon is even newer and the international facets of this research has practically just begun. One way to promote and enhance international exchange among practitioners and researchers in this domain is through international conferences and meetings. Such meetings are actually a necessity to start a dialogue among researchers, which should enable them to conceptualize self-help in its appropriate dimensions, taking into consideration the various aspects of this phenomenon discussed above. Yet, given the lack of an agreed upon definition of self-help, and given the various research traditions and orientations in different countries, such conferences should be very carefully planned and managed. Without getting into specifics, it would seem, for example, important to create forums for dialogue among researchers who may use different methodologies to study the same problem area in different cultural/national settings; or to create forums for dialogue among researchers from developing and developed countries who study different problems, in order to "extract" the common elements, etc.

This book is an attempt to bring together different traditions of research for the study of cross-cultural and intercultural self-help groups. Articles for this volume were selected from among the scientific presentations held at the International Conference on Self-Help/Mutual Aid in Ottawa in 1992. This international conference was the first of its kind and was organized by the Canadian Council of Social Development with the financial support of the Canadian Government. The conference was intended for people interested in self-help in the world and it favoured exchanges between members and representatives of various self-help associations. The conference organizers, Hector Balthazar and Ann Chudleigh among others, had chosen to welcome diverse experiences identified as self-help. Although most of the presentations revolved around self-help groups, experiences of co-counselling, peer-counselling, or setting up collective resources were also described. Numerous testimonies from self-help group members as well as workshops given by self-help specialists likewise were fruitful learning experiences. During the conference, a research track that emphasized the research carried out in many countries was planned. As we have already pointed out, the research component used a more stringent definition of self-help groups.

For the research track, a scientific committee consisting of Thomasina Borkman, Francine Lavoie and Benjamin Gidron was formed. In 1991, they proceeded to a call for papers among the international scientific comunity and self-help associations. A professional peer review procedure was used. The 65 submitted abstracts were reviewed by two external judges (French or English-speaking) and one member of the committee. Finally, 22 abstracts were accepted for the conference. The three co-editors then attended these presentations and invited some of the authors to present a written text. Once again, these texts were subjected to a process of evaluation. The following articles have thus been selected twice, a first time for the conference and second time for this special volume. The article by Lavoie, Farquharson and Kennedy, as opposed to the others, was solicited in order to acknowledge a workshop that took place the day before the conference and whose theme nicely completed the present volume. In a way, the selection procedure for the articles allowed us to leave the beaten path and transcend the limits of disciplines and countries.

The papers in Part 1 of the volume, highlight some of the major issues involved in the international study of self-help. Gidron and Chesler's paper provides a conceptual framework to study self-help internationally and interculturally, and draws, among other sources, on the authors' own experience in this domain. Borkman and Schubert's paper discusses some new and, to date, nonconventional methods to study self-help; methods that focus more on the process than the outcome, and depart from a strictly positivistic orientation to researching this phenomenon.

The following three papers in this section can serve as case studies of the previous two conceptual ones, where concrete examples of selected aspects of self-help outside North America are presented. Oka's paper discusses in detail the tremendous effect of the Japanese form of compliance on the nature of self-help in this country, the difficulties to establish it, and the difficult roles of professionals in this context. Von Appen presents a fascinating case of "inventing" self-help in a society that only recently acquired the freedom to organize (former East Germany), and where the population was used to get social and medical services from the authorities without questioning anything. The transformation both the population and the services have to undergo and the help they get from the self-help systems in the former West Germany is also highlighted in the paper. Wong and Chan's paper highlights Borkman's argument that self-help needs to be studied in more than one way. The action-research orientation of their reported study has helped not only to get important information on the size and nature of the phenomenon in Hong Kong, but has also led to create a coalition among those groups and the planning of some joint action on their behalf.

The next three papers assist us in understanding the real-life experience of particular cultural groups. Medvene, Lin, Wu, Mendoza, Harris and Miller, thanks to a comparison of Mexican American and Anglo American parents, allow us to grasp the cultural traits that may influence participation in self-help groups for parents of the mentally ill. In a longitudinal study, Humphreys, Mavis and Stöffelmayr wonder if twelve step self-help groups are useful to African Americans. Kennedy and Humphreys propose a new way of perceiving outcomes, they invite us to explore the transformations of worldviews of self-help group participants. But their contribution is not only in considering the worldviews of participants but mainly by studying them in accordance with naturalistic and narrative approaches.

The second section of the book examines inter-organizational and intra-organizational aspects. These themes have not yet been explored in the international literature, but the following articles, by the variety of their methods, point to interesting research leads for international or inter-cultural comparison studies. Inter-organizational issues, as it is well known, have been discussed since the beginnings of this social movement. Many papers can be found on the roles of professionals and the problem of the professionalization of self–help groups. But only lately has research been implemented in a rigorous fashion. Till now intra-organizational studies have focused mainly on outcomes or therapeutic processes and have proceeded from the perspective of self-help groups being an adjunct or an alternative to psychotherapy. In the first section of the book, Gidron and Chesler conceptualized self-help groups as "communities of interest," it is thus interesting to see that researchers in this second section consider mostly self-help groups as social organizations. Worldviews, leadership, and social climate are new emerging themes of research.

The first paper addresses inter-organizational topics. Stewart, Banks, Crossman and Poel propose a partnership model between self-help groups and professionals. This model was elaborated during an action-research that encouraged numerous exchanges between representatives of both points of view. By emphasizing the pitfalls but also the positive traits to be encouraged, the article allows us to understand what people involved in the field intuitively perceive as important determinants of collaboration.

The three other papers examine the intra-organizational level. Meissen and Volk in their study of burn-out in leaders of many self-help groups addresses a dimension that has been ignored until now. Meanwhile, Perkins, Lafuze and Van Dusen attempt to explain the perceived effectiveness of the Alliance for the Mentally Ill groups by the contribution of the social climate. Among other things, the authors cite the members' perception of support, leadership and quality of the organization. Lotery and Jacobs supply data on the attitudes of self-help groups as well as the roles perceived as appropriate for professionals.

The volume's last section allows us to initiate a reflection on the good practice of professionals in their ties with self-help groups and on certain methodological problems of experimental studies. The article by Lavoie, Farquharson and Kennedy presents the results from an international workshop that examined the points of view of self-help groups and professionals on problems in their relationships and on possible ways of improving these ties. This information may lay the foundation for the elaboration of ethical guidelines. Kaufmann, Schulberg and Schooler inform us on the participation in self-help groups for people with severe mental illness. They also help us to understand the difficulties associated with using an experimental schema to understand the participation in self-help groups.

This variety of themes and approaches clearly demonstrates the vitality of research in the field of self-help groups. Since 1976, great steps have been taken. It is now time, we believe, to integrate international and inter-cultural perspectives.

Francine Lavoie
Université Laval
Canada

Thomasina Borkman
George Mason University
USA

Benjamin Gidron
Ben Gurion University of the Negev
Israel

REFERENCES

Katz, A. H., & Bender, E. I. (1990). *Self-help groups in a changing world*, pp. 30-31. Oakland: Third Party Publishing.

Milofsky, C. (1988). Structure and process in community self-help organizations. In C. Milofsky (ed.), *Community organizations: Studies in resource mobilization and exchange*. NY: Oxford University Press.

Riessman, F. (1992). Redefining self-help: Implications for the professional. Conference presented at the First International Conference on Self-Help and Mutual Aid Groups, Ottawa.

Chapter 1

Universal and Particular Attributes of Self-Help: A Framework for International and Intranational Analysis

Benjamin Gidron

Ben Gurion University of the Negev

Mark Chesler

University of Michigan

SUMMARY. The growth in self-help activity in many countries in the past two decades, brings into focus the international nature of this social phenomenon. The paper deals with both the universal and particular aspects of self-help, and proposes a framework within which to analyze and conduct research on it. In analyzing the universal attributes of self-help, the concept "Community" is used. The use of this concept directs our attention to three *internal processes,* common to traditional communities and modern self-help frameworks: (1) the development of distinct cultures which shape individuals' identity; (2) the provision of social support to members, especially during times of crisis; and (3) the empowerment of members.

Address correspondence to Dr. Benjamin Gidron, Department of Social Work, Ben-Gurion University of the Negev, P.O. Box 653, Beer-Sheva 84105, Israel.

[Haworth co-indexing entry note]: "Universal and Particular Attributes of Self-Help: A Framework for International and Intranational Analysis." Gidron, Benjamin and Mark Chesler. Co-published simultaneously in *Prevention in Human Services* (The Haworth Press, Inc.) Vol. 11, No. 1, 1994, pp. 1-44; and: *Self-Help and Mutual Aid Groups: International and Multicultural Perspectives* (ed: Francine Lavoie, Thomasina Borkman, and Benjamin Gidron) The Haworth Press, Inc., 1994, pp. 1-44. Multiple copies of this article/chapter may be purchased from The Haworth Document Delivery Center [1-800-3-HAWORTH; 9:00 a.m. - 5:00 p.m. (EST)].

The paper then turns to discuss the particularistic attributes of self-help. The analysis of the differences among self-help groups focuses on their *structural properties*. Our analysis divides the self-help phenomenon into three key dimensions along which one can detail its wide variety: (1) the nation, its legal and administrative structure, which defines social relationships and the relationship between individuals and the state, (2) within nations, the different ethnic/racial cultures, which define norms of behavior with kith and kin and the place of individuals within communities and (3) the issues around which groups and organizations are formed.

As the issue at hand was hardly dealt with in the literature, the paper uses as its data base a review of indirect studies on the subject, as well as findings from the authors' own comparative study of self-help groups in Israel and the U.S.

INTRODUCTION

The 1970s and 1980s saw a major expansion in the scientific attention paid to the self-help phenomenon globally, and apparently a significant rise in the occurrence of self-help throughout the world. Several international conferences have included major sections dealing with self-help, and the recent International Conference on Self-Help/Mutual Aid (1992) included sessions with authors from Asia, Africa and South America, as well as Europe and North America. The presentations reflected a varied background of political and social traditions, but they all dealt with aspects of the same "newly discovered" phenomenon. In fact, an international review of self-help published in 1983 already was titled *Rediscovering Self-Help* (Pancoast, Parker & Froland, 1983). While social historians may speculate on the timing of this development, it is clear that we are dealing with a rediscovery rather than a discovery. This should not be surprising. One of the main theses of this paper is that self-help is based on natural modes of affiliation and bonding between human beings, a form of communal relationship that is both timeless and universal.

Because of the often informal nature of self-help, data about its expansion, and its particular forms, are difficult to obtain. However, many nations now are formulating social policies vis-à-vis self-help, are building coordinating structures to link self-help groups with other support and service systems, and are establishing clearing houses to further facilitate the use of this mode of mutual aid (Katz & Bender, 1990; Leventhal, Maton & Madara, 1988; Madara, 1985; Pancoast et al., 1983; Reynolds, 1982).

The focus of this paper is the international nature of self-help. We deal with both the universal and particular aspects of self-help, and propose a framework with which to analyze and potentially conduct research on this growing phenomenon. Next, we describe the methods used in constructing this analysis and this paper.

We also examine the universal attributes of self-help, some of which have been discussed widely. The recruitment and mobilization of peers in an informal and non-hierarchical setting, and the sharing of their common experiences, are the basic building blocks for almost all forms of self-help, in all nations and cultures. Under these conditions, all members have an opportunity to see their personal problems in a new light, to collectivize and legitimize their understandings and reactions, and to adopt active and empowered roles in coping with life dilemmas. The opportunity not only to receive help from others, but to provide it to others, also is empowering. Thus, self-help reemphasizes the importance and even the indispensability of the human bond among peers as a mechanism of communication around difficult issues, and as a mechanism with healing power. While different groups, and even different forms of self-help, emphasize different aspects of this process, in different ways and degrees, they almost all share this basic paradigm. We conceptualize all these self-help characteristics within the universal social framework of *community*.

Finally we explore the particularistic aspects of self-help. Our analysis divides the self-help phenomenon along three key dimensions which detail its wide variety: (1) the *nation*, its politico-economic and administrative structure, and the resultant social relationships and relationships between individuals and the state; (2) the different *demographic statuses and ethnic/racial cultures* within nations, which define norms of behavior with kith and kin and the place of individuals within communities; and (3) the *issues or problems* around which groups and organizations are formed.

Different nations have different visions of the proper relationship between individuals and the state, and organize these visions into different legal and politico-economic frameworks. These frameworks, which reflect the dominant culture in a society, help both to give meaning to human experience and to define the ways in which people should act on their experiences. Some societies promote notions of self sufficiency that cause people to rely solely on their own resources in times of crisis. Others promote a view of the general welfare that suggests citizens should look to and rely on the state–on public and formal resource systems–for assistance when they are in trouble. Still others promote a view of reliance upon small groups of kith and kin in such circumstances, and emphasize the importance of families, neighborhood units and other voluntary or informal associations for assistance to people in crisis.

Given the existence of demographic and ethnic or cultural variations within any nation, and the powerful effects of economic and ethnic stratification, within any nation there are various modes of self-help group organization, depending on the specific ethnic/racial culture, and where discriminatory practices exist, different degrees of access to all resources, including self-help groups.

The issues around which groups organize and define their members are: their economic and social location, kith and kin connections, their physical and mental situation, often their age and gender, the chronicity of their situation. The scope of this paper does not permit us to list and examine all the issues around which people organize to form self-help associations; such a list would be several pages long (however, see examples in Katz & Bender, 1990a; Katz & Bender, 1976; Killilea, 1976; Neighbors, Elliott & Gant, 1990; Powell, 1987; Trojan, Halves & Wetendorf, 1986). Suffice it to say, in many nations one can find self-help groups and/or organizations dealing with practically every social, personal or medical problem. Although groups often focus on common problems of economic deprivation or immigration, they also can focus on rare events and diseases, where the incidence in the population is very small or scattered through a wide geographic area. It is under these conditions that the normal economic apparatus or the formal medical or social service network, as well as family connections, are most likely to be inadequate. It also is not uncommon to find several groups focusing on the same (economic, social or personal) problem, either for somewhat different populations (e.g., people with sub-standard housing as well as homeless people, or family members of patients as well as patients), or with somewhat different ideological and programmatic preferences (e.g., economic cooperatives vs. unemployment support groups).

These three major differentiating factors (nation, demographic or cultural group, issue or problem) provide the contexts in which self-help operates, and therefore have major impact on it. The impact is on both: (a) the overall self-help sector in a nation, namely its size, the issues around which groups organize (and others around which they don't), and their relationships with human service professionals and formal service organizations; and (b) individual groups, in terms of their goals, resources, leadership patterns, organizational structures and activities or programs. The self-help sector in a nation can be large or small, with groups and organizations existing for many or a few issues, with close, loose or no contacts with formal helping agencies and professionals. Individual groups can focus primarily on goals of personal change of their members, or on social change, or on some combination thereof. Leadership patterns vary between groups which are led externally–mostly by professionals, or internally–by one or more members, or by some combination or shared pattern (Mellor, Rzetelny & Hudis, 1984; Borkman, 1990; Yoak & Chesler, 1985). The organizational structures of groups can be formal or informal, with or without elected officers, regular committees, budgetary procedures and rules of operation. Finally, different groups can engage in a variety of programs or activities, including emotional support, education (of members and of the public), advocacy, fund-raising, counselling, etc.

METHODS OF INQUIRY

In preparing this analysis two data bases and methods were used: (a) a synthetic review of the literature, a secondary analysis of prior work, much of which is only indirectly related to the issues at hand; and (b) an analysis of original empirical data from a recent study we conducted.

We conducted a review of the literature on self-help in different nations, with a special focus on those reports that were deliberately comparative. Part of the problem encountered in this review is that there are no studies that examine the same issues, in groups dealing with the same "problems" or "life conditions" in different nations. What we do find are: (1) theoretical, and often quite general and abstract, discussions of the probable impact of different national polities/economies and cultures on self-help processes and groups; (2) case study reports of self-help groups and processes in various nations and cultures, where the reader may extrapolate to internationally comparative conclusions; (3) a few instances of comparative studies of self-help groups and processes dealing with the same problem or condition within a single nation, but across cultural or demographic characteristics. In the absence of truly international comparative studies that are sufficiently well-designed and controlled we do the best we can with the above reports.

We also report here some findings from our own comparative study of self-help groups and processes in Israel and the United States (see Chesler, Chesney & Gidron, 1990; Gidron, Chesler & Chesney, 1991 for details). This study gathered data from self-help groups of parents of children with cancer (U.S.), parents of murdered children (U.S.), parents of persons with mental illness (Israel) and parents in families of new immigrants (Israel). Informants included people actively participating in these groups, as well as some persons experiencing these life crises who had not elected to join a self-help group.

In both countries nationwide convenience samples of groups were used. In the U.S., data were gathered from 111 parents in 8 groups dealing with childhood cancer, and from 104 parents in 5 groups dealing with murdered children. In Israel, data were gathered from 50 parents in 5 groups dealing with mental illness, and from 69 parents in 2 groups dealing with immigration. As a result of our prior study and knowledge of the variety and distribution of these groups (Gidron & Bargal, 1986; Yoak & Chesler, 1985), we are fairly confident that the group population is roughly similar to the national population of groups dealing with these issues.

The major research tool was a self-report questionnaire with structured and open-ended questions about various aspects of informants' lives and group experiences. The inquiry focus included social background characteristics, access to various types and sources of social support, coping strategies, perceived life-changes over the course of the illness, activities or programs of the self-help group, and benefits derived from self-help group membership. Each of these major areas of concern were assessed via several items and indices, all answered on 3, 4, or 5-point Likert type formats. Most items were selected from prior studies of families in crisis, as well as from self-help group inquiries, and were adapted to the relevant national culture and life condition, as well as language (Hebrew and English). Additional data on groups were gathered via in-depth interviews with a sub-sample of informants, field notes based on visits to local groups and perusals of their meeting minutes, published documents and records.

While we would have preferred to focus this research on similar types of family crises in both nations, problems of access made that impossible. Thus, unfortunately, these data also do not contain international comparisons of groups dealing with the same problem or condition, although they do utilize similar questions and variables with varying groups in the two nations. Thus, although these data, like some of the above literature, may at times approach a comparative perspective, they too fail to provide a well-controlled comparative framework. Because problems of access required the use of somewhat different procedures in the study of these four different types of groups, the data reported in most tables do not represent a single universe. Thus while we provide illustrative comparative data, we cannot provide tests of statistical significance of data drawn from different universes. Once again, we do the best we can. On the other hand, such a design enabled us to highlight the common elements of self-help, regardless of problem-areas and culture.

UNIVERSAL ATTRIBUTES OF SELF-HELP: THE COMMUNITY CONCEPT

One of the earliest social frameworks in the history of humanity is the geographic community (the "community of propinquity"). Some researchers relate it to similar frameworks that exist among animals and even plants. The way in which members of a common species cling together, and create a social unit, is prevalent in all cultures.

A functional analysis of community in traditional societies suggests that this unit has obvious economic and security functions, and that without it in some form individuals would have difficulty surviving. But in addition to promoting survival, the community performs other important social-psychological functions for its members. Although it is larger than the family, it has the capacity to support intimate and personal relationships. Therefore, it often serves as the first locus for individuals to take on complex and varied roles, ones not possible within the highly structured familial situation. Furthermore, as a stable social framework, it provides an ongoing and intergenerational identity for its members, an identity that has both social and personal implications.

Viewed from a collective perspective, this communal identity develops over generations into a unique culture. Being a part of such a social system creates member loyalty to the community and to other members, translating into support of them in times of need and crisis. The bonds of identity and loyalty, and the reciprocal nature of caring and support, can empower individual members and, on occasion, empower the entire community. By individual empowerment we mean a positive sense of self-esteem and the ability to cope competently and actively with one's life crises and situations. At the community level empowerment may be reflected in collective actions directed toward the external environment, such as efforts to build new norms and capabilities that may lead to change in the service system or a change in the relationship with the surrounding society.

Our analysis focuses on three social processes of traditional communities and their parallels in modern self-help groups.

1. Community as a locus for the development of distinct cultures and (new or altered) individual identities.
2. Community as a mechanism for providing social support to individuals, especially during times of crisis.
3. Community as an empowering mechanism.

Community as a Locus for the Development of Culture and Identity

The geographic community served for many generations as the basis for the development of distinct communal cultures. As the same group of people and their ancestors occupied a certain geographic area, a predominant economic and social style developed, based partly on what the particular geography had to offer. As such, unique cultures developed, ones derived in part from their ecological relationships–intense and lengthy interactions between a particular group of people and their particular material environment. Before the era of mass communication and mass mobility, the more geographically or socially isolated the community was, and the less interaction it had with outsiders, the more its culture was likely to be unique.

As a culture characterizes a community, individual community members act as carriers of that culture, both in their interactions with other community members (for instance, sharing in community rituals and festivities) and with outsiders (for example, being recognized by outsiders as belonging to a specific community by one's way of speaking or dressing). Thus, members come to identify with the community and to forge their personal identities (at least partly) in the image of the collectivity. As Sennett notes (1977, p. 22), community "is also a collective identity; it is a way of saying who we are . . . born from the union of shared action and a shared sense of collective self."

Similar to geographic communities, self-help groups develop distinct cultural attributes, such as language (words known only to insiders), norms of behaviors (how to behave in a group meeting where tragedy is being shared), customs (ways of starting or ending sessions), etc. Internally it means that the relationships individuals have with other community members reflect these norms, and often have a different quality than do their relationships with outsiders. Externally it means that others identify members and make assumptions about them and their community on the basis of these characteristics. Loyalty to the community as a whole, and to individual members, creates strong intragroup commitments. These attributes have implications both for persons' relationships with other community members and with outsiders.

The traditional community represented a total experience, and thus was capable of forging individuals' identities and loyalties; sharing a life crisis with others in the context of a self-help group also often is a total experience. In the context of a life crisis, as people's lives are altered in fundamental ways, they may need to find new ways of thinking and acting–a new identity. Belonging to a self-help group puts people in touch with others who share their life experience sufficiently to create and share a new identity based upon this experience. Thus, we argue, self-help is a novel form of community, created by individuals who discover a "need" for a new or special type of communal experience (Naisbit, 1982; Toffler, 1980). And many of the above characteristics of a community are universal elements of self-help.

Several scholars of self-help have identified aspects of this concept of community in noting some of the (relatively) universal characteristics of self-help groups. For instance, Borman (1992) and Mullan (1992) refer to the "instant identity" gained in a self-help group. This (new) identity is borne of the shared experience or "common problem" (Hedrick, Isenberg & Martini, 1992; Richardson, 1983) that creates immediate interpersonal "resonance" (Romeder, 1990) or "identification resonance" (Klass, 1992). An "identification with fellow travelers" (Klass, 1992) is seen to lead to validation of one's own experience and place in the world (identity) via the discussion of mutual problems and learning from others' modelling of distinctive role behaviors.

Borkman (1990) and Katz and Bender (1976) amplify this process by discussing the process of "identity change" that occurs in such an "experiential learning community" (Borkman, 1990). Bakker and Karel also discuss this identity change, suggesting that in order for people in crisis to cope positively with their changed life situation they need to find "a different way of experiencing (their) problems and situations (that) requires different interpretations" of their experience (1983, p. 162). The self-help group, Bakker and Karel argue, substitutes for the vanishing social structure of small isolated village communities. As Van Harberden notes, (1990, p. 215), such groups represent "a new form of solidarity in an atomistic society," and provide a feeling of community (Back & Taylor, 1976). Mack and Berman (1988) discuss the isolation and lack of community often experienced by parents of children with (rare) genetic diseases; they argue that the cohesion, or sense of community found in a self-help group plays a curative role in overcoming their sense of alienation.

Powell (1987) discusses another element of this process of community formation, drawing attention to the ways in which the self-help group may operate as a reference group for people, a setting in which they learn new values and behaviors, and adopt a different cultural frame or meaning system with which to interpret or make sense of their personal or collective situation. The process of identity (re)formation and (re)socialization into new beliefs and behaviors also is discussed by Weber (1982). Thus, self-help groups often can be considered as "communities of belief" (Antze, 1976), as well as communities of persons and shared experiences.

The positive utility of connecting to others with whom one can share perceptions, beliefs and experiences seems to be especially important when the life situation or illness people experience is stigmatizing or when it leads to their being labelled as deviant. One arena in which this often occurs involves mentally ill persons or families of mentally ill persons. Kaufman, Freund and Wilson (1989) discuss the positive social identity created in the supportive community of self-help groups for mentally ill persons, an identity that is "often distinct from their devalued (or alienated) status in most social groups outside of the self-help community" (p. 7). In a similar vein, Kurtz (1990a) reports how such groups (in this case for persons with NDMDA) help in "reconstruction of a positive identity for persons labelled as deviant" (p. 106).

The Community's Social Support Function: Helping People During Times of Crisis

Traditional communities have diverse customs which reflect their collective concern and responsibility for individual members. These customs are expressed especially when individuals undergo a crisis or problem. When such events occur, the individual may be "surrounded" by community members who offer comfort and attend to individual and familial needs–practical and emotional needs. For instance, in many cultures intimate mourners are given "time off," during which time they are exempted from work and normal social duties, while others, mostly neighbors and other family members, comfort them and take care of their chores. The importance of that "time off" for the mourner, in which he or she is allowed time to adjust to their new situation in an non-pressured way, has been widely documented (Silverman, 1974; see also Parsons' discussion of the "sick role," 1951). In some nations, formal social policy has buttressed this informal process of relief time.

Kropotkin (1972) argued that traditional communities indeed were characterized by mutual aid. He suggested that mutual aid was a "natural human force," where the social and economic needs of a community and its members were intertwined. The notion that the move away from the traditional and geographically distinct (and predominantly rural) community coincided with the move away from traditional values regarding mutual aid received a lot of attention in the 1960s and 1970s (see, especially, Fromm, 1968; Nisbet, 1960) However, an overly idealistic depiction of the joys of community life in the past also has been criticized (see, especially, Fischer, 1976; Suttles, 1972).

In a different approach to the issue of community support, Marris (1974) used the situation of grieving to generalize to other situations of major change in people's lives. Building upon his own as well as others' studies of diverse populations facing community breakup or transition, such as widows in England, tenants forced out of their neighborhoods, travelling Nigerian businessmen and American students, he observed that "the anxieties of change centered upon the struggle to defend or recover a meaningful pattern of relationships" (1974, p. 1). Marris makes two further points: (1) humans have a "conservative impulse," a deeply-seated resistance to change and unpredictability in their close relationships, especially changes that diminish their ability to interpret events in a communal framework; and (2) change involves an element of loss, and the ensuing period of adjusting to a new situation is much like grieving, where the need to adjust to change has to overcome the impulse to restore the past.

These notions of human conservatism or consistency are based upon social psychological principles affirming how pre-existing cognitive and emotional structures help define the meaning of events for persons and how they try to incorporate new events into these meaning systems. As Marris writes (p. 21):

> When a pattern of relationships is disrupted in any way for which we are not fully prepared, the thread of continuity in the interpretation of life becomes attenuated or altogether lost. The loss may fundamentally threaten the integrity of the structure of meanings on which this continuity rests, and cannot be acknowledged without distress. But if life is to go on, the continuity must somehow be restored.

But how can such continuity be maintained in the face of loss? Marris does not think individuals can manage this process by themselves. In traditional societies prescribed customs and intimate others who were close by facilitated this process. But now professionals, who are assumed to have substantial skill and objectivity in this regard, fill this role; kith and kin are, in Marris' view, too often insensitive or unskilled to help in this task of reintegration. Writing before the self-help "revolution" of the 1980s, such a conclusion is not surprising. Yet had Marris written now, after observing self-help groups in action, he might have added a discussion of the ways in which peers who have experienced similar losses can help others undergo such loss and change.

Community has importance and impact for individuals because of its potential for providing: (a) connection with others who have shared experiences; (b) ongoing interaction with a (relatively) stable group of others; and (c) the security of interdependence and mutual concern (Marris, 1974; Kropotkin, 1972). In times of illness, personal crisis or community disaster, when formal helping modes are nonexistent or inaccessible, these commitments are expressed in the form of mutual aid. Such aid finds expression in processes such as: emotional bonding, identification with the larger social entity, empathy, sharing of information and skills, sharing of material resources, opportunities for mobilization to pursue and realize self-interests.

The analysis of reports of initiation processes in self-help groups, or the introduction of new members into groups, indicates how sensitive most members are to helping each other cope with loss and change. Consistently, before suggestions are made for new behavior, elaborate discussion focuses on the crisis or loss at hand, and individuals' feelings and reactions to these situations. This is the stage when parents of a chronically mentally ill child speak about their dreams and hopes of seeing their child recover and get married, or when a grieving mother speaks about her child in vivid terms, as if he/she was alive. Others, too, "tell their tales," legitimizing and sympathizing with the feelings of new members. Thus, the "conservative impulse" is supported, and the stage is set for entry into the consideration of new behaviors and responses.

Several scholars of self-help discuss the ways in which these processes and groups also help establish a new social network which people can rely upon as they attempt to deal with and integrate the current crisis into their life experience (Borman, 1992; Hedrick et al., 1992; Humm 1984). Meeting other people who are willing and able to provide help is a central function of self-help groups (Borman, 1992; Katz & Bender, 1976; Klass, 1992; Richardson, 1983), and Mullan (1992) makes a particular point of indicating the ways in which "veterans" can help "rookies" interpret and respond to their loss.

Over time, Powell (1990) reports, self-help groups generally help expand both the size and density of individuals' social networks. Thus, not only may new people be encountered through this process, but established friends and contacts may be able to deepen and expand the intimacy and helpfulness of their relationships in this context. For instance, McWhirter, McWhirter and McWhirter (1988) discuss the ways in which self-help groups organized around a common religious tradition, and a social context of oppression, can create increased solidarity among neighbors. Their analysis of Christian Base Communities (CBC are self-help and mutual aid groups composed of members of local parishes that assist in alleviating the effects of poverty and powerlessness in Latin America) provides direct parallels between the mutual support available in self-help groups and communities.

In self-help groups such as The Compassionate Friends, Klass (1992) suggests, the organizational structure and interaction patterns, and the rituals and traditions of the group, provide an alternative meaning system which helps individuals make sense out of their new situations and relate them to their prior existences. These gains also are engendered by the deepened sense of support and intimacy often found in a self-help group; a form of relationship akin to that found in other, more established, loving connections (Borman, 1992; Hedrick et al., 1992). Such unconditional acceptance provides emotional bulwarks with which to deal with new and challenging situations. Several scholars have argued that the outcomes of the support provided in self-help groups include a stress-buffering effect on mental and physical health (Baider & DeNour, 1989; Cohen, Adler & Mintz 1983; Telch & Telch, 1986; Vugia, 1991), an improved capacity for solving the particular practical problems of daily life in new circumstances (Bakker & Karel, 1983; Kurtz, 1990b), and perhaps even improvements in physical health itself (Spiegel, Bloom, Kraemer & Gottheil, 1989).

The Community's Empowering Function: Improving Individuals' Skills and Social Services

A third sense of community relevant to self-help focuses on the nature of the community as a source (and agent) of empowerment for its members. One of the central purposes of a community is to provide the arena in which individuals can strive to meet their needs, pursue their interests and exert greater self-determination and control over their personal lives (Froland, Pancoast & Parker, 1983). They may accomplish these tasks in the community setting and/or utilize the community as a resource to discover and join with others who share their needs and interests. The collectivization of individual need and interest, and the mobilization of resources to pursue such interests, are central to the core of community life. At the holistic or macro level as well, communities of interest (as they substitute for communities of propinquity) themselves seek to be empowered as they try to guarantee and advance the welfare of their individual members.

A number of self-help scholars have addressed this aspect of self-help as an empowering community. Reliance on the experiential wisdom of veterans who have weathered and understood a crisis (as contrasted especially with the abstract wisdom of professionals) itself may be personally empowering. In this context the "common sense wisdom" of ordinary persons is validated as useful and relevant and helpful (Klass, 1992; Powell, 1987). Both Borkman (1990) and Marieskind (1984) discuss how this knowledge, and its public legitimation, becomes a source of power for people expressing it.

The recognition of such powerful knowledge, and the new social skills that may be learned and expressed as a consequence, also have been suggested as a hallmark of increased social efficacy (Katz & Bender, 1990a).

We have previously addressed the social support function of people providing help to one another. But several observers emphasize the reciprocal nature of this (self-) helping process, indicating that the act of helping others, and seeing oneself as useful and potent in this regard, can be therapeutic (or in our sense here, empowering) for the helper as well as the person being helped (Borman, 1992; Gartner, 1990; Hedrick et al., 1992; Klass, 1992; Riessman, 1965; Theirs, 1987; van Harberden, 1990). This is one of the most common and powerful dynamics in self-help groups, one which emphasizes the democratic nature of the helping process and the experiential knowledge base that lies at its heart.

This democratic tradition is developed further by the reliance of self-help groups on indigenous and grassroots leadership (Borman, 1992). As an adjunct or alternative to the professionally-dominated social service system, self-help groups often are consumer-initiated (Gartner, 1990), self or peer-governed by members (LeVeck, 1982; Levy, 1976; Steinman & Traunstein, 1976; Videka-Sherman, 1990), and more or less autonomous from the professional service system (Mellor et al., 1984). Even those self-help groups that permit professionals to be members or leaders generally establish a partnership or coalition that guarantees member and group autonomy and separate spheres of influence and self-control (Yoak & Chesler, 1985).

Further discussion of the empowering aspects of self-help groups has been provided by numerous scholars (Chesler & Chesney, 1988; Gidron, Guterman & Hartman 1990; Gutierrez, Ortega & Suarez, 1990; Haber, 1992; Hedrick et al., 1992; Mullan, 1992; Neighbors et al., 1990). One theme has centered on the personally empowering issues of proactive coping and "prosumer" orientations to care. The argument generally is that groups help increase members' self reliance (Marieskind, 1984), coping ability (Chesler & Chesney, 1988), personal responsibility for solving their problems (Borkman, 1990; van Harberden, 1990), personal responsibility for making changes in their lives (Hamilton, 1990; Katz & Bender, 1976), and a more educated consumerism (Mullan, 1992).

A second theme has centered on the collectively empowering and external social change focus of some self-help groups (Katz, 1981; Katz & Bender, 1976; Mellor et al., 1984; Neighbors et al., 1990; Videka-Sherman, 1990). Scholars have pointed to groups' and members' increased ability to "exert pressure on the environment" and "correct the service system" (Bakker & Karel, 1983, p. 163), by undertaking advocacy vis-à-vis the service system they deal with (Chesler, 1991; Romeder, 1990) or the public in general (Mullan, 1992). The increased knowledge gathered by parents active in these settings, and the bonds they establish with peers, are resources crucial to the organization and mobilization of any change effort or social movement activity (Chesler, 1991; Gamson, Fireman & Rytina, 1982; McCarthy & Zald, 1973; 1977). Obviously, as Smith and Pillemer note (1983, p. 215), self-help groups "differ among themselves in having varying degrees of social movement/social change orientation," but the potential for collective as well as individual empowerment, and for collective action, exists.

Self-help groups have utilized several common tactics to advocate and act upon their members' concerns: opening up clogged communication channels; engaging in collaborative problem solving that persuades decision-makers of the need for change, generating coercive challenges or protests to change policies and practices; mobilizing press and public opinion in support of their cause, etc. All these tactics require the exercise of some sort of power, and often the surfacing of structural conflict and/or the escalation of overt conflict–to gain attention, to engage collaboration, or to force new decisions (Chesler, 1991).

In a more general sense, Reynolds suggests (1982, p. 79) that self-help can be seen "as a medium of social and economic advancement in a society with limited resources." Bakker and Karel argue that (1983, p. 160), however subtly, all self-help "implicitly criticizes how the welfare state is organized" and operates. In this context, in particular, observers have cautioned against the pattern of state cooptation of self-help in the effort to diminish public and professional resources available to people in crisis (Withorn, 1980). Similarly, McWhirter et al., (1988) caution against the potentially pacifying role of the Christian Base Communities that they so strongly sympathize with. This is an especially important concern in an age when conservative national governments are attempting to cut back the welfare state system and promote the scarcity paradigm of limited expertise, love, resources and power.

In our international study comparing self-help groups across nations as well as issues, we found clear indications of some of these universal dynamics. Specifically, as Table 1 indicates, participants in all the U.S. and Israeli groups ranked the perceived benefits they derived from participation in self-help quite similarly: the rank-order correlation coefficient of benefits suggests that the ordering of benefits from group participants in both nations (Israel and the U. S.) was quite similar. The benefits most highly ranked in groups in both nations included: "meeting others with similar problems," "being part of a larger group," and "feeling freer to express my feelings." The rank-order correlation coefficient of benefits (Spearman's rho) was .89, indicating a relationship, such that the ordering of benefits from group participants in both nations (Israel and the U.S.) and dealing with four different types of life crises, was quite similar.

In another analysis, where people assessed the ways in which their lives had changed since the crisis began, the outcome of "personal empowerment," both at the intrapersonal (feeling competent and in control) and social (activism) levels, significantly distinguished self-help group participants and non-participants in both nations. Samples of participants and non-participants were available only with regard to the conditions of childhood cancer and children's mental illness, so Table 2 is limited to an analysis of the results from the groups dealing with these two sets of problems or issues. Although the concept of empowerment is measured so differently in different studies that it is hard to draw consistent interpretations of these comparative findings, the message generally is affirmed in much of the recent literature.

These data suggest that there may be some relatively universal characteristics (benefits, outcomes, and their corollary processes and functions) of self-help groups. As Biegel and Yamatani also argue (1987, p. 1197), "Self-help groups share a common helping focus regardless of the problem area." They come to this conclu-

TABLE I. Rank-Ordering of the Mean Benefits of Self-Help Groups for Parents*

Activity	United States		Israel	
	PCHCA (Cancer)	POMC (Murdered)	PMIC (Ment. Ill)	MFNI (New Imm.)
Informational				
Learning who's who on staff	8	6	9	10
Practical				
Coping with the family's problems	7	8	7	12
Learning to cope differently	6	7	6	5
Emotional				
Feeling freer to express feelings	3	3	4.5	3
Getting help from other parents	4	4.5	4.5	7
Coping with public attitudes	5	4.5	3	8
Social				
Meeting with similar others	1	1	2	2
Feeling part of a larger group	2	2	1	1
Self-empowering				
Developing self-confidence	9	9	8	6
Learning how to be a leader	11	12	12	11
Being active in the system	10	10	10	4
Changing the service system	12	11	11	9

*Spearman rho PCHCA × POMC is .97, PCHCA × PMIC is .96, PCHCA × MFNI is .64. Rho POMC × PMIC is .67, POMC × MFNI is .63. Rho PMIC × MFNI is .63.

TABLE 2. Changes in One's Life[a] (Since the Onset of Family Crisis) Reported by Participants and Nonparticipants in Self-Help Groups[b]

Life changes	U.S. parents of children with cancer		Israeli parents of persons with mental illness	
	Participants (N = 65)	Nonparticipants (N = 51)	Participants (N = 32)	Nonparticipants (N = 18)
Activism				
Willingness to join others to change things	2.7	2.1*	2.5	1.9*
Sense of what you can do as an individual	2.7	2.3*	2.2	1.7*
Personal identity				
Personal control over life	2.0	1.7*	1.4	1.4(NS)
Sense of who you are	2.6	2.4(NS)	2.0	1.6*

[a] Mean scores assessed on a 3-point scale (3 = better, 2 = same, 1 = worse).
[b] Limited to parents of children with cancer and groups of parents of mentally ill children because these were the only samples containing group participants and nonparticipants.
* Statistically significant at the .05 level, using an F test of mean differences in a one-way ANOVA *within* each of the two samples separately.

sion on the basis of two forms of evidence: (1) by analyzing the common activities and processes of 10 self-help groups for families of mentally ill people that they studied; and (2) by comparing the ordering of activities and benefits in these 10 groups with similar data from Levy's (1979) study of behavioral control and stress-coping groups. A priority on empathy, emotional catharsis, mutual affirmation, encouragement of sharing and normalization seem to be common across all these groups. Similarly, several other authors agree that it is "the opportunity to meet with others with similar problems that is the most beneficial aspect of group participation" (Hinrichsen, Revenson & Shinn, 1985, p. 67; also Chesler, 1991; Gottlieb, 1982; Kagey, Vivace & Lutz, 1981; Knight, Wollert, Levy, Frame & Padgett, 1980).

To summarize, while the traditional geographically bounded and isolated community is quickly vanishing in the light of modernization and development, humans' need for "community relationships" is still very much alive. As the modern geographic community no longer is able to provide its members with the type of informal support they require, alternative, non-geographic alternatives have been created to respond to this need. Humans have opted for a variety of other social units, such as the workplace, professional groups, political parties and "cause" groups, as well as self-help groups, and turned them into non-geographic communities. This conceptualization of the development of the self-help phenomenon in the 1970s and 1980s argues that self-help is a novel form of a modern day "community." Both communities and self-help groups share similar internal processes, outlined above, and often have similar effects. As community is a universal social framework, known to humans for hundreds of generations, viewing self-help within this framework helps explain the existence and expansion of the phenomenon internationally, and its similar forms across cultures and issue areas.

PARTICULARISTIC ATTRIBUTES OF SELF-HELP

But communities are diverse: there are major differences between communities and heterogeneity within them as well. While the origins of self-help may stem from the same human experience as community life, and result in similar social and personal processes, both communities and self-help groups exist within larger social contexts, contexts which define many of their structural attributes and possibilities. Different civic/political cultures, different social and economic histories, and different health and welfare systems mean that both communities and self-help groups will develop differently in different nations, in different ethnic, class or demographic groupings within nations, and around different issues. As people experience and advocate varied cultures and interests, and varying patterns of interaction and communication, so do the communities that they create vary. Thus, while there are universal or common characteristics of self-help groups, as discussed above, there also are important particularistic characteristics of these groups.

Three powerful factors appear to account for much of the variation in structures and processes, helping to explain the particularistic forms of self-help amidst and alongside the universalist tendencies discussed above. They include: (a) nation, (b) culture and/or sociodemographic status within a nation, and (c) problem or life situation around which organization occurs. In our view, the unique structural characteristics of self-help groups generally are determined by or derived from these three primary influences. That is, the literature and our own data indicate that these three factors, separately and in interaction, largely determine the ways in which self-help finds expression. Specifically, they determine:

- The size of the self-help sector
- The composition of the self-help sector, the issues around which groups are organized
- The predominant organizational structure of groups
- The predominant leadership and membership styles/patterns
- The characteristic programs and activities
- The relationships with professionals and with formal help systems

Nations

Different nations have different ideologies and different formal arrangements for caring for people in stressful life situations. Specifically, they differ in ideologies regarding the state's responsibility for people in need and thus the comprehensiveness and universality of public services. Some of these differences have been highlighted in the distinction between the Western industrialized world, where "specialized agencies of help, with professional providers who are believed to possess unique knowledge and technology" (Katz, 1984, p. 233) offer assistance, as contrasted with the developing countries, where mutual assistance is offered by kith and kin in traditional and basic form (Katz, 1992). In Katz' view, self-help in the industrialized nations may be driven by dissatisfied reactions to highly formal, alienating and bureaucratized services, whereas in developing nations it may reflect traditional forms of kinship and communal responsibility.

But the focus on developed vs. developing nations may mask other important differences. For instance, deCocq (1990) argues that the welfare state orientation of the Scandinavian and other Western European nations fosters a national commitment to help self-help groups, as a state responsibility for the provision of assistance to all citizens. In the United States, he argues, an anti-social-welfare, pro-entrepreneurial and voluntarist ideology helps self-help groups wish to be, and be seen as, freer of state interference and support. When the state supports the idea of self-help in the United States, it often is done as an explicit spur to voluntaristic and private alternatives to state activity and service (Asch, 1986; Withorn, 1980). In North America, for instance, self-help often is seen as a substitute for governmental service, or as an opportunity to pressure the state to provide services for a particular population. Within such a framework, self-help groups are more likely to be independent and even antagonistic to formal services, and in struggle with them for resources.

As an extension of this analysis, Leventhal et al.(1988) argue that the entire self-help sector in the United States is loosely organized, partly as a function of its voluntary and non (or anti-) state nature, and partly as a result of the state's stance of non-responsibility for self-help. Thus, the pattern of self-help groups that we primarily read about in the U.S. literature are initiated by indigenous people and sustained by them relatively independently of formal authorities; this is less common outside the North American continent.

In some other developed nations, the state may be much more active, even to the point of organizing and enlarging the self-help sector. Van Harberden (1990) affirms this distinction implicitly, as he describes how the Dutch government actively supports self-help as a state responsibility. Thus, in Holland self-help is not seen as a substitute for formal and state-provided services. Van Harberden and Raymakers comment further (1986, p. 28):

> Findings indicate that a majority of self-help groups consider help by and for fellow sufferers as complementary to professional care and not as an alternative. To put it differently, many people have a shortage consciousness, the feeling that existing helping resources (professional care and/or neighbor and family help) leave them out in the cold, but this doesn't mean that they want to banish these helping resources completely.

Another illustration of the active role of the state in self-help comes from nations where governments provide financial support to self-help groups (Katz, 1984; Gidron, 1991) and their incorporation into social welfare programs (especially in England, West Germany and the Netherlands: Humble & Unell, 1989; van Harbarden, 1990). For instance, according to one report from a local Council of Voluntary Organizations in the U.K.(Unell, 1987, p. 5).

> Councils for voluntary service and other local development agencies have begun to recognize the contribution made by self-help groups by making available resources to enable and support their development. Their aim has been to smooth the path between groups and the resources they need, to enable them to make more informed choices about their goals and to improve the local climate of opinion about the value of self-help. The rationale for providing this support is clear. The task of a local development agency, expressed in its most general terms, is to enable people to participate more fully in the life of their communities by furthering the possibilities of voluntary action. Involvement in a self-help group is a type of voluntary activity which promotes the participation of some of the most vulnerable and isolated members of society.

Despite this optimistic local picture, however, there is not always an explicit governmental policy vis-à-vis self-help which translates into concrete support, and it often "falls between the chairs" of several ministries (see van Harberden & Raymakers, 1986).

Further, Trojan (1983) suggests some differences (and similarities) between the French and West German experiences with self-help. The most striking difference, he argues, is that in West Germany there are many more discussion-oriented self-help groups than in France, while in France there appear to be more action-oriented groups and organizations of groups. He does not speculate on the nationality-based reasons for such differences, except to indicate that "Institutionalized rights for the participation of consumers in decision-making processes or provision of health and social services do not exist in West Germany" (Trojan et al., 1986, p. 22). Perhaps this gap explains the slow (or low level of) development of advocacy-oriented and well organized self-help groups in West Germany. But even these close links do not negate the existence of social change-oriented and advocacy groups, some of which co-exist along side of or even within traditional support-oriented groups.

Katz suggests that in Europe there is less interest on the part of self-help groups in working harmoniously with state services, and more interest in altering the service delivery system, and indeed the social structure of the society, than in the United States' groups (Katz, 1984). Early research into self-help groups in the United States would seem to support this view of a priority on a personal change versus a social change agenda; however, more recent work suggests that more self-help groups in the United States are undertaking local and even national change agendas.

Moreover, the nature of self-help also is influenced by the civic culture and legal framework that encourages or discourages people from forming or joining voluntary organizations. These are translated into structural encouragements or limitations for such endeavors. Thus for example, in countries where groups are required to formally register with the State authorities or where a certified professional must be available in group meetings, lay people will be less inclined to initiate or sustain independent groups. Such legal patterns make certain assumptions about the need, the right, and the organizational know-how to form citizens' organizations (see Cnaan, Perlmutter & Kang, 1992).

Sidel's (1976) report on the People's Republic of China's represents a different and even cynical concept of self-help. She observes that the government used China's communal, family-oriented, mutual aid tradition to organize workers' cooperatives and work gangs in rural areas. Such organizations were built on the traditional affinities of people from the same geographic community and used grassroots organizing methods, but had to comply with state directives and a "watchful eye" from above. This combination of the traditional communal culture and a bureaucratic national framework also was used to organize communes and residents' committees in urban areas. A similar theme in China's self-help framework occurs in therapeutic settings with mental patients and criminals, where people are paired in order to share feelings and thoughts and to analyze and discuss their behavioral options. Within such institutions, "patients . . . participate in regular study sessions, using the writings of Mao-Tse-Tung to analyze their own illnesses and points of view and to remold their attitudes" (p. 226). Thus, the government has used traditional cultures and lifestyles, but has added a new ideological framework and supervisory mandate. The result is an encouragement of grassroots activity and freedom to organize on the one hand, and constraints on the issues and procedures with which self-help functions on the other.

Another example of a self-help framework introduced "from above," yet integrated into communal and workplace situations, is reported by Barath (1990). Hypertension Clubs in Croatia (when it was part of Yugoslavia) were initiated by general practitioners as part of a prevention program. At the same time, these clubs were part of the "socio-political organizing structure of a local or labor community," and they worked with the "intensive cooperation of health workers" (p. 207). Once again, we see freedom to organize and design activities, but within a limited focus on reducing members' blood pressure–presumably by traditional treatment methods–and with the close supervision of professionals (and state officials).

In nations where comprehensive and universally accessible services are provided, the population may come to expect that authorities will deal with social and individual problems through formal, generally state-supported, professional mechanisms; these mechanisms also are readily available, and tend to intervene (preventively/proactively or reactively) when required. The general relevance of the overall political and economic context within which self-help groups are formed and operate, as well as the potential for change in this context, is stressed in Gidron and Bargal's (1986) account of the Israeli experience. Gradually, what was a very centralized system, dominated by a large public sector, has become a more open and decentralized system, with a consequent increase in independent self-help groups and organizations in Israel.

Under circumstances of expanded state services and support for self-help, professionals are likely to generate and play potent roles in self-help activities and groups, and groups are likely to work in conjunction with public providers. Parker, Pancoast and Froland (1983) note that researchers in West Germany and the United Kingdom "found a widespread acceptance of the usefulness of self-help groups among professionals" (p. 280). On the other hand, other researchers have indicated an "uncertain" and "not especially enthusiastic" (p. 279) response by professionals to the role of self-help groups in the United States, France and the United Kingdom. These contradictions may reflect international differences, intranational differences, or simply interresearcher differences.

Data examining the existence of national differences in self-help group experiences and activities are available from our study. Since informants in the two nations studied also experienced different family crises, we conducted an analysis that maintained the separateness of the four life crises of the samples of people from the two nations. These comparisons illuminate some of the differences between the two nations' samples, possibly in light of the differences in their economic, political and social service systems. In general, U.S. informants reported that they coped with family crises by sharing their feelings with others and by publicly seeking help from informal sources more often than did Israeli informants. Israelis, on the other hand, tended to rely more than did their U.S. counterparts on the formal service system for help. In addition, they reported that they received more help from a variety of sources. They also more often reported making positive life changes as a result of their efforts to deal with their family illness. This evidence of general national differences provides a useful background to our effort to understand how self-help group processes and activities may differ in the two nations. For instance, despite the fact that the self-help group participants' rank-ordering of benefits was quite similar in the two nations, the mean frequencies of their reports of activities and the mean value of reported benefits received did differ by nation. The data in Table 3 suggests differences in the reported frequency of various self-help group activities and benefits, respectively, in the two nations. The strongest national differences in group activity patterns occur in the areas of getting information about treatments, sharing emotional feelings and making changes in the social service system: U.S. informants reported that their groups conduct more of each of these programs. In addition, U.S. parents consistently report higher levels of benefit from group involvement than do Israeli parents, despite the commonality of the ranking of these benefits (as shown in Table 1).

Another clear national difference is reflected in members' reports of the roles professionals played in these different self-help groups. In both of the U.S. samples, parents of children with cancer and parents of murdered children, members reported the following professional roles as most common:

- Refer new parents to the group
- Provide information
- Refer parents for special help
- Consult with the group on problems
- Advocate the group's existence and function

On the other hand, the following roles were reported as least commonly played by professionals:

- Train parents in how to lead the group
- Set the agenda for the group
- Plan group activities
- Supervise the group's operations

In marked contrast, members in both of the Israeli groups, parents of mentally ill people and parents in families of new immigrants, reported the following professional roles as played most commonly:

- Lead the group
- Set the group's agenda
- Plan group activities

And they reported the following roles as least common:

- Raise or provide funds
- Attend social functions/activities

Whereas professionals linked to the U.S. groups most commonly played advisory or consultative roles, and desisted (or were prevented) from controlling or supervising functions, the reverse often was true in the Israeli groups. Self-help groups in Israel appear to be much more dependent upon professional direction than are groups in the United States. This does not mean that the U.S. groups operate without or in opposition to professional assistance, but that assistance takes different forms and is delivered in a different manner than it is in Israeli settings. These findings are consistent with some of the literature suggesting that the more elaborate and professionalized social service and state welfare system in Israel would extend into active state and professional involvement in self-help groups. In the U.S., with a less extensive social welfare and social service apparatus, and with a strong tradition of voluntary activity, self-help groups appear to operate with greater autonomy from professional control and direction.

Demographics and Ethnic Status

In addition to the international diversity discussed above, intranational differences also are sources of self-help group particularities. Different sociodemographic groups within a nation may have different cultural beliefs and traditions about the responsibility of person, family, community and nation in dealing with stressful life situations, different traditions about local and grass-roots mobilization of kith and kin, and differential access to state-supported services.

Pancoast, Parker and Froland (1983), in general, and Richardson (1983) in particular, discuss some of these differentiating characteristics. Several other authors studying a variety of self-help groups

TABLE 3. Comparative Reports of the Mean Incidence of Activities and Benefits of Self-Help Groups for U.S. and Israeli Members

Activity(a)	United States		Israel	
	PCHCA (Cancer)	POMC (Murd. Chi.)	PMIC (Ment.Ill)	MFNI (N. Imm.)
Informational/educational				
Discuss recent advances in treatment, enforcement, and so on	3.08	3.29	2.63	2.51
Sharing/dealing with feelings				
Talk about family stresses	3.50	3.40	3.30	2.11
Talk about personal feelings	3.12	3.51	3.28	2.29
Deal with emotional issues	3.21	3.26	3.40	2.44
Fund-raising				
Raise funds for needy families	2.48	1.59	1.65	3.00
Social events				
Plan to get together socially	3.00	2.00	1.72	3.93
Making change				
Give feedback to staff	2.52	2.57	2.30	1.82
Plan to change the systems of care	2.10	2.89	1.67	1.04
Maintenance				
Plan group activities	3.17	2.36	1.44	3.84
Discuss recruitment of new members	2.52	2.06	1.62	2.73

	United States		Israel	
Benefit(b)	PCHCA (Cancer)	POMC (Murd. Chi.)	PMIC (Ment. Ill)	MFNI (N. Imm.)
Informational				
Learning who's who on staff	3.08	3.20	1.57	1.48
Practical				
Coping with the family's problems	3.09	3.01	2.52	1.33
Learning to cope differently	3.23	3.16	2.75	2.00
Emotional				
Feeling freer to express feelings	3.46	3.51	3.00	2.43
Getting help from other parents	3.42	3.30	3.00	1.68
Coping with public attitudes	3.25	3.30	3.17	1.62
Social				
Meeting with similar others	3.70	3.78	3.61	2.91
Feeling part of a larger group	3.48	3.53	3.77	3.65
Self-empowering				
Developing self-confidence	3.00	2.91	2.21	1.88
Learning how to be a leader	2.72	2.50	1.33	1.42
Being active in the system	2.83	2.77	1.54	2.03
Changing the service system	2.22	2.58	1.42	1.53

(a) Activity items were rated by group members on a four-point scale ranging from *a lot* (4) to *never* (1). Higher scores indicate greater incidence.
(b) Benefit items were rated by group members on a four-point scale ranging from *much benefit* (4) to *no benefit* (1). Higher scores indicate greater benefit.

within a given nation report the great differences they observed: Trojan in West Germany (1989), Levy in England (1982), Gidron and Bargal in Israel (1986), Neighbors and Jackson in the Black community in the United States (1984), and Pilisuk and Minkler in the elderly community in the United States (1980) are but the tips of this iceberg emphasizing intranational and even intracultural particularism.

Weber (1982) emphasizes how a group's culturally determined beliefs about the nature of their common problem (due to fate, their own agency, identifiable actions of others, etc.) impacts on their views and practices of self-help. And Cohen (1982) also emphasizes the ways in which local cultural contexts influence beliefs in self-help. He also notes the importance of economic class, suggesting that inasmuch as certain beliefs may be tied to class origins and location they, too, may be considered in the same manner as cultural variables. Biegel and Yamatani (1987) report that the membership of the 10 self-help groups for families of mentally ill persons that they studied were almost exclusively made up of people who were white, female and middle class. Vine and Beels (1990) also examined groups for family members of mentally ill persons, and affirm the class bias in group membership. They attribute this to the group's attractiveness to highly verbal people, who have higher education and more resources, and who are intolerant of and ready to advocate resistance to the trend toward deinstitutionalization of the mentally ill. Evidence regarding the largely white and middle class (and often female) dominated membership of a great variety of self-help groups seems to support these observations (Battaglino, 1987; Borman, 1982; Edwards, 1966; Lieberman & Borman, 1976; Medvene & Krauss, 1989; Videka-Sherman, 1982).

Others (Hamilton, 1990; Hedrick et al., 1992) argue that, in the United States for instance, most organized self-help groups do not reach adherents in the barrios and ghettos. Hedrick et al. (1992) also suggest that older citizens are not often included either. Bartalos (1992) generalizes this perspective, suggesting that many groups that are underserved by the formal social service apparatus also are underrepresented in self-help groups–the very old, the very young, the very poor, and people with severe disabilities. This is not to suggest that self-help as such does not exist in these classes and culturally diverse settings, but that the formally organized self-help group often discussed in the literature is not evident. Much more evident in these communities are informally developed networks of kith and kin involved in mutual help and support.

Thus, involvement in formally organized groups is not the only culturally appropriate self-help framework available. Neighbors et al. (1990) argue that the unique cultural and material position of Blacks in the United States leads to their special focus on the use of informal help systems. They argue that it is not possible to separate African-Americans' involvement in voluntary self-help group activities from their larger struggle for freedom, equal rights and a meaningful role in the U.S. society. In their view, Black churches and fraternities, as well as political advocacy groups, are the historic agencies of this community's self-help efforts. This view is affirmed by Rodgers and Tartaglia (1990), who also discuss the growth of the United Black Fund as a culturally unique form of self-help activity aimed at community self-improvement and self-empowerment, especially in the face of elite white control of social services and charitable resources.

In another case study of a self-help process within an ethnic community in the U.S., Gutierrez et al. (1990) discuss the incompatibilities between the Anglo cultural priority on functional independence and individual autonomy and the Latino orientation toward collectivism and social harmony. They assert that self-help is quite compatible with the Latino culture, but with an emphasis on neighborhood and family oriented "mutual aid": in times of crisis Latinos do use their own indigenous and familial communal aid networks, which include the extended family, church, merchant and social clubs. (see also, DeAnda & Becerra, 1984). The authors also analyze why Latinos are minimally inclined to join existing (mainstream and Anglo) self-help groups: distance from their residence, language differences, awkwardness with white-led ventures, experiences of prejudice and discrimination, and a host of other instrumental difficulties (baby-sitting, time and energy, etc.).

One may also count as another example of the workings of culture the role of the professional culture, or as Borkman calls it, the professional "frame of reference" (Borkman, 1990). The chapter authors in Pancoast, Parker and Froland (1983) discuss the varied reactions of policy-makers and professionals to self-help groups and processes. To the extent that professional socialization and commitment (developed through both pre-professional and on-the-job socialization) represents a coherent belief system, a professional ideology about service, service provision and service reception, it may represent a distinctive culture (or subculture), one often at odds with lay cultures–and certainly with the often aprofessional (or even antiprofessional) ideology of self-help group organizers and members (Chesler, 1991). Moreover, to the extent that this professional culture reflects and advances values that are dominant in the Anglo and middle or upper-middle class community, it may represent a culture at considerable variance from that of Black, Latino, Asian and Native American peoples and communities.

Unfortunately, there is not sufficient variation in our samples of self-help group members to conduct analyses that would differentiate, on the basis of race and class, intra-national differences on these cultural and/or demographic factors.

Problem Situation or Life Condition

The common life situation or problem people in a particular group may experience also creates differentiation within the larger phenomenon of self-help. For instance, the nature of the problem situation (age of impact, chronicity, medicalness, seriousness, probability of personal or social explanation/blame, etc.) affects, by definition, the potential membership of the group. Specifically it determines the age and social status strata from which members are drawn, the length of their need or attraction to self-help, their skill and energy for local initiative and leadership, their experience with and thus openness to professional leadership, their energy, their personal and group goals, and their readiness to invest in collective action. All these factors also find expression in organizational characteristics as well, such as in their types of activities, resources, leadership patterns, average length of membership involvement, etc. Thus, the specific problem at issue will account for much of the variation of self-help groups within a given nation and even within a given culture, sub-culture or demographic category.

Emerick extends this argument, noting that (1990, p. 401):

> Some structural factors may be generic to all self-help groups, but conditions that facilitate or impede the establishment of partnerships between self-help groups and health care professionals vary with the type of group–that is, with the nature of the problem the group addresses.

Thus, he argues, groups for people with physical health problems (cancer, AIDS) will differ from groups for people dealing with mental health problems, (schizophrenia, NDMDA), which in turn will differ from groups for people dealing with life cycle transitions (divorce, death), precisely because they are dealing with professionals with very different philosophies of care.

Brickman and his colleagues (1983) interpret some of the dynamics of any helping process (lay or professional) in terms of two kinds of responsibility: (1) the degree to which the individual is responsible for having created the situation; and (2) the degree to which the individual is responsible for managing a recovery. The situation a person is not responsible for causing, but is responsible for recovering from, is one which is most amenable to help from others; these people are most deserving of sympathy, they have not done this to themselves, and help will be most effective to them because they can play a role in their own recovery. Clearly, various problem situations (physical disease such as cancer, drug and alcohol abuse, accidental injury and murder, self-inflicted damage, mental illness, immigration) may vary on these perceptions of responsibility, and so will the sympathy and willingness to help the afflicted.

Numerous scholars have attempted to categorize self-help groups in terms of the problem situations or life conditions to which they respond (Katz & Bender, 1976; Neighbors et al., 1990; Trojan et al., 1986; Powell, 1987; among others). Any and all of these categorizations can be very helpful in creating a typology of self-help groups that may integrate the structural properties of the problem around which the group organizes, and that problem's likely impact on personal and organizational characteristics.

Data are available from our studies to examine some of these issues. For instance, within the U.S. samples there are substantial differences between the parents of murdered children and the parents of children with cancer with regard to their coping styles, receipt of support from various sources and life changes. Table 4 also shows differences in the rank-ordering of the mean incidence of activities between the two groups studied in the U.S. Despite these programmatic differences in the groups, however, Table 1 indicated that there are minimal differences between these populations in their reported rankings of the benefits of their self-help groups. Within the Israeli sample, there also are differences between the parents of mentally ill persons and the parents in immigrant families with respect to their coping patterns, receipt of support and life changes and, as Table 4 indicates, also in the rank-ordering of the mean incidence of their activities. Once again, such differences are not sustained in participants' rankings of group benefits.

CONCLUSIONS

This paper focuses on comparative aspects of self-help, with a special emphasis on international comparisons, an aspect of self-help often overlooked in other discussions, analyses and empirical studies of groups and processes. The other two comparative (and differentiating) factors of (sub-) culture or demographic grouping and problem or issue also appear to have powerful potential impact on the nature and extent of self-help. This comparative perspective helps place an emphasis on, and differentiates between, the internal processes of self-help groups and activities and the external or contextual factors within which self-help operates.

The conceptualization of self-help within the "community" framework relates the modern phenomenon of self-help to a historic and universal framework, and thus to a fundamental pattern of bonding among people. It also sets the stage for explanations of some of the differences in self-help, especially differences between cultures that reflect different communal traditions and histories. In this sense, the international and cross-cultural study of self-help is an especially good vantage point from which to view a variety of social and psychological aspects of human activity.

Given the low level of empirical data that is directly relevant to many of these issues, the conclusions drawn from the literature and our own data are quite tentative. We hope to generate further

TABLE 4. Rank-Ordering of the Mean Incidence of Activities of Self-Help Groups for U.S. and Israeli Members*

Activity	UnitedStates		Israel	
	PCHCA (Cancer)	POMC (Murd. Chi.)	PMIC (Men. Ill)	MFNI (New Imm.)
Informational/educational				
Discuss recent advances in treatment, enforcement, and so on	5	3	4	5
Sharing/dealing with feelings				
Talk about family stresses	1	2	2	8
Talk about personal feelings	4	1	3	7
Deal with emotional issues	2	4	1	6
Fund-raising				
Raise funds for needy families	9	10	8	3
Social events				
Plan to get together socially	6	9	6	1
Making change				
Give feedback to staff	7.5	6	5	9
Plan to change the systems of care	10	5	7	10
Maintenance				
Plan group activities	3	7	10	2
Discuss recruitment of new members	7.5	8	9	4

* Spearman rho PCHCA × POMC is .57, PCHCA × PMIC is .57, PCHCA × MFNI is .09. Rho POMC x PMIC is .25, POMC × MFNI is –.38. Rho PMIC × MFNI is –.53. *None* of these rhos is statistically significant at $p < .05$.

inquiry and debate on what often have been unasked, let alone unanswered, questions. Indeed, we hope that the next step will be taken to engage in international comparative studies of this fascinating and vital human social phenomenon.

Adequate international or cross-cultural studies in the area of self-help are extremely hard to conduct. Indeed, our own efforts reflected in the data tables reported in this article illustrate some of the difficulties:

1. Gaining access to similar or different groups, in ways that provide a similar sampling frame, so that definitive comparisons can be made.
2. Gaining access to groups focussing on the same life crisis, in different cultures and nations and demographic groupings.
3. Designing instruments and items that mean the same in different cultures and languages.
4. Gathering the resources that permit international colleagues to talk, work, write and otherwise communicate and collaborate in ways that create truly cooperative ventures.

BIBLIOGRAPHY

Antze, P. The role of ideologies in peer psychotherapy organizations. *Journal of Applied Behavioral Science*. 1976, 12(3), 323-346.

Asch, A. Will populism empower the disabled? *Social Policy*. 1986, 16(3), 12-18.

Back, K., & Taylor, R. Self-help groups in Western society: History and prospects. *The Journal of Applied Behavioral Science*. 1976, 12(3), 295-309.

Baider, L., & De-Nour, A. Group therapy with adolescent cancer patients. *Journal of Adolescent Health Care*, 1989, 10(1), 35-38.

Bakker, B. & Karel, M. Self-help: Wolf or lamb? In Pancoast, Parker and Froland (eds.), *Rediscovering Self-Help–Its Role in Social Care*. Beverly Hills: Sage, 1983.

Barath, A. Hypertension clubs in Croatia, Yugoslavia. In Katz and Bender (eds.), *Helping One Another*. Oakland: Third Party Publishing, 1990, (pp. 205-214).

Bartalos, M. Illness, professional caregivers and self-helpers. In Katz, Hedrick, Isenberg, Thompson, Goodrich, & Kutscher (eds.) *Self-Help: Concepts and Applications*. Philadelphia: The Charles Press, 1992 (pp. 68-77).

Battaglino, L. Family empowerment through self-help groups. In A. Hatfield (ed.), *Families of the Mentally Ill: Meeting the Challenges*. San Francisco: Jossey-Bass, 1987.

Biegel, D., & Yamatani, H. Help-giving in self-help groups. *Hospital and Community Psychiatry*, 1987, 38(11), 1195-1197.

Borkman, T. Experiential, professional and lay frames of reference. In Powell (ed.), *Working with Self-Help.* Washington: NASW Press, 1990.

Borman, L. Kalmuk resettlement in America. In Weber & Cohen (eds.), *Beliefs and Self-Help: Cross-cultural Perspectives and Approaches,* New York: Human Services Press, 1982. (pp. 31-74).

Borman, L. Introduction: Self-help/mutual aid groups in strategies for health. In Katz, Hedrick, Isenberg, Thompson, Goodrich, & Kutscher (eds.), *Self-Help: Concepts and Applications.* Philadelphia: The Charles Press. 1992.

Brickman, P., Kidder, L., Coates, D., Rabinowitz, V., Cohn, F., & Karuza, L. Help: Making it fair and effective. In Fisher, Nadler & DePaulo (eds.), *New Directions in Helping, Vol. I.* New York: Academic Press, 1983.

Chesler, M. Mobilizing consumer activism in health care: The role of self-help groups. *Research in Social Movements, Conflict and Change.* 1991, 13, 275-305.

Chesler, M., & Chesney, B. Self-help groups: Empowerment attitudes and behaviors of disabled or chronically ill persons. In Yuker (ed.), *Attitudes Toward Persons with Disabilities.* New York: Springer Publications, 1988.

Chesler, M., Chesney, B., & Gidron, B. Israeli and U.S. orientations toward self-help groups for families in crisis. *Nonprofit and Voluntary Sector Quarterly,* 1990, 19(3), 251-262.

Cnaan, R.A., Perlmutter, R.D. & Kang, C.H. Voluntary associations: Societal variations in response to human needs. Paper presented at the 3rd International Conference of Research on Voluntary and Nonprofit Organizations, Indianapolis, March, 1992.

Cohen, C., Adler, A., & Mintz, J. Network interventions on the margin: A service experiment in a welfare hotel. In Pancoast, Parker & Froland (eds.), *Rediscovering Self-Help.* Beverly Hills: Sage Publishing, 1983.

Cohen, L. Cross-ethnic comparisons. In Weber & Cohen (eds.), *Beliefs and Self-Help: Cross-Cultural Perspectives and Approaches.* New York: Human Services Press, 1982 (pp. 337-354).

De Anda, D. & Becerra, R.M. Support networks for adolescent mothers. *Social Work,* 1984, 31(6).

de Cocq, G. European and North American self-help movements: Some contrasts. In Katz & Bender (eds.), *Helping One Another: Self-Help Groups in a Changing World.* Oakland, CA: Third Party Publishing Company, 1990 (pp. 199-203).

Edwards, G. Who goes to Alcoholics Anonymous? *Lancet.* 1966, 2, 382.

Emerick, R. Self-help groups for former patients: Relations with mental health professionals. *Hospital and Community Psychiatry,* 1990, 41(4), 401-407.

Fischer, C. *The Urban Experience.* New York: Harcourt, Brace Jovanovich, 1976.

Froland, C., Pancoast, D., & Parker, P. Introduction. In Pancoast, Parker & Froland (eds.), *Rediscovering Self-Help: Its Role in Social Care,* Beverly Hills: Sage Publications, 1983.

Fromm, E. *The Revolution of Hope*. New York: Harper & Row, 1968.
Gamson, W., Fireman, B., & Rytina, S. *Encounters with Unjust Authorities*. Homewood, IL: Dorsey Press, 1982.
Gartner, A. A typology of women's self-help groups. In Katz & Bender (eds.), *Helping One Another: Self-Help Groups in a Changing World*. Oakland: Third Party Publishing Company, 1990.
Gidron, B. & Bargal, D. Self-help awareness in Israel: An expression of structural changes and expanding citizen participation. *Journal of Voluntary Action Research*, 1986, 15(2), pp. 47-56.
Gidron, B., Chesler, M., & Chesney, B. Cross-cultural perspectives on self-help groups: Comparison between participants and nonparticipants in Israel and the United States. *American Journal of Community Psychology*, 1991, 19(5), 667-681.
Gidron, B., Guterman, N., & Hartman, H. Participation in self-help groups and empowerment among parents of the mentally ill in Israel. In T. Powell (Ed.), *Working With Self-Help*. Washington, D.C.: NASW Press, 1990 (pp. 267-276).
Gidron, B. Stress and coping patterns of parents of the mentally ill in Israel. *International Social Work*, 1991, 34, 159-170.
Gottlieb, B. Mutual help groups: Members' views of their benefits and of roles for professionals. *Prevention in Human Services*, 1982, 1(3), 55-67.
Gutierrez, L., Ortega, R. & Suarez, Z. Self-help and the Latino community. In T.J. Powell (ed.). *Working with Self-Help*. Silver Spring: NASW, 1990 (pp. 218-236).
Haber, D. Self-help groups and aging. In Katz, Hedrick, Isenberg, Thompson, Goodrich, & Kutscher (eds.), *Self-Help: Concepts and Applications*. Philadelphia: The Charles Press, 1992.
Hamilton, A. Self-help and mutual aid in ethnic minority communities. In Katz & Bender (eds.), *Helping One Another: Self-Help Groups In a Changing World*. Oakland, CA: Third Party Publishing Company, 1990 (pp. 47-61).
Hedrick, H., Isenberg, D., & Martini, C. Self-help groups: Empowerment through policy and partnerships. In Katz, Hedrick, Isenberg, Thompson, Goodrich, & Kutscher (eds.), *Self-Help: Concepts and Applications*. Philadelphia: The Charles Press, 1992 (pp. 3-55).
Hinrichsen, G., Revenson, T., & Shinn, M. Does self-help help? An empirical investigation of Scoliosis peer support groups. *Journal of Social Issues*, 1985, 41(1), 65-87.
Humble, S. & Unell, J. *Self-Help in Health and Social Welfare: England and West Germany*. London: Routledge, 1989.
Humm, A. The changing nature of lesbian and gay self-help groups. In Gartner & Riessman (eds.), *The Self-Help Revolution*. New York: Human Sciences Press, 1984 (pp. 33-39).
International Conference on Self-Help/Mutual Aid. Ottawa: Canadian Council on Social Development. 1992.
Kagey, J., Vivace, J., & Lutz, W. Mental health primary prevention: The role of

parent mutual support groups. *American Journal of Public Health*, 1981, 71(2), 166-167.

Katz, A. Self-Help and mutual aid: An emerging social movement. *Annual Review of Sociology*, 1981, 7, 129-155.

Katz, A. Self-help groups: An international perspective. In Gartner & Riessman (eds.), *The Self-Help Revolution*. New York: Human Science Press, 1984.

Katz, A. Professional/self-help group relationships: General issues. In Katz, Hedrick, Isenberg, Thompson, Goodrich, & Kutscher (eds.), *Self-Help: Concepts and Applications*. Philadelphia: The Charles Press, 1992 (pp. 56-60).

Katz, A. & Bender, E.(eds.) *The Strength in us: Self-Help Groups in the Modern World*. New York: New Viewpoints/Vision Books, 1976.

Katz, A. & Bender, E. (eds.) *Helping One Another*, Oakland, Third Party Publishing. 1990.

Katz, A., & Bender, E. Social learning and group dynamics in self-help. In Katz & Bender (eds.), *Helping One Another*. Oakland: Third Party Publishing. 1990a.

Kaufman, C., Freund, P., & Wilson, J. Self-help in the mental health system: A model for consumer-provider collaboration. *Psychosocial Rehabilitation Journal*, 1989, 13(1), 5-21.

Killilea, M. Mutual help organizations: Interpretations in the literature. In Caplan & Killilea (eds.), *Support Systems and Mutual Help*. New York: Grune & Stratton, 1976 (pp. 37-93).

Klass, D. The dynamics of self-help in healing parental grief: The role of the compassionate friends. In Katz, Hedrick, Isenberg, Thompson, Goodrich, & Kutscher (eds.), *Self-Help: Concepts and Applications*. Philadelphia: The Charles Press, 1992 (pp. 231-249).

Knight, B., Wollert, R., Levy, L., Frame, C. & Padgett, V. Self-help groups: Members' perspective. *American Journal of Community Psychology*, 1980, 8(1), 53-65.

Kropotkin, P. *Mutual Aid: A Factor in Evolution*. New York: New York University Press, 1972.

Kurtz, L. Twelve-step programs. In T. Powell (ed.), *Working With Self-Help*. Silver Spring: NASW Press, 1990a (pp. 93-119).

Kurtz, L. The self-help movement: Review of the past decade of research. *Social Work with Groups*, 1990b, 13(3), 101-115.

LeVeck, P. Self-help in a manic depressive association. In Weber & Cohen (eds.), *Beliefs and Self-Help: Cross-Cultural Perspectives and Approaches*. New York: Human Services Press, 1982 (pp. 235-265).

Leventhal, G., Maton, K., & Madara, E. Systemic organizational support for self-help groups. *American Journal of Orthopsychiatry*, 1988, 58(4), 592-603.

Levy, L. Self-help groups: Types and psychological processes. *Journal of Applied Behavioral Science*, 1976, 12(3), 310-322.

Levy, L. Processes and activities in self-help groups. In Lieberman & Borman (eds.), *Self-Help Groups for Coping with Crisis*. San Francisco: Jossey-Bass, 1979.

Levy, L. Mutual support groups in Great Britain: A survey. *Social Science in Medicine*, 1982, 16, 1267-1275.

Lieberman, M., & Borman, L. Epilogue: Self-help and social research. *Journal of Applied Behavioral Science*, 1976, 12(3), 455-463.

Mack, S., & Berman, L. A group for parents of children with fatal genetic illnesses. *American Journal of Orthopsychiatry*, 1988, 58(3), 397-404.

Madara, E. The self-help clearinghouse operation: Tapping the resource development potential of I & R Services. *Information and Referral: The Journal of the Alliance of Information and Referral Systems*, 1985, 7(1), 42-58.

Marieskind, H. Women's self-help groups. In Gartner & Riessman (eds.), *The Self-Help Revolution*. New York: Human Sciences Press, Inc., 1984, pp. 27-32.

Marris, P. *Loss and Change*. New York: Pantheon, 1974.

McCarthy, J. and Zald M. Resource mobilization and social movements: A partial theory. *American Journal of Sociology*, 1977, 82:1212-1241.

McCarthy, J. and Zald, M. *The Trend of Social Movements in American: Professionalization and Resource Mobilization*. Morristown, N.J.: General Learning Press, 1973.

McWhirter, B., McWhirter, E., and McWhirter, J. Groups in Latin America: *Comunidades Eclesial de Base* as mutual support groups. *Journal for Specialists in Group Work*, 1988, 13, 70-76.

Medvene, L, & Krauss, D. Causal attributes and parent-child relationships in a self-help group of families of the mentally ill. *Journal of Applied Social Psychology*, 1989, 19, 1413-1430.

Mellor, M., Rzetelny, H., & Hudis, I., Self-help groups for caregivers of the aged. In Gartner & Riessman (eds.), *The Self-Help Revolution*. New York: Human Sciences Press, 1984.

Mullan, F. Rewriting the social contract in health. In Katz, Hedrick, Isenberg, Thompson, Goodrich, & Kutscher (eds.), *Self-Help: Concepts and Applications*. Philadelphia: The Charles Press, 1992 (pp. 61-67).

Naisbit, J. *Megatrends*. New York: Warner, 1982.

Neighbors, H., & Jackson, J. The use of informal and formal help: Four patterns of illness behavior in the black community. *American Journal of Community Psychology*, 1984, 12(6), 629-644.

Neighbors, H., Elliott, K. & Gant, L. Self-help and black Americans. In T. Powell (ed.). *Working with Self-Help*. Silver Spring: NASW. 1990 (pp. 189-217).

Nisbet, R. Moral values and community. *International Review of Community Development*, 1960. No. 5.

Pancoast, D., Parker, P., & Froland, C. (eds.), *Rediscovering Self-Help: Its Role in Social Care*. Beverly Hills: Sage Publications. 1983.

Parker, P., Pancoast, D., & Froland, C. Wheels in motion. In Pancoast, Parker & Froland (eds.), *Rediscovering Self-Help*. Beverly Hills: Sage Publications, 1983.

Parsons, T. *The Social System*. Glencoe: The Free Press, 1951.

Pilisuk, M., & Minkler, M. Supportive networks: Life ties for the elderly. *Journal of Social Issues*, 1980, 36(2), 95-116.

Powell, T. *Self-Help Organizations and Professional Practice.* Silver Spring: NASW. 1987.
Powell, T. Social networks and self-help organizations. In Powell (ed.), *Working with Self-Help.* Silver Spring, MD: NASW, 1990 (pp. 71-92).
Reynolds, J. Water for Karas: Harambee In West Pokot, Kenya. In Weber & Cohen (eds.), *Beliefs and Self-Help: Cross-cultural Perspectives and Approaches.* New York: Human Services Press, 1982 (pp.75-125).
Richardson, A. English self-help: Varied patterns and practices. In Pancoast, Parker, and Froland (eds.), *Rediscovering Self-Help: Its Role in Social Care.* Beverly Hills: Sage Publications, 1983 (pp. 203-221).
Riessman, F. The "helper-therapy" principle. *Social Work*, 10, 2, 1965, 27-32.
Rodgers, A., & Tartaglia, L. Constricting resources: A black self-help initiative. *Administration in Social Work*, 1990. 14(2), 125-137.
Romeder, J. *The Self-Help Way: Mutual Aid and Health.* Ottawa: Canadian Council on Social Development, 1990.
Sennett, R. *The Fall of Public Man.* New York: Knopf, 1977.
Sidel, R. Self-help and mutual aid in the People's republic of China. In Katz & Bender (eds.), *The Strength in Us.* New York: New Viewpoints, 1976 (pp. 216-228).
Silverman, P. et al. *Helping Each Other in Widowhood.* New York: Health Sciences, 1974.
Smith, D., & Pillemer, K. Self-help groups as social movement organizations: Social structure and social change. In Kriesberg, (ed.), *Research in Social Movements, Conflict and Change.* Greenwich, CT: JAI Press, Vol. 5, 1983, 203-233.
Spiegel, D., Bloom, J.R., Kraemer, H.C., & Gottheil, E. Effect of psychosocial treatment on survival of patients with metastatic breast cancer. *Lancet*, 1989, 2, 888-891.
Steinman, R., & Traunstein, D. Redefining deviance: The self-help challenge to the human services. *Journal of Applied Behavioral Science*, 1976, 12(3), 347-361.
Suttles, G. *The Social Construction of Communities.* Chicago: University of Chicago Press, 1972.
Telch, C., & Telch, M. Group coping skills instruction and supportive group therapy for cancer patients: A comparison of strategies. *Journal of Consulting & Clinical Psychology*, 1986, 54, 802-808.
Theirs, N. Self-help movement gains strength, offers hope. *Guidepost*, 1987, 30(9), 1, 8, 16.
Toffler, A. *The Third Wave.* New York: William Morrow & Co., 1980.
Trojan, A. Groupes de sante: The users' movement in France. In Hatch & Kickbush (eds.) *Self-Help and Health in Europe: New Approaches in Health care.* Copenhagen: WHO, 1983.
Trojan, A., Halves, E. and Wetendorf, H.W. Self-help groups and consumer participation: A look at the German health care self-help movement. *Journal of Voluntary Action Research*, 1986, 15(2), 14-23.

Trojan, A. Benefits of self-help groups: A survey of 232 members from 65 disease-related groups. *Social Science and Medicine*, 1989, 29(2), 225-232.

Unell, J. *Help for Self-Help*. London: Bedford Square Press/NCVO, 1987.

van Harberden, P. Self-help behind the dikes. In Katz & Bender (eds.), *Helping One Another.* Oakland: Third Party Publishing, 1990 (pp. 215-223).

van Harberden, P. & Raymakers, T. Self-help and governmental policy in the Netherlands. *Journal of Voluntary Action Research*, 1986, 15(2), 24-32.

Videka-Sherman, L. Effects of participation in a self-help group for bereaved parents: Compassionate Friends. *Prevention in Human Services*, 1982, 1, 69-78.

Videka-Sherman, L. Bereavement self-help organizations. In T. Powell (ed.), *Working With Self-Help.* Silver Spring: NASW Press, 1990 (pp. 156-174).

Vine, P., & Beels, C. Support and advocacy groups for the mentally ill. In Herz, Keith & Docherty (eds.), *Handbook of Schizophrenia, Vol. 4: Psychosocial Treatment of Schizophrenia.* Elsevier Science Publishers, 1990 (pp. 387-405).

Vugia, H. Support groups in oncology: Building hope through the human bond. *Journal of Psychosocial Oncology*, 1991, 9(3), 89-105.

Weber, G., Self-help and belief. In Weber & Cohen (eds.), *Beliefs and Self-Help: Cross-cultural Perspectives and Approaches.* New York: Human Services Press, 1982 (pp. 13-30).

Withorn, A. Helping ourselves: The limits and potentials of self help. *Social Policy*, 1980, 11(3), 20-28.

Yoak, M., & Chesler, M. Alternative professional roles in health care delivery: Leadership patterns in self-help groups. *Journal of Applied Behavioral Science*, 1985, 21(4), 427-444.

Chapter 2

Participatory Action Research as a Strategy for Studying Self-Help Groups Internationally

Thomasina Borkman
Marsha Schubert

George Mason University

SUMMARY. Cultural phenomena in which individuals and groups develop their own meaning systems and practices are vitally implicated in considering research on self-help groups internationally or interculturally. Qualitative participatory action research (PAR) is described as an appropriate research strategy for gaining indepth knowledge and insight into cultural phenomena associated with self-help groups. PAR as defined here draws on the traditions of action science (used by William Foote Whyte and others) in studying industrial organizations and on participatory research (used by L. David Brown and Rajesh Tandon and others) in studying communities in Third World countries. PAR involves a form of applied social research. The participants share at least some power and ownership

---

The authors thank Mark Chesler, Keith Humphreys, Benjamin Gidron, and Maria Parisi for their thoughtful reviews of an earlier draft of this paper.

Address correspondence to Thomasina Borkman, Department of Sociology, George Mason University, 4400, University Drive, Fairfax, VA USA 22030.

[Haworth co-indexing entry note]: "Participatory Action Research as a Strategy for Studying Self-Help Groups Internationally." Borkman, Thomasina and Marsha Schubert. Co-published simultaneously in *Prevention in Human Services* (The Haworth Press, Inc.) Vol. 11, No. 1, 1994, pp. 45-68; and: *Self-Help and Mutual Aid Groups: International and Multicultural Perspectives* (ed: Francine Lavoie, Thomasina Borkman, and Benjamin Gidron) The Haworth Press, Inc., 1994, pp. 45-68. Multiple copies of this article/chapter may be purchased from The Haworth Document Delivery Center [1-800-3-HAWORTH; 9:00 a.m. - 5:00 p.m. (EST)].

of the research with the researcher through their involvement in the design, data collection, analysis and action phases. The characteristics of PAR are described. A case study that illustrates the use of PAR in studying the experiential knowledge created by a group of parents with gifted and learning disabled children is presented. The usefulness of PAR for cross-cultural and intercultural research is outlined.

INTRODUCTION

In their conceptual framework for studying international and intercultural aspects of self-help groups (SHGs) in this volume, Gidron and Chesler distinguish three levels of analysis: the national societal level, racial/ethnic/religious or demographic differences within a society, and the focal problem for which the SHG is formed. All three levels importantly involve cultural phenomena in which individuals and groups develop and use their own meaning systems. As we know from anthropology, cultural phenomena are easily misunderstood and interpreted by observers if they are not studied intensively and appropriately (Geertz 1973). The question arises then as to what are appropriate methodological paradigms for studying SHGs internationally and interculturally.

In this paper we propose qualitative participatory action research (PAR) as an appropriate methodological strategy for studying the cultural aspects of SHGs. Participatory action research is proposed as one suitable approach to researching SHGs. First, we will discuss some of the culture constructing aspects of SHGs, including experiential knowledge. The inadequacies of conventional quantitative approaches toward understanding SHGs will be manifest; instead, special qualitative methods that allow one to capture the meanings of actions and words in all their richness are necessary. Second, we describe PAR as a methodological strategy, and contrast it briefly with more positivistic ones that primarily utilize quantitative techniques. Third, we will present a case study of PAR to illustrate the approach and its fruitfulness for capturing meaning systems. The case study will illustrate how PAR was used in a project to identify the experiential knowledge developed within a SHG for parents of intellectually gifted and learning disabled children. Fourth, we will conclude with some general ideas about the utility of PAR as a strategy in studying SHGs internationally and interculturally.

SELF-HELP GROUPS AS CULTURAL MEANING SYSTEMS

Recent research has turned to exploration of the cultural aspects of SHGs by which we mean the special experiential knowledge, meaning systems, customs, rituals, ideologies or world views, and languages developed and used by SHGs. Nearly twenty years ago Antze (1976) suggested the importance of the belief systems that SHGs develop about their common problems, but little attention was paid to it until recently. Now SHGs are being defined as "communities of interest" (Gidron & Chesler, in press) or "communities of belief" (Kennedy & Humphreys, in press) which spotlights their cultural aspects. As many papers in this volume demonstrate, SHGs are being explored as culture creating and transmitting groups that develop their own worldviews and accompanying experiential knowledge of their problem and its resolution. It has been recently recognized that worldviews are expressed through personal stories and narratives about the problem and its resolution by group members (Rappaport, in press; Humphreys, in press; Kennedy & Humphreys 1993). Experiential knowledge (Borkman 1976a, 1993), while regarded as valuable, has not been empirically researched until recently (Schubert 1991, Schubert & Borkman, in press).

SHGs usually evolve naturally within a geographical community and are intimately linked with their immediate locale. The participants who volunteer their time and resources choose their intensity, frequency and duration of involvement with the group. Accordingly, there are many patterns of participation and involvement among attendees. The cultural aspects of SHGs are both similar to the surrounding society of which they are a part and different from it. The SHGs' perspective of their problem(s) and how to resolve it is often discrepant from professionals' perspectives on the problem and/or with the lay public (Borkman 1990).

Accompanying the recent interest in the cultural aspects of SHGs has been a dawning recognition of diversity among self-help organizations even for the same problem and the same general meaning system [e.g., various local units of Alcoholics Anonymous (see Hoffman, 1984 or Mäkelä, 1993) or National Alliance for the Mentally Ill (see Perkins, Lafuze & Van Dusen, in press; Medvene and colleagues, in press)]. Diversity is even more likely across SHGs for different problems or with members from different demographic backgrounds or cultures. Neither the cultural features nor the diversity of groups has been researched to any extent within a society, much less cross-culturally. Moreover, when the focus is on international differences, we know almost nothing empirically about how the cultural aspects of SHGs for a specific problem are similar to and different from their equivalent SHGs in other societies. As we propose that more international and intercultural research be conducted, it is fortuitous and fortunate that the cultural aspects and diversity of SHGs are simultaneously being recognized and highlighted in this volume. The cultural aspects and resulting organizational diversity require methodological approaches that tap the richness and particularity of meanings and beliefs in groups. Given the potentially large amount of variation across cultures and problems in SHGs, it seems prudent to develop research strategies that are likely to discern this variation.

PARTICIPATORY ACTION RESEARCH AS A METHODOLOGICAL STRATEGY

In this section we first describe the characteristics of PAR (Chesler, 1991) as a strategy appropriate for the study of SHGs. The description is followed by a brief history of two traditions of PAR over the past 20 years. Then, PAR as defined here is discussed as falling more naturally under the naturalistic paradigm (Lincoln & Guba, 1985) which has also been proposed for the study of SHGs (Kennedy & Humphreys, 1993; Kennedy, Humphreys & Borkman, in press). The section concludes by contrasting PAR with positivistic strategies showing why the latter are less appropriate for studying SHGs cross-culturally.

PAR is a relatively new strategy that is still not widely known or used. PAR is a form of applied social research similar to action research in that the findings of research are used to change the group or to empower them to work for changes in their environment. PAR is a special form of action research in which some of the people in the community or group under study participate actively with the researcher throughout the research process and action phases of the project (Whyte, 1991, p. 20).

One objective of PAR is to obtain information that is closer to the participant's own experience than to that of the "objective" observer.

> Without collaborative and participatory procedures, not only are group members' interests easily violated but researchers increase their distance from the immediate experience of group members so substantially that they risk being out of touch with the reality of local knowledge and experience. (Chesler 1991, p. 764)

A second objective is to design the research process in a manner that will result in findings useful to the participants as well as in contributions to social science knowledge of the phenomena. The researcher is not claiming to be "objective" but takes a value stance and commitment to conduct the research in a manner that will produce results that can raise the consciousness and change the group or help the group change its external environment.

Participatory action research (PAR) or participatory research (PR) has developed out of differing traditions. Two major traditions will be considered here: one exemplified by Brown and Tandon (1983) and one represented by Whyte (1984, 1991). Brown and Tandon (1983) and Tandon (1988) come from a "participatory research" tradition that evolved from research on oppressed people in Third World countries. Freire's (1970) well known approach to adult education that engages people in critical analysis and organizes action to improve their situation is part of this tradition. The tradition assumes a conflict model of community relations in which the community power and resource distributions are not viewed as legitimate by the lower level participants.

The ideology and political economy of participatory research (Brown & Tandon, 1983) differs from Whyte's definition of PAR which evolved from the action research tradition. Whyte's early work (1984) with industrial organizations was in the action research tradition developed by Kurt Lewin, Chris Argyris, and others coming out of World War II research in the United States. In action research the legitimacy of national authorities is not questioned and social scientists focus on solving practical problems. They assume consensus models in which all parties to a situation could find mutually agreeable solutions to problems.

In 1991, Whyte edited a book titled *Participatory Action Research* which drew on earlier work on industrial organizations (Whyte, 1984) as well as recent work on agricultural development in Third World countries. Whyte defined PAR as a type of applied social research in which "some of the people in the organization or community under study participate actively with the professional researcher throughout the research process from initial design to final presentation of results and discussion of their action implications" (1991, p. 20). He contrasted PAR with the expert model in which the researcher controls the entire research process and the subjects' role is to consent to being involved in the research and to provide information as structured by the researcher.

In 1983, Brown and Tandon found that the two traditions of participatory research and action research were not in contact with each other based upon references in major bibliographies of each tradition. They attributed this mutual ignorance to differences in ideology and political economy. In 1991, Whyte and his contributors, including Argyris, referenced the action researchers such as Lewin, but did not reference the participatory researchers Brown, Tandon or others. Thus, there still seems to be little communication among the two traditions.

Whyte's definition of PAR will be used here as the basis of an expanded definition. What is missing from Whyte's 1991 definition is recognition of the range of involvement and related power and ownership over the research process that participants can have in relation to the researcher.

Chesler (1991) is the first to describe PAR as an alternative methodological strategy that is appropriate for the study of SHGs. Chesler (1993), in a personal communication, suggested that there is a continuum of forms of PAR that vary in the extent to which the participants share power and ownership of the research process with the researcher.

A simplified model of three categories of power and ownership of participants in the research process are distinguished here: slight, moderate and extensive. *Slight* power refers to the conventional model of the researcher as professional expert in which the subjects' power lies primarily in the right to refuse to participate or in their unwillingness to cooperate in completing data collection in good faith by answering honestly and accurately. *Moderate* power refers to participatory research in which all participants, including participants at lower levels of the organization or community, are involved with the researcher somewhat in decision making about the project's design, data collection, analysis and actions for change based on the results. *Extensive* power refers to research in which the participants, including lower level participants, share equal power and ownership of the project with the researcher. There is another degree of power which is excluded here in which lower level participants totally control the project and engage the researcher as a professional expert to work under their direction and control–this seems to circle back to the conventional model (of slight power) except that the people in power are at the bottom, not the top of the organization or community.

Only the moderate and extensive power forms of research would be categorized as PR (Brown & Tandon, 1983) or PAR (Whyte, 1991) in that the participants share at least some power and ownership in the research decision-making. Chesler's PAR in relation to SHGs (Chesler, 1991) did not distinguish between degrees of shared power but it is compatible with the proposed continuum described here.

Both traditions of PR and PAR have been developed during the past 20 years. Cancian and Armstead (1990) developed a partly annotated bibliography of the various topical areas in which PAR had been used by 1990: in addition to the PR tradition stemming primarily from research and adult education efforts in the Third World (Brown & Tandon, 1983; Tandon, 1988); and from feminist researchers (Bookman & Morgan, 1988; Maquire, 1987); studies of industrial societies include the social empowerment of citizens in communities (Gaventa, 1988), workplace relations (Sacks, 1988; Whyte, 1991), and education and health (Freire, 1970; Mies, 1983; Maquire, 1987).

Chesler (1991) contrasted PAR with the positivist paradigms that rely extensively on researcher controlled studies and that assume an "objective" observer whose exemplar is the classical experimental-control design using standardized measures that emphasize quantitative and statistical approaches. Recently a number of other strategies or paradigms have been proposed as alternatives to positivistic ones for studying SHGs including naturalistic inquiry (Kennedy & Humphreys, 1993; Kennedy, Humphreys & Borkman, in press), collaborative research (Rappaport and colleagues, 1985), and action research (Lavoie, 1984).

PAR as defined here falls under the naturalistic paradigm (see Kennedy & Humphreys, 1993; Kennedy, Humphreys & Borkman, in press). Naturalistic inquiry (Lincoln and Guba, 1985; Guba, 1990) is defined as a philosophical level paradigm that assumes that objectivity is impossible because human beings filter their observations through their culturally learned lenses; therefore, there are multiple realities constructed by human groups and individuals all of which are valid. Hence, universal generalizations about human behavior are impossible. Qualitative methods that can delve into local particular meanings, language, beliefs, etc., are necessary to adequately understand and study individuals and groups.

Both PAR and naturalistic inquiry make largely similar assumptions and have similar criticisms of positivism as an inappropriate approach to studying SHGs. Three major assumptions that importantly characterize naturalistic inquiry and PAR are that: (1) objectivity by a researcher is impossible to achieve; (2) the value orientation of the observer affects what and how s/he conducts research and needs to be admitted and dealt with throughout the research process; and (3) the status difference between the researcher and the participants is decreased because the participant's knowledge and views are respected as valuable.

Both PAR and naturalistic inquiry use similar methodological approaches that emphasize qualitative techniques providing intensive "thick" (Geertz, 1973) descriptions of the local situation and context. These qualitative approaches yield deep and rich understandings of the language, meanings, and perspectives of the people/group being researched–all of which are necessary for studying cultural aspects of SHGs. For example, often used techniques include indepth focused interviewing, participant observation, ethnographic field studies, participant's stories and personal narratives or oral histories, questionnaires, retrospective histories of the groups, and reviews of written materials produced by the groups. Quantitative methods could be used if they were grounded in and developed on the basis of the meanings of the local contexts. Standardized measuring instruments developed in and for other contexts would not usually be used.

An exemplar of the positivistic paradigm that has been applied inappropriately to SHGs (Lieberman & Bliwise, 1985; Levitz & Stunkard, 1974) is controlled psychotherapy effectiveness research (see Kennedy, Humphreys & Borkman, in press). SHGs do not meet the assumptions underlying controlled clinical trials with random assignment making these positivistic methodologies inappropriate. Controlled studies of psychotherapy make the assumption that treatment is a relatively specific intervention (like a drug dosage) that is administered over a relatively limited and calculable time period. You can measure the "subject's" initial status before and after the treatment. There is the assumption that there are no significant characteristics of "subjects" that affect their outcomes when they are randomly assigned to experimental and control conditions; in effect, treatment is assumed to have a measurable main effect regardless of the "subject's" motivation or type of involvement. There are, of course, other forms of treatment evaluation research that make assumptions closer to the ones we make.

In contrast to these assumptions, participation in SHGs is self-selective; only a small proportion of the people with a problem go to SHGs (Regier et al., 1993). Participation in SHGs is not a discrete event like attending a therapy session; instead, it can and often does include meetings before and after the "formal meetings," telephone calls, social events and often a social network of friends and support. Persons choose how extensively, with what frequency, and for what duration they will participate in the group. In addition, their participation also varies over time. Some self-helpers participate in a group for many years, and therefore there is no "outcome" because "treatment" never ends. Participants receive different benefits depending on their level of motivation, their intensity and frequency of participation (Borkman, 1976b). The researcher cannot control assignment to the group, extent of participation, or the nature of the intervention or it is not self-help mutual aid. The characteristics of SHGs, thus, are contrary to the characteristics of "treatment." Positivistic approaches designed for treatment effectiveness research are thus inappropriate for studying SHGs.

CASE STUDY OF RESEARCH ON EXPERIENTIAL KNOWLEDGE ABOUT PARENTING GIFTED AND LEARNING DISABLED CHILDREN

This case study is presented to illustrate the PAR approach and its fruitfulness for capturing meaning systems in SHGs. The project from which this case study was drawn was a doctoral dissertation by Marsha Schubert. The senior author was her dissertation co-adviser. Schubert's doctoral project followed a PAR approach although not initially named as such. The project would be classified as moderate on the continuum of power and ownership of participants described above.

Schubert had worked with exceptional children for approximately 15 years, primarily as a special education teacher of students with learning disabilities, some of whom were also intellectually gifted. She collaborated extensively with the SHG for parents of gifted and/or talented/learning disabled (GT/LD) children from its inception in 1987 for four years until 1991. Throughout the case study the researchers' involvement and attitudes are described because objectivity is considered impossible and we want to acknowledge the dispositions and potential biases of the researchers.

The case study is described in terms of five phases. We will briefly summarize each of the phases in terms of its objectives and the nature of the collaboration between the researchers and the parents and other participants of the SHG. Readers who are interested in more details about the rationale and specifics of some phase of the research process should see Schubert (1991) or Schubert and Borkman (in press). Phase 1 deals with how the SHG for parents of LD/GT children was developed including Schubert's role in the group. Phase 2 shows how the research, initiated by the researcher, was jointly planned with leaders and members of the group. Phase 3 describes how the first phase of data collection delineated the elements of experiential knowledge created by the group. Phase 4 chronicles how the second phase of data collection, a questionnaire survey was developed and administered. Phase 5 shows how study findings were fed back to the group for action purposes.

Development of the Group

The first stage describes how and why the group developed during its first four years from 1987-1991. Although Schubert was a cofounder of the group, her initial role was as an interested special education teacher who attended but did not lead the group.

Federal legislation mandates a free, appropriate public education for any United States student with a disability. Since state laws and school district policies must reflect this requirement, agencies, school districts and colleges have developed identification procedures, assessment practices and programs to provide the required services for these individuals, the majority of whom are diagnosed as learning disabled (LD). In addition, many states and school districts have developed methods of identifying and serving children who are intellectually gifted (GT) and/or talented, although these services are not ordained by federal law.

Students who are both LD and GT often encounter problems in obtaining the promised appropriate education because of three circumstances: (1) students' LD problems interfere with their academic performance to such an extent that they cannot meet eligibility requirements for GT programs, (2) students' intellectual abilities mask their LD problems so that they are not identified as disabled; instead, low achievement is often blamed on attitude or laziness, and (3) even if they are placed in an LD and/or GT program, the interaction of their disabilities and their giftedness results in needs which are not met in programs designed for either GT or LD students. Thus, parents of LD/GT students find no programs designed specifically for their children. Although such students are legally entitled to an individualized education, in most cases, their schools have failed to provide one.

Over the years, Schubert became aware that some of the students in her LD classes were extremely bright and needed special help. She worked with parents of these children to help solve their children's problems. After learning about the value of SHGs, Schubert and a parent co-founded the group for parents of GT and LD children in 1987. The SHG was formed largely to help these individuals understand the abilities and needs of their children, and to assist them in ensuring their children were provided the educational services to which they were legally entitled. The goals of the group were to provide families with support and information, to increase educators' awareness of the GT/LD population and its problems, and to pressure local schools into providing services and/or programs which better met the needs of these individuals.

The founders initially agreed that (1) the group should be run for and by parents rather than by professionals, as is typical in SHGs, (2) a list of attendees with pertinent information about them would be maintained to facilitate communication, (3) major portions of all meetings would be devoted to the sharing of information by attendees on an informal level, and (4) group leaders would make note of questions and topics of discussion related to parenting and/or educating children diagnosed as GT/LD at meetings or in other interactions.

Once meetings began, officers were selected. Schubert attended, took notes of meetings and provided technical information upon request, but had no official leadership role. The group meeting format was simple. The two-to-three hour monthly meetings began with an informal sharing time when people had a chance to talk, have refreshments and look at available materials in the group's collection. This was followed by a planned program of some sort–a presentation by a professional working in a field related to the problem, a panel discussion of parents or students, small group discussions of some aspect of a problem, a video, etc. Parents actively engaged presenters by questioning, debating, offering examples, challenging and/or supporting speakers, whether those speakers were professionals, self-helpers, or even a panel of their own members or of students who were GT/LD. Group leaders and some members took notes of issues raised at meetings. The meeting ended with more informal discussion time.

Over a three year period, the group's mailing list grew from 18 to 249. There were no criteria for attending meetings or joining the SHG. Registration lists show that attendance ranged from 15 to nearly 100, with the average falling between 25 and 30. Except for the officers and a few regulars, most members only attended meetings of interest to them and/or when they had a problem they wished to address.

The SHG was located in the northern part of Virginia, in a suburb of Washington, D.C. The group was largely comprised of middle-class, white women, but also included a number of parent couples and a few men. All members were high school graduates, and most had attended college; many had college degrees. Some members were professionals in fields related to the problem on which the group focused. Almost all members were parents or guardians of children considered to be simultaneously intellectually GT and LD.

Planning the Study

Schubert became interested in identifying the content and use of experiential knowledge (Borkman, 1976a) created by the group for her dissertation project after having worked with the group as an informal consultant about technical aspects of special education programs and an attendee for two years. Schubert's ongoing involvement with this group and her ready access to its records and attendees made it a logical subject for a proposed study on the experiential knowledge of such a group. Schubert shared parents' interest in building understanding of the GT/LD syndrome and in getting schools to more adequately address the needs of this special population. Because of her interest and her continuous involvement, she was an accepted part of the group and was actively involved in its activities.

Schubert approached leaders and active members of the group about the proposed study. After several informal discussions, they became very interested in having Schubert conduct the study and several volunteered to help her with it.

The study was designed to be conducted in two sequential phases. First, the content and categories of experiential knowledge that the group had created would be identified and verified with the participant volunteers. Through a content analysis of notes of meetings, newsletters, and the other written materials from the group, the elements of experiential knowledge would be identified and categorized into a manageable set of topics. Second, a survey of all attendees would be done to verify the elements of knowledge found in the first phase, and to see the relative use of experiential knowledge of parents in comparison with that of professionals. A questionnaire would be designed for the survey based on the results of the content analysis.

Although the leaders and members who were consulted generally endorsed the idea of generating new knowledge about SHGs and were willing to assist someone they considered a colleague and/or friend, their major rationale for agreeing to be involved in the study was that its outcomes would support their group goals of increasing membership and providing relevant information about the group. They were more interested in the outcomes of the research than in the process of conducting it. Specifically, they felt that the results of the study possibly could be used: (1) to organize and to articulate the knowledge of the group so that it might be more efficiently shared, particularly with non-group members like educators; (2) to identify areas or concerns which people felt needed to be addressed by the group; (3) to facilitate planning for future programs and events to make them more relevant to the needs of group members; and, (4) to increase the membership of the group and hopefully its influence in the schools.

The participants who volunteered to help the researcher were leaders and frequent attendees. Several parents who were leaders of the group or had attended meetings for at least two years assisted in planning, conducting, and evaluating the study. Among these were mothers of elementary and high school aged GT/LD children, a parent who was also a psychologist familiar with assessment techniques and school policy regarding LD/GT students, and a parent who came to the group looking for information about legal requirements of the schools and ideas for approaching school personnel. These and other self-helpers spent hours conferring with the researcher, critiquing the survey instrument, making follow-up phone calls, and sharing copies of their notes from meetings and other materials for the content analysis. The researchers took final responsibility for decisions made but the participants' ideas and recommendations were usually followed and they were partners in all phases of the study.

Delineating the Elements of Experiential Knowledge

The first phase of the study was to identify the elements of knowledge created by the group and to categorize them into a limited set of mutually exclusive categories. For this study, the best source of data about experiential knowledge was the content of personal interactions among group members or members and presenters. The most efficient means of collecting information was note taking by the researcher and by other members who had volunteered to help. These notes included brief summaries of conversations before and after the actual meetings, notations of topics of phone conversations when people called asking for advice or sharing some aspect of the problem, questions asked during presentations, remarks made during sharing sessions, and ideas for future programs.

This group was unusual in that note taking during meetings was a commonly accepted practice from its beginning and no one paid much attention to anyone who took notes during meetings. Officers, the researcher and other members had taken notes of issues raised, questions asked, and suggested solutions during meetings. Some officers and members made their personal notes available to Schubert.

Sources of data for the content analysis included researcher and members' notes, the group's newsletter (which often contained such items as meeting summaries and suggestions for such activities as aiding students with their homework), and the group's records–minutes of meetings, pamphlets describing the group, registration sheets, etc.

After the collection of information, the next step was to look for patterns within the collected data. A content analysis of the notes and records described above was done using the techniques of coding and indexing described by Bogdan and Bliken (1982). The combination of notes and documents yielded approximately 300 pages of typed material.

An inductive approach that follows the naturalistic paradigm was used to develop coding categories from the 300 pages of documented material and from the experiential knowledge of members. Schubert went through this material line by line to develop coding categories. Her attempts to develop a small number of workable categories were only partly successful until after she met with three officers asking for their suggestions. She showed them her work to date, including those instances that did not fit her preliminary categories. The result of the collaborative meeting was the development of eight categories into which data could be sorted. Once the data had been coded and indexed, Schubert made a list of items grouped by the eight categories. She again set a meeting asking four members to review the categories to determine if they agreed that the data categories were relevant, to ask if others should be added, and so on. The members concluded that the list was very inclusive and adequate.

Survey of the Use of Experiential Knowledge

Next, Schubert presented her proposed second phase of data collection to group members. Since only a small proportion of people on the mailing list attended meetings, a mailed questionnaire would reach more people who had children who were GT/LD, thus potentially adding to the information available there.

In developing the survey instrument, Schubert worked with several members who volunteered to furnish materials, advice and time to the project. A draft instrument was constructed according to the researcher's objectives; items were based on the results of the content analysis from Phase 3. Next, the draft was critiqued by a panel of reviewers–four members mentioned earlier and researchers who had used questionnaires in work with SHGs. A number of suggestions were made by reviewers. For example, one member suggested that the proposed questionnaire include data about private as well as public school enrollment and about parent comfort levels in talking to professionals. Because of these comments, the questionnaire distinguished among different kinds of professionals which in turn led to one of the major findings of the study.

The instrument was revised to incorporate most of the members' and other reviewers' suggestions. Two new sections included items related to relationships between group members and professionals and to the value placed on different types of knowledge. One section sought information regarding members' comfort levels when interacting with professionals, self-helpers and lay persons. The other section presented respondents with hypothetical situations and asked them to indicate the person they would most likely turn to for help or support: professionals with specialized knowledge, general educators, parents who had a child with similar problems, or close friends or family members. The purpose of this section was primarily to see how these self-helpers valued experiential knowledge compared to specialist or generalist professional, or to lay knowledge. The final questionnaire contained quantitative Likert-scale ratings as well as open ended questions for narrative answers.

Leaders and members enthusiastically advertised the survey, encouraging attendees and members to complete the survey when they received it. The survey was announced in the newsletter. The questionnaire was mailed to every person/couple who had been registered as having attended a meeting of the parent group from the time the group was founded in 1987 to 1990. Thus, the population was self-selected, as it has been in many other studies of SHGs (e.g., Jacobs & Goodman, 1989; Powell, 1985).

Schubert mailed out 249 questionnaires accompanied by a cover letter signed by her and a self-addressed, stamped return envelope. After one month, 141 people had returned their questionnaires. Several members volunteered to telephone all those who had not responded. A final total of 181 questionnaires (73%) were returned after these follow-up phone calls. Among the 64 dues-paying members, 97% responded. Thus, the members' help in encouraging participation initially and with the follow-up resulted in a higher response rate for the survey.

Feedback Findings to the Group for Action Purposes

Upon final analysis of the questionnaire data and collection of input from group members and advisors, Schubert (1991) concluded the study had four major sets of findings. This paper discusses only selected findings dealing with the members' use of experiential knowledge, the professional knowledge of specialists (e.g., private practitioners such as psychologists or psychiatrists or special education teachers in schools) and of generalist (e.g., public school personnel and family physicians) professionals. See Schubert (1991) for the remaining findings.

The distinction between specialist and generalist professionals, which was identified during the construction of the survey, led to a major finding. The self-help literature had many references to the strained relationships between self-helpers and professionals (e.g.,

Chamberlin & Rogers, 1990; Powell, 1987, 1990; Suler, 1984). Indeed, this group had decided that professionals could not hold leadership roles in the group–only parents. Some self-helpers felt that public school personnel and private practitioners had responded differently to their problems. The results of the study, however, revealed a somewhat different division–one between generalists and specialists who worked with these children. We found that participants relied on the professional knowledge of specialists almost as much as they did on the experiential knowledge of veteran parents. But generalist professionals (and families and friends) were viewed as much less helpful sources of support and suggestions than specialists or experienced parents.

The results of the survey indicated that specialists within the schools were appreciated as well as those in the private sector. In addition, generalists in the private sector (i.e., family physicians, tutors) were often considered problematic by self-helpers; this was especially true when those practitioners charged money but seemed unable to be of any real assistance to the child or the family.

The members used this information for taking action. First, they indicated they would be more willing to talk with and refer others to specialists in the public schools, especially those who had been helpful to other parents. They began to consider higher-level administrators in special education and the staff of the parent resource center as potential sources of help in dealing with middle management school level personnel who seemed to hinder rather than assist in the provision of special education services. They also discussed ways in which they might provide information to generalists or even to involve them in the group itself. A few people, for example, invited their children's teachers to group meetings, and at least one person paid membership dues for both her son's teacher and his principal. Thus, this finding led group members to valuable sources of assistance and eased the confrontational attitude some held toward the public schools. In doing so, the self-helpers enjoyed a moderate degree of power and ownership as participants in this research.

This study, based on PAR, was productive in several ways. One positive outcome of this project was the information which the group wanted in addition to that which was of interest to researchers. When the final results were presented to group leaders, they gained some ideas for making the group more valuable for current and potential members. They also obtained a categorized summary of areas in which individuals had developed knowledge based upon their concerns for and experiences with their children with GT/LD problems. Finally, they stated that they had a better idea of how to plan future meetings based upon the handwritten comments in the questionnaires and the indications of the value of information from people who had "been there" as well as from specialists.

The study yielded procedural information about how a researcher could go about exploring the nebulous and concrete entity of experiential knowledge. Although the PAR process described herein is demanding in some ways, particularly in requiring close association with the group being studied, extensive time, and often complex logistics to assemble the members to collaborate with the researcher, it exemplifies one way in which research in experiential knowledge could be approached.

Finally, it generated a number of findings, only some of which were presented here. Of these, perhaps the most intriguing involves the distinction these self-helpers made between specialist and generalist professionals. This finding, as well as the others, could easily lead to other research projects which would hopefully continue to expand our understanding and appreciation of the experiential knowledge produced by SHGs.

DISCUSSION AND CONCLUSIONS

This paper suggests that PAR is an appropriate strategy for studying SHGs interculturally and internationally. PAR has been discussed as a form of action research based on naturalistic inquiry, a philosophical level paradigm that subsumes PAR. PAR (and naturalistic inquiry) involves a radically different stance toward "objectivity" and the people and groups being researched in positivistic paradigms. Individuals and groups, including researchers, are seen to create their own version of social reality grounded in their values, beliefs, previous experiences, and training, etc. Since all observers are constructing their own versions of reality, the researchers' version is not inherently superior to that of the participants. The

PAR researcher views ordinary people as knowledgeable and/or capable of learning; their everyday experience and feelings are a major source of knowledge. The PAR researcher respects people as valuable assets and partners and shares power with them at every stage of the research. In contrast, the positivistic researcher is the "professional expert" who assumes that there is no proactive participation of subjects in the study or that they have little or no valuable knowledge to contribute.

In the case study presented here, the researcher's objective was to identify the experiential knowledge created and used by the SHG for parents with learning disabled and gifted children. She assumed that the group not only had developed experiential knowledge about dealing with their children's common problems, but that it was different from professional knowledge of the same topic. The leaders and some members of the group co-planned and jointly implemented the study with the researcher partly for their self-interest–they wanted information that would help them improve the functioning of their group. Without the self-helpers as partners, the study's objective could not have been accomplished since the self-helpers were the only ones with the experiential knowledge.

The case study also shows how the SHG benefitted from the skills and expertise of the researcher and from the results of the study. Members were unlikely to learn what they did about their group without the disciplined methods of inquiry applied by the researcher. The group then used the results of the study to improve their programs, recruitment, and activist efforts to improve services their children received from the school system. From a scholarly point of view the most interesting finding of the study was the distinction between specialist and generalist professional which has not been made in empirical research before in the literature on SHGs. This useful distinction arose out of the interaction between the researcher and the self-helpers, and it is unlikely that it would have been detected if a more positivistic approach were used in this research.

Approaching this research as an interested member, Schubert was able to introduce and guide the research while SHG members shared somewhat in the decision making throughout the various phases of the project. This case study falls in the moderate category of power and ownership of the participants as described in the section on PAR as a methodological strategy.

PAR seems to be a very appropriate approach for intercultural and cross-cultural research because it captures the richness and particularity of meanings, language and beliefs, that is, the very stuff of culture. In addition to this technical appropriateness, however, PAR is politically and socially appropriate for cross-cultural and intercultural research. Most research on SHGs has been done in a few countries such as United States, Canada, England and Germany–all developed, industrialized countries. In international research there are sensitive political and social issues about the potential imperialism of researchers from the developed countries imposing their beliefs and paradigms on those from countries with less developed research infrastructures. Similarly, in intercultural research PAR is a strategy that avoids some of these potential problems because of its assumptions about the research process. Instead of the elite structure of positivistic approaches in which the researcher is regarded as an expert, in PAR the researcher and the self-help participant are regarded as partners in the process.

Some obstacles to using PAR are apparent from the case study, and other obstacles need to be identified. The case study suggests that identifying cultural aspects of a SHG through PAR is very labor intensive and time consuming on the part of the researcher. In addition, the researcher needs to have a special relationship of trust and acceptance with the group which may take a long time and special circumstances to nurture. We do not think that the case study implies that only researchers who are cofounders and intimately involved with the group over a long time period are appropriate for PAR. In our experience, there are a large number of researchers who are basically sympathetic and involved with the groups they research. Some have personally experienced the problem of the group that they study (Chesler, 1991) while others have not. Another obstacle is the potential problem of positivistically trained researchers attempting to use PAR without having the consciousness to relinquish their elite status and to sincerely regard self-helpers as partners in the research enterprise (see Kennedy, Humphreys & Borkman, in press).

In conclusion, PAR has been introduced as one methodological approach to studying SHGs interculturally and internationally. It has raised a few but by no means all of the issues that need to be discussed about conducting cross-cultural research. Hopefully this paper will serve to open a dialogue about appropriate methodologies for studying SHGs internationally.

REFERENCES

Antze, P. (1976). The role of ideologies in peer psychotherapy organizations: Some theoretical considerations and three case studies. *Journal of Applied Behavioral Science*, 12, 323-346.

Bogdan, R. C., & Bliken, S. K. (1982). *Qualitative Research for Education: An Introduction to Theory and Methods*. Boston: Allyn & Bacon, Inc.

Bookman, A., & Morgen, S., Eds. (1988). *Women and the Politics of Empowerment*. Philadelphia: Temple University Press.

Borkman, T. (1976a). Experiential knowledge: A new concept for the analysis of self-help groups. *Social Science Review*, 50, 445-455.

Borkman, T. (1976b). Participation patterns and benefits of membership in a self-help organization of stutterers. Pp. 81-90. In Katz, A. H. & Bender, E.I. (eds.), *The Strength in us: self-help groups in the modern world*. NY: Franklin Watts.

Borkman, T. (1990). Experiential, professional and lay frames of reference. In T. J. Powell (ed.), *Working with Self-Help* (pp. 3-30). Silver Spring, MD: NASW Press.

Brown, L.D., & Tandon, R. (1983). Ideology and political economy in inquiry: Action research and participatory research. *Journal of Applied Behavioral Science*, 19, 277-294.

Cancian, F. & Armstead, C. (1990). *Participatory Research: An Introduction*. Irvine, CA: Department of Sociology, UC-Irvine. (mimeo).

Chamberlin, J., & Rogers, J.A. (1990). Planning a community-based mental health system: Perspective of service recipients. *American Psychologist*, 45, 1241-1244.

Chesler, M. (1991) Participatory action research with self-help groups: An alternative paradigm for inquiry and action. *American Journal of Community Psychology*, 19, 757-768.

Chesler, M. (1993). Personal communication.

Freire, P. (1970). *Pedagogy of the Oppressed*. NY: Seabury Press.

Gaventa, J. (1988). Participatory research in North America. *Convergence*, 21 (2/3), 41-46.

Geertz, C. (1973). *The Interpretation of Cultures*. NY: Basic Books.

Gidron, B., & Chesler, M. (1994). Universal and particular attributes of self help: A framework for international and intranational analysis. In F. Lavoie, B. Gidron, & T. Borkman (eds.), Special issue on international self-help. *Prevention in Human Services* 11(1).

Guba, Egon (ed.). 1990. *The Paradigm Dialog*. Newbury Park, CA: Sage.
Hoffman, F. (1984) Transcultural adaptation of Alcoholics Anonymous to serve Hispanic populations. Unpublished paper.
Humphreys, K. (1993). *World view transformation in adult children of alcoholics mutual help groups*. Doctoral dissertation, University of Illinois, Urbana.
Jacobs, M. K., & Goodman, G. (1989). Psychology and self-help groups: Predictions on a partnership. *American Psychologist*, 44, 1-10.
Kennedy, M. & Humphreys, K. (1993, June). *Promises and perils of naturalistic research with mutual help groups*. Paper presented at the Fourth Biennial Conference on Community Research and Action, Williamsburg, VA.
Kennedy, M. & Humphreys, K. (1994). Understanding worldview transformation in members of mutual help groups. In F. Lavoie, B. Gidron & T. Borkman, eds. Special issue on international self-help. *Prevention in Human Services*.
Kennedy, M., Humphreys, K. & Borkman, T. (In press). The naturalistic paradigm as an alternative approach in research with mutual help groups. In T. Powell (ed.), *Understanding self-help organizations: Frameworks and findings*. Newbury Park, California: Sage.
Lavoie, F. (1984). Action research: A new model of interaction between the professional and self-help groups. In A. Gartner & F. Riessman (Eds.), *The Self-Help Revolution*. New York: Human Sciences.
Levitz, L.S., & Stunkard, A.J. (1974). A therapeutic coalition for obesity: Behavior modification and patient self-help. *American Journal of Psychiatry*, 131, 423-427.
Lieberman, M.A., & Bliwise, N.G. (1985). Comparisons among peer and professionally directed groups for the elderly: Implications for the development of self-help groups. *International Journal of Group Psychotherapy*, 35, 155-175.
Lincoln, Y., & Guba, E. (1985). *Naturalistic inquiry*. Beverly Hills: Sage.
Mäkelä, Klaus (1993). Implications for Research of the cultural variability of Alcoholics Anonymous. In B.S. McCrady & W.R. Miller (eds.), *Research on Alcoholics Anonymous: Opportunities and Challenges* (pp. 189-208). New Brunswick, NJ: Rutgers Center on Alcohol Studies.
Maquire, P. (1987). Doing participatory research: A feminist approach. Amherst, MA: Center for International Education, Univ. of Mass.
Medvene, L.J., Lin, K-M., Wu, A., Mendoza, R., Harris, N. & Miller, M. (In press). Mexican American and Anglo American parents of the mentally ill: Attitudes and participation in family support groups. In Lavoie, F., Gidron, B., & Borkman, T. (eds.) Special issue on international self-help. *Prevention in Human Services*.
Mies, M. (1983). Toward a methodology for feminist research. In Gloria Bowles and Renate D. Klein (eds.), *Theories of Women's studies*, pp. 117-139. London: Routledge and Kegan Paul.
Orefice, P. (1988). Participatory research in Southern Europe. *Convergence*, 21: 39-48.
Perkins, D.V., Lafuze, J. E., & Van Dusen, C. (In press). Social climate correlates of effectiveness in Alliance for the Mentally Ill groups. In F. Lavoie, B.

Gidron, & T. Borkman (eds.), Special issue on international self-help. *Prevention in Human Services.*

Powell, T. J. (1985). Improving the effectiveness of self-help. *Social Policy*, 16 (2), 22-29.

Powell, T. (1987). *Self-help organizations and professional practice.* Silver Spring, Maryland: National Association of Social Workers.

Powell, T. J. (1990). Self-help, professional help, and informal help: Competing or complementary systems? In T. J. Powell (ed.), *Working with Self-Help.* Silver Spring, MD: NASW.

Rappaport, J. (In press). Narrative studies, personal stories, and identity transformation in the mutual help context. (*JABS*, Tom Powell (ed.), special issue on self-help).

Rappaport, J., Seidman, E., Toro, P., McFadden, L., Reischel, T., Roberts, L., Salem, D., & Zimmerman, M. (1985). Collaborative research with a mutual help organization. *Social Policy*, 15(3), 12-24.

Reiger, D.A., Narrow, W.E., Rae, D.S., Manderscheid, R.W., Locke, B.Z., & Goodwin, F.K. (1993). The de facto US mental and addictive disorders service system. *Archives of General Psychiatry*, 50, 85-94.

Sacks, K. (1988). Caring by the hour. Urbana: Univer. of Illinois Press.

Schubert, M. A. (1991). Investigating experiential knowledge in a self-help group. Unpublished doctoral dissertation, George Mason University.

Schubert, M. A. & Borkman, T. (1994). Identifying the experiential knowledge created by a self-help group. In T. Powell (ed.), *Understanding self-help organizations: Frameworks and findings.* Newbury Park, California: Sage.

Suler, J. (1984). Role of ideology in self-help groups. *Social Policy*, 14 (3), 29-36.

Tandon, R. (1988). Social transformation and participatory research. *Convergence*, XXI (2/3), 5-15.

Whyte, W. F. (ed.), (1984). *Learning from the field: A guide from experience.* Newbury Park, CA: Sage.

Whyte, W. F. (ed.), (1991). *Participatory Action Research.* Newbury Park, CA: Sage.

Chapter 3

Self-Help Groups in Japan: Trends and Traditions

Tomofumi Oka

Sophia University

SUMMARY. Western concepts of self-help were developed in unique Western culture: in Judeo-Christian, individualistic, and pluralistic culture. To use these concepts in Japanese culture effectively, we remove peculiar cultural factors from them, and identify basic elements and processes of self-help groups which are universally effective in various cultures. They are sponteneous sharing [wakachiai], individual independence [hitoridachi], and emancipation from suppression [tokihanachi]. However, Japan's long history of isolation and feudal suppression generated peculiar groupism or group-oriented culture. The basic elements and processes of self-help groups are prone to be distorted by Japan's group-oriented culture, which values emotional cohesiveness, non-individualism, homogeneity, hierarchy, and the particular patterns of their social behaviors. Additionally, we identify political obstacles to the development of self-help groups in Japan–they are lack of pluralism and centralization of administrative power. People avoid becoming polit-

The author would like to thank Dr. Benjamin Gidron and Mrs. Shirley St. John for their comments on the manuscript.

Address correspondence to Tomofumi Oka, Department of Social Welfare, Faculty of Humanities, Sophia University, 7-1, Kioichi, Chiyoda-Ku, Tokyo, 102 Japan.

[Haworth co-indexing entry note]: "Self-Help Groups in Japan: Trends and Traditions." Oka, Tomofumi. Co-published simultaneously in *Prevention in Human Services* (The Haworth Press, Inc.) Vol. 11, No. 1, 1994, pp. 69-95; and: *Self-Help and Mutual Aid Groups: International and Multicultural Perspectives* (ed: Francine Lavoie, Thomasina Borkman, and Benjamin Gidron) The Haworth Press, Inc., 1994, pp. 69-95. Multiple copies of this article/chapter may be purchased from The Haworth Document Delivery Center [1-800-3-HAWORTH; 9:00 a.m. - 5:00 p.m. (EST)].

ical minorities under the cultural pressure, and they have respect for the governmental authorities.

INTRODUCTION

Group-Orientedness in the Isolated Country and Communities

Japan is geographically isolated by sea. The Straits of Tsushima, which is between Japan and Korea, is much larger and difficult to cross than the Straits of Dover. "Throughout most of its history Japan has been perhaps the most isolated of all the major countries of the world" (Reischauer, 1988, p. 31). Sea and raging waves protected Japan from alien invaders. Japan is a rare country, which had no experience of being occupied by people of different races in its recorded history until the end of World War II. Additionally, Japan had more than two centuries of self-imposed seclusion until various Westerners came by ship in the 1850s. Clark (1977, pp. 228-231) states that the origins of Japanese uniqueness were based on this fact: in its own territory, Japan had been free from serious conflicts with people of other races within its recorded history. Furthermore, Japanese people never experienced the migration of a nation, and had few frontiers. This history of isolation produced an extremely homogeneous society in Japan.

Not only Japan but also small Japanese communities themselves were isolated from and shut off from each other in the feudal age. From the 17th century to the 19th century, Japanese peasants, who constituted most of the total population, were bound to their very small pieces of land without freedom of movement, and people were forced to pay tax on collective responsibility, as groups of people living on the same piece of land. They were compelled to unite and help each other. Under such circumstances, people had many kinds of groups. Many of them were organized under the age-grading system. The age-grading system has operated not only in Japan, but also in East Africa, the northeast and central parts of India, parts of the Pacific Islands, and parts of southern Brazil. This system is strong in societies where blood relationships are weak, and it produces strong horizontal affiliation among the age-mates of the same age-grade (Takahashi, 1977). Not only men, but also women, had such peer groups in traditional Japanese societies, according to their familial status–such as daughter-in-law (young mother), housewife, and retired woman (Ôtsuki, 1968). These traditional groups did not permit people to join or leave voluntarily and their membership was decided by traditional rules (Hasegawa, 1986, p. 89). These traditions partly remain in modern Japanese communities, and people tend to form groups according to age-grade and/or familial status. These traditional groups were often used as mutual-watch mechanisms by rulers. By fixing interlocking responsibilities upon the people, the rulers manipulated these mutual-watch mechanisms to oppress and control people for hundreds of years. Groups were ordered to bear group taxation and to prevent any one of the members from committing crimes.

In 1868, during the Meiji Restoration, Japan escaped from the long feudal age and started to develop into a modernized and industrialized country. The very short and quick process of industrialization was prompted by the centralized government, not by the bourgeosie and the middle class. This short process did not destroy the functioning of many traditional groups in Japanese communities. Present Japanese people still live in many traditional groups and/or those which were reproduced by traditional ways of organizing.

Traditional Values for Self-Help

Four short years after the Meiji Restoration, when the Japanese knew little about Western values, the magnum opus of Samuel Smiles (1812-1904), *Self-Help*, with illustrations of Character, Conduct and Perseverance was translated and published, and became a bestseller in Japan (Reischauer, 1988, p. 129). Samuel Smiles is one of the two great writers (the other is Peter Kropotkin) who presented basic models of self-help in Western countries (Froland, Pancoast & Parker, 1983, pp. 11-12). The fact that this translated book of Smiles' excited many Japanese people means that Japanese people already had similar values in their indigenous culture (Fujiwara, 1986). These values were developed by Baigan Ishida (1685-1744), and his followers endeavored to spread their value system of frugality, deligence, honesty, and filial piety among Japanese people, including those of low social classes (Yasumaru,

1974). They presented human models of diligence and conscience, as Samuel Smiles did.

About half a century after the Meiji Restoration, several national self-help organizations were formed among stigmatized people, such as blind people in 1909 (Yokota, 1972, pp. 36-37), deaf people in 1915 (Fujimoto, 1971, pp. 16-17), and Buraku people (those who were in the lowest class in the feudal system) in 1922. In 1926, lepers formed the first self-help group in Japan (Osa, 1978). However, these liberation movements were completely oppressed by the rise of militarism and fascism in the 1930s. During World War II, small groups were again used as mutual-watch mechanisms, and people were severely ordered to watch each other's anti-government actions and ideas (Akimoto, 1974).

Group Movements in the Postwar Period

In the 1950s, Japanese people began to have small group movements, which were called "circle" movements in Japan. This movement was created mainly by four kinds of small groups: (1) learning groups, (2) chorus groups, (3) Writing-Daily-Life groups, and (4) hobby groups (Sasaki, 1956; Senzaki, 1957, pp. 66-72). The learning groups usually read textbooks about Marxist theories (Kokumin Bunka Chôsakai, 1956, p. 185). The chorus groups gave young people the opportunity for psychological relaxation, which had been diminished by the fascist education and poverty (Fukutake & Watanuki 1960, pp. 348-353). The Writing-Daily-Life groups involved a great number of people in communities, and influenced the civil movements of the next decade. People of these groups wrote about their everyday lives, and read each other's writings. By this way of sharing, people obtained an opportunity to exchange their feelings and ideas about their daily lives, and get social insights into their problems (Sasaki, 1956). The movement first began among young workers and housewives, and thereafter, spread among the socially disadvantaged, such as disabled people and patients. Those days, many patients and people with physical disabilities published haiku (a type of Japanese poem) books. Exchanging and sharing haiku and other writings among stigmatized people pushed their liberation movements forward (Hanada, 1990). Buraku people made full use of this movement, not only to raise their social consciousness, but also to abolish illiteracy (Nakamura, 1990; Ozawa, 1990; Motoki & Uchiyama, 1992).

It is after the mid-1960s that patients and people with disabilities started active social actions (Tsuda, Kida, Yamada & Saitô, 1977, p. 44; Osa, 1978, p. 158). They organized many national organizations in the 1970s. In the 1980s, Japanese self-helpers began to participate in various international organizations, and learned many Western concepts such as self-help groups and independent living.

THE UNDERLYING ASSUMPTIONS OF SELF-HELP AND THE TRADITIONAL JAPANESE CULTURE

The Underlying Assumptions of Self-Help

We should remember that Western concepts of self-help have been developed in unique Western culture: in Judeo-Chiristian, individualistic, and pluralistic culture (Oka, 1990). On the other hand, Japanese culture is non-Judeo-Chiristian, non-individualistic, and non-pluralistic. At least, Japanese people have no counterpart of a Judeo-Christian tradition of group confession, which is a basis of Western self-help groups (Hurvitz, 1976).

To use Western concepts of self-help in Japanese culture effectively, we should remove peculiar cultural factors from these concepts, and identify basic elements of self-help concepts which are universally effective in various cultures. However, it is almost impossible to identify such elements as long as concepts of self-help groups are used in limited areas of the world. Instead, we identify basic processes and qualities of self-help groups, which are very important and prone to clash with Japanese predominant culture. They are sponteneous sharing, individual independence, and emancipation from suppression (Oka, 1992).

"Sponteneous Sharing" [wakachiai] is the first basic process in self-help groups. By this, people spontaneously and freely exchange their feelings, ideas and information with each other as equals. Sharing has several ways: talking, writing, "chatting" on line, and so on. Sharing includes free talking and exchanging letters among members, and peer telephone counseling service. "Individual independence" [hitoridachi] means that individuals hold autonomous self-control of their own lives with experiential knowledge (Borkman, 1990) and information, which they obtain by sharing in self-help groups, and that they participate in the society as complete members through their self-help groups. "Emancipation from suppression" [tokihanachi] includes psychological group processes to destigmatize socially disadvantaged people and recover their self-esteem, and social activities to improve the environment for their human rights and welfare.

These three qualities and processes are prone to be distorted by Japanese group-oriented culture, which values emotional cohesiveness, homogeneity, and hierarchy, and the particular patterns of their social behaviors.

Japanese Group-Oriented Culture

Emotional Cohesiveness in Groups

Japanese long history of isolation and feudal suppression generated peculiar groupism or group-oriented culture. Reischauer (1988) states "certainly no difference is more significant between Japanese and Americans, or Westerners in general, than the greater Japanese tendency to emphasize the group at the expense of the individual" (p. 128). Taylor (1983) also notes "one of Japan's most prominent national characteristics is the individual's sense of the group" (p. 67). What are the characteristics of Japanese groups in the group-oriented culture? Social scientists point out the emotional cohesiveness of Japanese groups (Nakane, 1984, pp. 9-23; Takagiwa, 1987, pp. 82-83).

In other words, Japanese groups and human relations are not formed by contracts. Though contracts hold together societies of free individuals, "Japanese society is characterised by an extreme looseness of the notion of contract" (Dore, 1990, p. 183). Westerners consider contracts important in human groups and relations, because they have Judeo-Christian ideas, where God and human beings have contracts. Japanese gods have no contracts with human beings.

Rules do not form Japanese groups. As Kenrick (1990) points out, "Western fraternities, corporations and societies are bound by formalised and often iron-clad rules. Japanese fraternities . . . have their rules which . . . are rarely stated in words which do not leave room for alternative interpretations" (p. 31). Therefore, newcomers have to be dependent upon veterans to know what behaviors are proper in groups. Lack of clear rules in groups strengthen the hierarchical structure in the groups, where newcomers are at the bottom and older members hold higher positions.

Neither ideology can generate Japanese groups. According to Clark (1977), while Westerners, Chinese, and Korean people value ideologies, Japanese do not. Instead of ideology, the Japanese appreciate emotional relations more.

Blood relationship is not an important binder of Japanese groups. Japanese blood relationship is traditionally weak (Nakane, 1977, pp. 44-47). The Japanese are much more free from blood relationship than other Asian people, such as Chinese and Korean people.

Without contracts, rules, ideology, or blood relationship, Japanese groups are maintained by the feeling of oneness (Lebra, 1976, p. 25) and emotional cohesiveness. This emotional cohesiveness in Japanese groups makes it difficult for a person to move from one group to another, or to belong to plural groups at the same time (Nakane, 1967, p. 67). Each group has a strong psychological barrier against outsiders. If you attended a meeting of a Japanese group, you would be treated as a guest or an outsider, not a member or an insider. You would have to wait a long time before the members began to accept you emotionally as a member. If the group was formed by a contract, a rule, or an ideology, you could more quickly become a true member by accepting the contract, rule or ideology of the group.

We should remember that this emotionalism does not lead to free expression of emotions. Conversely, people are inhibited in groups, because individual free expression of emotions disturbs the emotional oneness of the whole group. As Reischauer (1988) states, "the Japanese actually are a deeply emotional people, but they strictly hide their emotions as much as possible" (p. 138).

Homogeneous Groups

If you are in an emotionally cohesive group, it is undesirable to let the other members of your group know that you are different from them, because great differences may expel you from the emotional oneness of the group. Emotional relation is sometimes strong, but weak in a sense that the basis of the relation is obscure. The most simple fact that causes emotional oneness is that "we are the same." In what point are we the same? Nobody knows. Therefore, groups of young Japanese boys and girls want to wear the same clothes, speak in the same manner, eat the same food, and play with the same toys. You should remove any difference in yourself, or hide it; otherwise, you would be isolated and alienated. After the severe socialization for homogeneity, the feeling of differences sometimes generates intense guilt in the Japanese mind (Maniwa, 1990, p. 164). To maintain the emotional oneness, individual differences are punished psychologically, for example, by neglect and a cold smile from other group members. Consequently, Japanese people always feel the "tension of mutual watching" (Frost, 1987, pp. 69-70) in groups. This is a mechanism for Japanese people to maintain extremely homogeneous and other-directed societies through numberless groups.

Even if you were excluded and expelled from one group, you would have no problems as long as you could join another group. However, this kind of transfer is not easy in Japan, because independent groups try to be in harmony with each other, and each group tends to reject a person who is rejected by other groups (Sakuta, 1959, p. 15). Consequently, it is difficult for those who are isolated and alienated in their groups to find other groups which accept them. Their fear of isolation is much more increased by this kind of inextricable structure of the group-oriented society. People cannot help becoming obedient to group pressure and suppressing their individuality in groups.

Fate-Sharing Groups

Because freedom to move from one group to another is suppressed and the opportunity to choose a group is curtailed, and additionally, homogeneity in a group is emphasized and appreciated, people feel that they are fated to belong to a group and share the same fate (Minami, 1983, pp. 11-12). The unquestioning and self-sacrificing loyality to the group is often required. Therefore, if a member tries to leave the group, she or he is severely criticized for desertion of the group. Not only older, but also younger people have this sense of ethics. For example, when Japanese university students desert their groups such as sports clubs and volunteer clubs, they often have a bitter time because they are reprimanded by the group members. A strategy of modern Japanese management is to exploit this value system. Managers make all workers have the feeling of sharing the same fate and believe that a worker's fate is all other workers' fate and his or her company's fate (Odaka, 1967, p. 67; Woronoff, 1979, pp. 55-92; Christopher 1987, pp. 239-265; Morita 1987, p. 130). A member's welfare is the whole group's welfare, and vice versa. In such fate-sharing groups, the members' individuality is repressed and despised.

Inclusiveness, Exclusiveness, and Hierarchy

Nakane (1984) classifies human groups by two criteria. "One is based on the individual's common attribute, the other on situational position in a given 'frame'. . . . 'Frame' may be a locality, an institution or a particular relationship which binds a set of individuals into one group" (p. 1). According to her observation, "the group consciousness of the Japanese depends considerably on this immediate social context, 'frame'" (p. 2). Groups based on "frames" include all the people in the "frames." An example of Japanese community life is a neighborhood organization. When you move anywhere in Japan, a representative of a neighborhood organization asks you to pay a membership fee without asking whether you want to join the organization. People have no legal obligation to belong to it. However, this sort of neighborhood organization is supposed to have all the inhabitants of the neighborhood area as its members. It is a socially recognized custom in Japan (Hendry, 1987, pp. 55-61; Dore, 1962, pp. 214-234). These organizations cover almost all the neighborhoods of Japan.

Such inclusive organizations accord with the emotional oneness: everyone in an immediate social context ("frame") is a member, and nobody is an outsider. Inclusive organizations can exist nowhere but in a homogeneous society. If people were completely different, how could they all enter only one organization?

However, different people exist in the most homogeneous society. How are they treated? They are repressed at the bottom of the society. This society has a strong hierarchical structure. Different people are treated as members low in the hierarchy and excluded from the main area of the society. With this hierarchy system, groups can be inclusive and exclusive at the same time; some people are included as low in the hierarchy, and excluded from the main area where only those high in the hierarchy enjoy themselves. According to Maniwa (1990, p. 27), this is the nature of many Japanese groups; in Japanese groups, the inclusiveness and the exclusiveness are united and controlled by the hierarchical structure.

Patterns of Interaction in Groups

This group-oriented culture influences people's patterns of social interaction. People maintain an inhibited attitude for their individual needs and feelings. They are unskillful speakers, and sensitive to hierarchy.

Inhibited Attitude for Individuality

Japanese appreciation of emotional oneness in groups is related to the fact that individual assertiveness is suppressed in Japanese groups. For individuals in groups, it is important not to express individual needs or opinions, but to dissolve in the group, as salt dissolves in water. As a matter of fact, many people place a negative image on individualism. They have no clear idea of the difference between individualism and self-assertive selfishness (Dore, 1990, p. 189), lack of self-discipline (Kenrick, 1990, p. 53), or "personal gratification and the pursuit of pleasure at the expense of social obligation" (Frost, 1987, p. 75). As Rieschauer (1988) states, "the word 'individualism' . . . has always been in ill repute in Japan" (p. 160). Actually, the Western notions of 'individual' were very difficult for Japanese intellectuals in the 19th century to understand and translate into the Japanese language (Saitô, 1977, pp. 229-249, Yanabu, 1982, pp. 23-42).

By suppressing individuality, Japanese people tend to understand their basis of personal identification as part of some larger group (Condon, 1984, p. 64). If you go to Japanese drinking houses, you find many groups laughing and talking loudly. Japanese people usually have a party to make sure that they belong to the same group. Their "party are characterized by group drinking and group games rather than by tête-à-tête conversations with shifting partners, as at Western dinners and cocktail parties" (Reischauer, 1988, p. 135).

Sensitive Attitude for Hierarchy

If you identify yourself as part of a group, you become sensitive to your position or rank in the group. In comparison between Japanese and American society, Reischauer (1988) finds "the much greater Japanese emphasis on hierarchy" (p. 149). Taylor (1983) also states, "All societies establish hierarchy. In few societies, however, are they so widespread or important as in Japan" (p. 42). As a matter of fact, in Japanese eyes, every room (traditional Japanese rooms have no chairs) has a hierarchical system of place (Wakamori, 1954, pp. 185-192). The highest place is usually the farthest from the door, and the lowest one is next to the door. In formal meetings, the younger members, and sometimes aged women who were trained to behave modestly, struggle to obtain this lowest place, because it is shameful for them to sit in higher places. This kind of value system prevents young people or newcomers from talking in free and relaxed ways in front of older or veteran people in groups. For people low in the hierarchy, just sitting in proper places is difficult. How much more difficult it is for them to talk properly! Japanese language has an extremely complicated system of honorifics. Consequently, people low in the hierarchy prefer fixed patterns of communication more than free conversation. As Neustupny (1987) states, in traditional Japanese parties, "participants take turns in making speeches, singing, or similar activities" (p. 52). Recently, "standing parties" of the Anglo-Saxon type have also become popular. "However, a number of Japanese will prefer a party at which they can sit together and enjoy listening to a monologue rather than engaging in conversation" (ibid.).

Japan, in principle, keeps a meritocracy (Gibney, 1987, p. 65), and very little privilege is inherited (Taylor, 1983, p. 44). It has realized a relatively classless society (Reischauer, 1988, p. 152; Kenrick, 1990, p. 7). Instead, there is a rigid hierarchy in the society. Historically, people associate this sense of hierarchy with the sense of social positions in the feudal class society. In the feudal class society, behaving properly according to one's social position was a basic code of ethics (Sakurai, 1949, pp. 97-136). This ethical code remains in modern Japan (Lebra, 1976, pp. 67-89), and maintains the hierarchical human relations in Japan.

In these human relations, those high in the hierarchy are expected "to show a sort of benign paternalism to those further down on the scale" (Reischauer, 1988, p. 156). As Dore (1990) states, "the principle of hierarchy is so well respected in Japan that superiors do not have to behave in an authoritarian way" (p. 182). On the other hand, those low in the hierarchy are allowed to be dependent on those higher up. This sort of dependence in vertical human relations is socially acknowledged and sometimes appreciated (Doi, 1973).

Undeveloped Talking Skills

Not only the inhibited attitude and hierarchical structure, but also their traditional contempt for talking and undeveloped talking skills prevent Japanese people from enjoying free conversation in groups. Kenrick (1990) summarized typical Japanese opinions about talking as follows: " 'The wise do not talk. The talkative are not wise' . . . Silence is a sign of honesty and trustworthiness"(p. 105). Kuwabara (1947, pp. 177-178) also writes that Japanese language has a much greater number of words to make people silent than Western languages. The Japanese emphasize the importance of "communion of heart with heart" and despise verbal communication (Honna & Hoffer, 1989, pp. 224-226). Condon (1984, p. 65) makes a comparison between the communication style of American people and that of Japanese people. Among American people, emphasis is on expressive forms–speaking and to a lesser extent writing. On the other hand, the Japanese emphasize perception, receptiveness, and observation skills; listening, reading and writing skills are valued more than public speaking ability.

The reason why the Japanese have despised and disdained speaking is, probably, historical. First, Japanese people had been almost deprived of the freedom of speech for a long time. Second, they had been confined to small communities in the extremely static society without seeing strangers. They did not need to speak.

Even present Japanese young people seemingly consider verbal communication less important. For teachers of social work, it is difficult to teach the importance of verbal communication to young students. They tend to refute, "We can communicate without talking!" However, silence makes it hard to make friends. Reischauer (1988) states "Japanese on the whole are less inclined than Westerners to enter into casual contacts and are likely to seem forbiddingly formal in any new encounter. Pauses in conversation can be agonizingly long, at least to the Western participant" (p. 147).

Secretive Attitude About Family Problems

Another great cultural factor which blocks spontaneous sharing in Japanese groups is a secretive attitude about family problems. In Japan today, small families are extremely isolated because of weak kinship and neighborhood relations. Their degree of isolation is also great in comparison with families in other societies such as the American, British, Indian, or Chinese (Nakane, 1977, pp. 153-166). In Japan, the institution of extended compound families, which is prevalent in the other Asian countries, essentially dissolved in the 17th century (Kawamura, 1982, p. 25). With few visitors, Japanese families can easily keep secrets such as familial violence, incest and child abuse. A strong and traditional ethical code of the Japanese is "Don't let the others know your family's shame." In particular, mental and/or rare diseases and disabilities are often considered to be due to bad actions of the parents or ancestors in traditional Japanese religions. This idea prevents people from making contact with self-help groups to express their problems, which they regard as their family's shame.

CULTURAL AND POLITICAL OBSTACLES TO THE DEVELOPMENT OF SELF-HELP GROUPS IN JAPAN

Japanese people have a strongly group-oriented culture. This makes it very easy to form groups among various sorts of people, including stigmatized persons. However, many stigmatized persons' groups are not real self-help groups. They lack three basic qualities and processes of self-help groups: "spontaneous sharing" [wakachiai], "individual independence" [hitoridachi], and "emancipation from suppression" [tokihanachi]. Why do they not become real self-help groups? What are obstacles to the development of self-help groups in Japan? We show two sorts of obstacles: cultural and political.

Cultural Obstacles

Homogeneity

The difficult first step to self-help groups. Group-oriented society emphasizes homogeneity among the members, because group life is easy for homogeneous people to live. This means that the group-oriented society is making people homogeneous. By oppressing and suppressing different people, the homogeneous society maintains itself. In such a society, people avoid becoming different from the others, and it is very difficult for them to acknowledge that they have different problems. Being different (and having different problems) is not only shameful and embarrassing, but also generates troubles and dangers. Different people, especially stigmatized people, are severely discriminated against. Therefore, different people are compelled to conceal their stigmas and/or great differences. Nevertheless, starting to participate in self-help groups necessitates their acknowledging that they are different or have different problems. Consequently, this first step to self-help groups is very hard and sometimes dangerous for people to take in the homogeneous society. Informing others that you are a member of a self-help group of 'different' people is to be exposed to the danger of isolation and alienation from the rest of the society. Asserting your difference is much more dangerous than having the original stigma. If you just lived with the original stigma, you could operate successfully at the bottom of the society by pretending to have no differences from the rest of the society.

Fear of being excluded from inclusive groups. In the homogeneous society, people fear becoming minorities–being minorities is identified with being excluded from the main area of the society and sinking to the bottom. Homogeneity is found not only in qualities, but also in behaviors. People are required to behave in the same way as other people do. If other people join a group, you should join it; otherwise, you would be regarded as a dropout in the group-oriented society; they would disturb the emotional oneness of the immediate social contexts ("frames") as different persons, and their behaviors would be regarded as being against social norms. Consequently, numerous inclusive groups are formed in numerous "frames" in the society.

For example, you find groups of patients with the same diseases in hospitals, and groups of parents of users in day care centers. Are they self-help groups? As a matter of fact, they may have no professional leaders. In many cases, the participation of the members is not compulsory. Nevertheless, we find it difficult to regard many of these groups as real self-help groups, because many members are actuated not by their own will, but by group pressure or cultural-social norms. In the strongly group-oriented culture, they are conditioned to join a group each time they hear they are eligible. However, their participation is often in name only; people seldom attend the meetings, or they do that to fulfil their social obligation. In these groups, people have little opportunity for spontaneous and free sharing [wakachiai].

In addition, because the groups are formed in immediate social contexts ("frame"), the members cannot keep their anonymity. Before sharing in group meetings, they know each other's name, address, and family members. They are using the same agency and day centers and seeing the same social workers. Under such circumstances, it is difficult and sometimes dangerous for them to freely express their feelings and ideas in the group meetings. For example, can a person express bad feelings toward the social worker in a group where other members know the same social worker very well? Can a female member talk about troubles in her marriage in a group where several members privately know her husband? These groups provide people with little opportunity for spontaneous sharing [wakachiai].

Segregation of people excluded from the homogeneous society. The homogeneous society excludes different and stigmatized people from the main area of the society, and these people cannot help working and/or living together in places isolated from communities. If you emphasized the importance of sharing feelings and personal information among people with the same disabilities and problems in front of such people, they might say that they were fed up with people with the same disabilities, because some of them are segregated and required to go to special nurseries and schools. After graduating from these schools, they work and/or live in asylums. Though Japanese people with disabilities are now struggling against these segregation systems, the development of normalization is, so far, very slow in Japan. These asylums sometimes have inclusive groups for users or families of users. We should not expect these groups to be a place where people can spontaneously share personal feelings.

Non-Individualism

By emphasizing homogeneity among group members, the individuality of the members is suppressed. Additionally, Japanese people were historically compelled to undertake collective and interlocking responsibility. This form of responsibility infiltrates the present Japanese mind. Consequently, self-help groups tend to be considered as groups for collective responsibility or a fate-sharing groups; a member's failure is a whole group's failure. In such groups, it is difficult to maintain the individual independence of each member: you may be expected to work as parts of the group. Real self-help groups do not suppress each member's individuality. They provide an opportunity to share feelings, ideas, and information among independent individuals, not among parts of a group. They propel not interdependent relationships among members, but members' individual independence [hitoridachi].

This individuality in self-help groups is not easy to understand for Japanese people in the group-oriented culture. To explain this nature of self-help groups to Japanese people, you can use the following analogy: Traditional Japanese mutual-help groups are like mass calisthenics. Each member plays a different part, and members' unification is important. On the other hand, self-help groups are like a gymnasium, where each person practices individually, but they exchange ideas and information, observing each other's practice. Another analogy is: In traditional Japanese festivals, a group of naked men carry a portable shrine. Being naked, men show the audience that they are the same without any differences, and that they are closely united. On the other hand, Western festivals have parades, where individuals dance individually, sometimes with different clothes. Parades have a route, which leads the dancers in the same direction. This route is like a program of a self-help group.

Hierarchy

Professionals as high in the hierarchy. Because of their great liking for hierarchy, Japanese clients usually maintain an obedient attitude toward professionals, who are regarded as high in the hierarchy of the professional-client relationship. Believing in the communion of heart with heart [ishindenshin], without using verbal communication, clients try to understand what the professionals have in mind; they obey not only professionals' words but also what the clients suggest the professionals think. This is a great virtue in the hierarchical society. Under such circumstances, it is very difficult, and sometimes impossible to distinguish self-help groups and professionally-run support groups, because even professionals who have no intention to supervise groups have a great influence on these groups. The group members obey "unspoken words" of the professionals, and professionals can "lead" a group without "leading." For example, many patients groups have meetings in hospitals without professionals' intervention. However, as long as they are working psychologically within the hierarchical relations between professionals and clients, we can hardly regard them as real self-help groups, because it is difficult for them to make social actions against, or to discuss various problems as equals with, medical authorities high in the hierarchy, to improve medical and social services for their patients' rights. The groups which are restrained by hierarchical structures lack one important quality of real self-help groups: emancipation from suppression [tokihanachi].

Hierarchy in groups. Not only in professional-client relationships, but also among group members, there is a hierarchical structure. Japanese obsession with hierarchy can spoil the egalitarian atmosphere of self-help groups. For example, Riessman's helper-therapy principle (Riessman, 1965), which is well known among Japanese professionals by a translated and published book of Gartner and Riessman (1977), can be distorted by Japanese liking for hierarchy. In a hierarchical structure of a group, "helper" tends to be regarded not as an unfixed and flexible role but as a fixed upper position or rank in groups. In place of the helper-therapy principle, we may identify the 'position'-therapy principle. As a Japanese proverb says, "Positions make persons good." However, fixed positions in the hierarchy block sponteneous sharing [wakachiai] processes in self-help groups. Moreover, conflicts over higher positions among members of Japanese groups may be unavoidable.

Communication Skills

Vague contracts between professionals and consumers. The belief in the communion of heart with heart [ishindenshin] makes the Japanese despise contracts and lets them be vague. This influences the relationship between professionals and consumers of their services–they do not spend enough time in discussing what the professionals do for the consumers. Consequently, when the professionals say that they support consumers' groups, both the professionals and the consumers usually have no clear idea about which sort of groups they are committed to, self-help groups, professionally-run support groups, or intermediate groups such as "hybrid self-help groups" (Powell, 1987, pp. 30-33) or "professionally facilitated self-help groups" (Comstock & Mohamoud, 1990). Some Japanese professionals make presentations in academic conferences, whose titles are "supporting self-help groups," and talk about their practice of substantially professional group work, emphasizing self-help and mutual-aid among the group members. It is not only because they confuse concepts of self-help groups with those of professional practice, but also because they and their consumers have no clear contracts about their helping relationship. Therefore, the groups are swinging between self-help groups and professionally-run groups without clear ideas and purposes.

Unpleasant silence in groups. Undeveloped talking skills generate unpleasant silence in face-to-face groups. As a matter of fact, Japanese group workers in the social work field often experience a very long silence among their clients. Their undeveloped talking skills and culture despising speaking may create great difficulties in keeping Japanese face-to-face groups therapeutic without professional involvement. Additionally, while Hurvitz (1976) states that the American movements of peer self-help psychotherapy groups were developed by a tradition of the Judeo-Christian group-confession and the popularization of psychotherapy, Japan has nothing like such religious traditions or social phenomena. Therefore, those who talk about their private matters among unfamiliar group members tend to be regarded as too talkative and socially naive in Japan. Sharing feelings about problems in face-to-face groups is often considered meaningless mutual-confort, which is shameful to Japanese ideas.

Sharing through writings. Talking is not the only way of sharing; sharing through writing is another way. As writing-daily-life movements prove, writing and reading, instead of talking and listening, is an important way of sharing among Japanese people. To share individual and private matters in face-to-face peer groups, Japanese people have several obstacles: hierarchical structure of communication, psychological barriers between insiders and outsiders, undeveloped talking skills, tension of mutual-watch, conformist group pressure, strong group-orientedness over individuality and so on. However, sharing through writings is free from such obstacles. Though Reischauer (1988, p. 138) states that "the Japanese have a strong aversion to most open displays of feelings," he doubtless refers to Japanese behaviors in face-to-face human relations. Through their writings, Japanese people express their feelings openly. As a matter of fact, a great number of patients' groups and disabled persons' groups have developed not through face-to-face talking, but through exchanging their individual writings in their journals (Hanada, 1990).

Studies of Japanese literature and writings prove that it has characteristics effective to share personal and private information, feelings, and ideas in groups. First, Japanese writings maintain a tradition of writing about private daily life (Kuno & Tsurumi, 1956, p. 104). Second, they historically emphasized subjectivity, not objectivity, and tended to describe feelings, not facts (Keen, 1983, p. 115). Third, they had a tradition of group writing (Keen, 1983, p. 116). An example is linked verse. Linked verse was considered a method to express the communal feelings of the meeting, and facilitate their deep interaction of feelings (Yamamoto, 1960). Fourth, they were traditionally written in private words, as in private letters to intimate friends (Saitô, 1939, p. 65). Japanese self-help groups' newsletters are full of private words; they are often boring and nonsense to those who don't know the writers privately. Fifth, Japanese poetry had such simple forms that people of low classes enjoyed it (Saitô, 1939, pp. 58-59; Tsuda, 1964). Simple forms of poetry, such as haiku, enable many people, including undereducated ones, to compose poems.

Political Obstacles

Lack of Pluralism and Control by Inclusive Organizations

From a political point of view, the homogeneous society is considered to lack pluralism. Although this homogeneity was caused by a long history of isolation of this country and its communities, we should notice that political powers contribute to the continuity of the homogeneous society; it is easier to dominate homogeneous people than heterogeneous people. Homogeneous people can be easily united and organized to make an inclusive group. By controlling this inclusive group, rulers can govern all the people. Japanese rulers had historically made full use of these groups as mutual-watch mechanisms. These mechanisms are still used by local self-governing bodies, though their use is much more moderate than that of the feudal rulers.

For example, after the end of World War II, the New Constitution of Japan was promulgated, which guarantees the right to live. With fear of inflation of people's demands, local self-governing bodies started to organize self-help inclusive organizations of recipients of social services, such as single mothers, physically disabled persons, and families of dead soldiers. They were inclusive in the sense that they automatically or semi-automatically included any eligible individuals in each district as their members. In those days, the right of confidential private information was not socially recognized. The local self-governing bodies gave the names and addresses of social service recipients to community leaders, and these leaders persuaded them to organize self-help inclusive organizations of the recipients. Because the people in those days regarded receiving social services not as a civil right, but as a favor of the government authorities, they obediently joined those self-help inclusive organizations. A political purpose of these inclusive organizations was to prevent communists and left-wing activists from organizing these recipients and causing the inflation of their demands in a state of disorder after the war (Oka, 1991).

These days, this sort of inclusive organization does not attract people, and has many members in name only. However, these organizations are often expected to distribute the financial support of local self-governing bodies to various self-help groups and to control their use of social resources. For example, people with disabilities start a new self-help group. They ask the local self-governing body to support them financially. Their reply is, "we cannot help your group specifically. We should be neutral among various groups. You can join your district's self-help (inclusive) organization of disabled people. This is open to any voluntary groups like yours. Our financial aid system is to give all the money to this (inclusive) organization and let it distribute the money to the member groups." Their logic is, the local self-governing body should be politically neutral, and they should not support groups of particular political ideology; any politically neutral groups can unite with each other, and the consequently united groups become the inclusive organization; therefore, the local self-governing body supports only the inclusive organization. However, as a fact, inclusive organizations tend to hesitate to include new self-help groups as their members, because increasing the number of member groups is to reduce each member group's share. In particular, inclusive organizations often reject politically active groups. Consequently, inclusive organizations work as mutual-watch/restraint mechanisms to prevent each other from becoming politically active.

The local self-governing bodies entrust many leaders of inclusive organizations to a job of "public adviser." Concerning physical disabilities, since 1967 public advisers have been chosen among leaders of inclusive organizations of people with disabilities. Through this system, inclusive organizations and the lower offices of the local self-governing body have united (Oka, 1991).

Under such circumstances, political pluralism around self-help groups is prevented. However, political pluralism is needed to promote the human emancipation [tokihanachi], which is an important purpose of self-help groups. Inclusive organizations usually function as mutual-watch/restraint mechanisms against self-help groups.

Centralization of Administrative Power

Some leaders of inclusive organizations say that their inclusiveness is due not to the political pressure by the local self-governing body but to their strategy against the centralized administrative power. Japan is a centralized country, where you need to organize as many as possible into one organization in order to pressure the administrative power. Nothing but the number of the members is the force of the organization against the centralized power. Therefore, many self-help organizations, which started as face-to-face small discussion groups, change into political pressure organizations which try to include as many people as possible at the expense of the friendly atmosphere of small groups. If Japan had developed decentralization systems, it would be possible for relatively small various self-help groups to have the opportunity to participate in the decision-making process of community policy.

Fear of Political Minorities and Respect for the Governmental Authorities

Despite the lack of pluralism, some self-help groups survive as political minorities. However, Japanese people, who have continuously had the conservative national government since 1948, exercise precautions not to be involved in political minorities. These precautions prevent some people from joining self-help groups.

For example, recently, many public health centers help patients start self-help groups, which it is often impossible to distinguish from professionally-run support groups due to cultural reasons mentioned above. Many of these groups are reluctant to cooperate with other independent patients' movements. We can understand this phenomenon by using a logic of "frame": these groups are disinclined to extend beyond the boundary of their "frame" (a public health center). Another explanation is political and more plausible: these groups regard independent patients' movements as political minorities. People remember that communists were cruelly crushed in prewar and wartime Japan and that they were again purged in the postwar time by the occupation army (Fujiwara, 1989, pp. 103-104). People know that being involved in political minorities may cause trouble.

Additionally, Japanese people, whose government has played the major enlightening role in the society, have the deep-rooted idea [kan-son-min-pi] that government organizations and personnel [kan] are respectable [son] and that non-government organizations and personnel [min] are unrespectable [pi]. Due to this notion, some people prefer connections with the government to those with independent voluntary movements. Likewise, some patients choose to belong to public health centers sponsored by the government rather than to independent patients' movements.

This respect for government organizations and fear of political minorities are mixed to make people adhere to government organizations. Those groups which adhere to government authorities can hardly make social actions for their human rights and emancipation [tokihanachi] against the government authorities.

CONCLUSION

Japanese history of a long isolation created a strongly group-oriented culture. This culture makes people form groups everywhere in the society. Consequently, there are also numerous groups of stigmatized people in Japan. However, these groups are not necessarily self-help groups, because they often lack basic processes and qualities of real self-help groups: sponteneous sharing [wakachiai], individual independence [hitoridachi], and emancipation from suppression [tokihanachi]. Several cultural and political obstacles prevent these groups from developing into real self-help groups: first, group-oriented culture encourages people to join inclusive groups in their immediate social contexts, and people, without making a choice of groups or with fear of being excluded from groups, participate in these groups. Without anonymity and by group conformity and hierarchical pressure, the members can hardly enjoy sponteneous sharing [wakachiai]. Their undeveloped talking skills and cultural contempt for talking also block sponteneous sharing in face-to-face groups. Second, by too much emphasis on the importance of group solidarity, the group-oriented culture makes it difficult for members to maintain their individual independence [hitoridachi] in groups. Respect for vertical and hierarchical human relationship develops dependent attitudes of those low in the hierarchy. This generates the relationship between paternalistic professionals and dependent consumers' groups, and obscures the substantial differences between self-help groups and professionally-run support groups. Third, mutual-watch/restraint mechanisms of the group-oriented culture, which have been used politically, hinder the emancipation [tokihanachi] process of self-help groups. Respect for hierarchy also discourages social actions against professionals and government authorities.

REFERENCES

Akimoto, R. (1974). *Sensô to Minshû* [People and Wars].Tokyo: Gakuyo Shobo.

Borkman, T.J. (1990). Experiential, Professional, and Lay Frames of Reference. In T.J. Powell (ed.), *Working with Self-Help* (pp. 3-30). Silver Spring: National Association of Social Workers.

Clark, G. (1977). *The Japanese Tribe: Origins of a Nation's Uniqueness*. Tokyo: Simul Press.

Christopher, R.C. (1987). *The Japanese Mind: The goliath explained*. Tokyo: Charles E. Tuttle.

Comstock, C.M. & Mohamoud, J.L. (1990). Professionally Facilitated Self-Help Groups: Benefits for Professionals and Members. In. T.J. Powell (ed.), *Working with Self-Help* (pp. 177-188). Silver Spring: National Association of Social Workers.

Condon, J.C.(1984). *With Respect to the Japanese*. Tokyo: Yohan.

Doi, T. (1973). *The anatomy of dependence: the key analysis of Japanese behavior*. Tokyo: Kodansha International.

Dore, R.P. (1962). *City life in Japan: A study of a Tokyo Ward*. (Aoi, K. & Tsukamoto, T. Trans.). Tokyo: Iwanami Shoten. (Original work published 1958.)

Dore, R.P. (1990). *Will the 21st century be the age of individualism?* Tokyo: Simul Press.

Froland, C., Pancoast, D.L. & Parker, P. (1983). Introduction. In D.L.Pancoast, P. Parker & C. Froland (eds.), *Rediscovering Self-Help: Its Role in Social Care* (pp. 9-23). Beverly Hills: Sage Publications.

Frost, E.L. (1987). *The New U.S.–Japan Relationship*. Tokyo: Charles E. Tuttle.

Fukutake, N. & Watanuki, J. (1960). Soshiki to Ningen (Organizations and Human Beings). In H. Odagiri (ed.), *Kindai Nihon Shisôshi Kôza* (Vol. 6) (pp. 303-355). Tokyo: Chikuma Shobo.

Fujimoto, T. (1971). Senzen no Rôa Undô. [The Prewar Movements of Deaf People]. In Zen Nihon Rôa Renmei Shuppankyoku (ed.), *1908-1971 Rôa Undô no Ayumi* (pp. 15-19). Tokyo: by the Editor.

Fujiwara, A. (1989). *Nihon no Rekishi: Sekai no nakano Nihon* [A History of Japan: Japan in the World]. Tokyo: Shogakkan.

Fujiwara, N. (1986). *Nihon ni okeru Shominteki Jiritsuron no Keisei to Tenkai* [The Formation and Development of Thoughts for Self-Reliance of Japanese Populace]. Tokyo: Perikan Sha.

Gartner, A., & Riessman, F. (1977). *Self-Help in the Human Services*. San Francisco: Jossey-Bass.

Gibney, F. (1987). *Japan: The Fragile Super Power* (Second Revised Edition). Tokyo: Charles E. Tuttle.

Hanada, S. (1990). *Nihon no Shôgaisha* [Japanese People with Disabilities]. Tokyo: Kozue.

Hasegawa, A. (1986). *Nôson no Kazoku to Chiiki Shakai* [Japanese Families and Communities]. Tokyo: Ochanomizu Shobo.

Hendry, J. (1987). *Understanding Japanese Society*. London: Croom Helm.

Honna, N., & Hoffer, B. (1989). *An English Dictionary of Japanese Ways of Thinking*. Tokyo: Yuhikaku.

Hurvitz, N. (1976). The Origins of the Peer Self-Help Psychotherapy Group Movement. *The Journal of Applied Behavioral Science, 12*(3), 283-294.

Kawamura, N. (1982). The Modernization of Japanese Society: 1986-1945. *Orientation Seminars on Japan (Vol. 10)*. Tokyo: The Japan Foundation Office for the Japanese Studies Center

Keen, D. (1983). *Nihonjin no Shitsumon* [Questions of Japanese People]. Tokyo: Asahi Sinbunsha.

Kenrick, D.M. (1990). *Where Communism Works: the success of competitive-communism in Japan*. Tokyo: Charles E. Tuttle.

Kokumin Bunka Chôsakai.(1956). *Sayoku Bunka Sensen* [Cultural Movements of Left Wing]. Tokyo: Seiko Sha.

Kuno, O. & Tsurumi, S. (1956). *Gendai Nihon no Shisô* [Thoughts of Modern Japan]. Tokyo: Iwanami Shoten.

Kuwabara, T. (1947). *Gendai Nihon Bunka no Hansei* [Reconsideration for Modern Japanese Culture]. Tokyo: Hakujitsu Shoin.

Lebra, T.S. (1976). *Japanese Patterns of Behavior*. Honolulu: University of Hawaii Press.

Maniwa, M. (1990). *Nihonteki Shûdan no Shakaigaku* [Japanese Groups and Sociology]. Tokyo: Kawaide Shobo Shinsha.

Minami, H.(1983). *Nihonteki Jiga* [Japanese Ego]. Tokyo: Iwanami Shoten.

Morita, A. (1987). *Made in Japan: Akio Moria and SONY*. New York: Fontana.

Motoki, K. & Uchiyama, K. (1992). *Shikiji Undô towa* [What is the Anti-Illiteracy Campaign?]. Osaka: Kaiho Shuppansha.

Nakamura, K. (1990). Kokusai Shikijinen to Kaihô Kyôiku [The International Literacy Year and Education for Liberation]. *Kaiho Kyoiku, 265*, 18-27.

Nakane, C. (1967). *Tate Shakai no Ningen Kankei* [Human Relations in a 'Vertical' Society]. Tokyo: Kodansha.

Nakane, C. (1977). *Kazoku wo Chûsin to shita Ningen Kankei* [Family-Centered Human Societies]. Tokyo: Kodansha.

Nakane, C. (1984). *Japanese Society*. Tokyo: Charles E. Tuttle.

Neustupny, J.V. (1987). *Communicating with the Japanese.* Tokyo: The Japan Times.

Odaka, K. (1967). *Nihonteki Keiei* [Japanese Management]. Tokyo: Chuko Shinsho.

Oka, T. (1990). Social and Historical Backgrounds to Concepts of Self-Help Groups in Europe and North America. *The Journal of Osaka City University-Society for Social Welfare Studies, 7,* 47-58.

Oka, T. (1991). Shûsenngo Kessei sareta Nihon no ikutsukano Jijoteki Sôgo Fujo Soshiki ni tsuite [Japanese Self-Help/ Mutual-Aid Organizations established after the War]. *Jôchi Daigaku Shakai Fukusi Kenkyû, Heisei 2 Nendo Nenpo* 22-66.

Oka, T. (1992). The Three Qualities of Japanese Self-Help Groups: Personal Interaction, Individual Independence, and Development of a Liberation Movement. *Science of Social Welfare, 33*(2), 118-136.

Osa, H. (1978). *Kanja Undô* [Patients' Movements]. Tokyo: Keiso Shobo.

Ôtsuki, H. (1968). On Social Education Given to Girls in Kô-groups in the Edo Era. *The Scientific Researches (The School of Education, Waseda University), 17,* 51-82.

Ozawa, Y. (1990). Gendai Sekai ni okeru Shikiji Undô [The Anti-Illiteracy Campaign in a Modern Society]. *Kaiho Kyoiku, 265,* 58-73.

Powell, T.J. (1987). *Self-Help Organizations and Professional Practice.* Silver Spring: National Association of Social Workers.

Reischauer, E.O. (1988). *The Japanese Today.* Tokyo: Charles E. Tuttle.

Riessman, F. (1965). The "Helper"–Therapy Principle. *Social Work, 10,* 27-32.

Saitô, K. (1939). *Nihonteki Seikaku no Bungaku* [The Characteristics of Japanese Literature]. Tokyo: Shibun Shobo.

Saitô, T. (1977). *Meiji no Kotoba* [Words in the Meiji Period]. Tokyo: Kodansha.

Sakurai, S. (1949). *Nihon Hôken Shakai Ishiki Ron* [The Theory of Japanese Feudal Consciousness]. Tokyo: Nikko Shoin.

Sakuta, K. (1959). Kodoku na Ningen [Lonely People]. In R. Hidaka (ed.), *Ningen to Shakai* (pp. 1-35). Tokyo: Yuhikaku.

Sasaki, A. (1956). "Circle" Undô no Rekishitekina Imi [The Historical Meanings of the "Circle" Movements]. *Chûo Kôron, 813,* 248-257.

Senzaki, K. (1957). *Sâkuru Katsudô Nyûmon* [Introduction to Circle Movements]. Tokyo: San' ichi Shinsyo.

Takahashi, T. (1977) Nenrei Shûdan (Age-Groups). In S. Itô et al. (eds.), *Hikaku Bunka (Vol. 6. Nihonjin no Shakai)* (pp. 41-66).Tokyo: Kenkyu Sha.

Takagiwa, H. (1987). *Nihonjin nitotte Wa towa nanika* [What is the Harmony for Japanese People]. Tokyo: Sotekku Sha.

Taylor, J. (1983). *Shadows of the Rising Sun: A Critical View of the "Japanese Miracle."* Tokyo: Charles E. Tuttle.

Tsuda, M., Kida, K., Yamada, E., & Saitô, M. (1977). *Shôgaisha no Kaihô Undô* [Liberation Movements of People with Disabilities]. Tokyo: San' ichi Shobo.

Tsuda, S. (1964). *Tsuda Sayukichi Zenshû* [The Complete Works of Sayukichi Tsuda]. (Vol.10). Tokyo: Iwanami Shoten.

Wakamori, T. (1954). Nihonjin no Ken'ikan [Japanese Sense of Authority]. In K. Yanagida (ed.), *Nihonjin* (pp. 172-198). Tokyo: Mainichi Shinbunsha.
Woronoff, J. (1979). *Japan: The Coming Economic Crisis.* Tokyo: Yohan.
Yamamoto, K. (1960). Bashô. In: T. Wakamori, M. Takasaki, Y. Ikeda & K. Yamamoto (eds.), *Kinsei Bungei to Minzoku* [Modern Literature and Folk-ways]. (pp. 35-52). Tokyo: Kobundo Shinsha.
Yanabu, A. (1982). *Hon' yakugo Seiritsu Jijô* [The Situations of Formations of Translated Words]. Tokyo: Iwanami Shoten.
Yasumaru, Y. (1974). Minshû Shisô no Tenkai [The Development of the Thoughts of Populace]. In M. Kanai (ed.), *Nihon no Shakai Bunka Shi (Vol.2)* (pp. 391-460). Tokyo: Kodansha.
Yokota, Z. (1972). Nihon no Môjin no Ayumi. [The History of Japanese Blind People]. In Sekai Mojin Hyakka Jiten Henshû Iinkai (ed.), *Sekai Môjin Hyakka Jiten* (pp. 24-42). Tokyo: Nihon Raito Hausu.

Chapter 4

The Development of Self-Help in Germany's New Provinces (Former East Germany): The Case of Schwerin

Ursula von Appen

Informational and Advicement Centre for Self-Help Groups

SUMMARY. Self-help is a young concept in the New Provinces (former East Germany) of the Federal Republic of Germany. The development of self-help groups or organizations in one of the provinces is detailed, with emphasis on the work of an institution playing the role of a clearinghouse. This is an occasion to witness the birth of such a movement in a society experiencing a radical transformation from a socialist ethos to a free-market orientation.

INTRODUCTION

The content and objectives of self-help are always determined by the given social framework within which people discover the need to help themselves in order to assume control of their lives.

The author thanks Methew Harris, who translated the paper, and Mrs. H. Rauch and Mrs. G. Zentsch, Paritätischer Wohlfahrtsverband Mechlenburg-Vorpommern for typing the manuscript.

Address correspondence to Ursula von Appen, Paritäetischer Wohlfahrtsverband, Pappelgrund 10, 2758 Scherwin, Germany.

[Haworth co-indexing entry note]: "The Development of Self-Help in Germany's New Provinces (Former East Germany): The Case of Schwerin." von Appen, Ursula. Co-published simultaneously in *Prevention in Human Services* (The Haworth Press, Inc.) Vol. 11, No. 1, 1994, pp. 97-116; and: *Self-Help and Mutual Aid Groups: International and Multicultural Perspectives* (ed: Francine Lavoie, Thomasina Borkman, and Benjamin Gidron) The Haworth Press, Inc., 1994, pp. 97-116. Multiple copies of this article/chapter may be purchased from The Haworth Document Delivery Center [1-800-3-HAWORTH; 9:00 a.m. - 5:00 p.m. (EST)].

In contrast to the long years of dedicated service in the field of self-help and mutual aid programs in Germany and in the Western world as a whole, such programs must be regarded as a novelty in the new provinces of the Federal Republic of Germany.

This paper will analyze the process by which self-help is being introduced to one community, Schwerin, in Germany's new provinces. It will also describe the special measures taken and the responses of groups, of potential members and of professionals. It will also report the work of the contact-center (clearing house) in Schwerin and its importance for the formation and evolution of self-help groups in that city.

SELF-HELP IN THE FEDERAL REPUBLIC OF GERMANY BEFORE 1989: AN OVERVIEW

Before unification, the self-help movement in the Federal Republic (formerly West Germany) had experienced steady growth. The movement developed in the 1970's, receiving inspiration from similar projects in the United States. This growth has been attributed to radical cultural changes occurring in a post-industrial society of services (Olk, 1992a). In this new social context, many people with similar societal and health-related difficulties felt the lack of beneficial medical, professional and institutional services. They came together in groups to solve their problems. The self-reliance required to act in this manner stemmed from the readiness and the capability to thematicize one's own ego or socio-psychological condition, and social acceptance of this attitude (Olk, 1992b).

Social changes have led to increasing numbers of small two-generation families, persons living alone, and single parents, as well as to a high divorce rate, loneliness following urbanization, and subsequent lack of relationship. As a result of these social developments, there was a corresponding lack of support systems for such events as illness, old age and helplessness. All of these factors provide reasons for the increasing importance of the self-help movement and the necessity to promote self-help and mutual aid by implementing policy through the activity of government or professionals in the field. An important means of fostering self-help in this way was to institute district clearing houses.

The concept of self-help is well-known to the population of the former Federal Republic. The people accept self-help and mutual aid, and organize and make use of this help in different forms: as small self-help discussion groups based on the needs of the individual; as self-help initiatives and projects; and as a means of helping oneself and others.

SELF-HELP IN THE NEW GERMAN PROVINCES AFTER UNIFICATION

What developments have we seen in the past few years in the self-help movement in the new German provinces? The formation of the "Schwerin Contact-Center for Self-Help Groups" can serve as one example to compare with similar efforts in other new provinces. (The term "contact-center" is very nearly synonymous here with "clearing house.")

The Socio-Psychological and Economic Situation

Schwerin is the capital of Mecklenburg West-Pomerania, which as the northernmost of Germany's six new provinces, lies along the Baltic Sea, stretching from Schleswig-Holstein in the west to the Polish border in the east. It is a beautiful region with many lakes and forests; it has an agricultural economy supplemented by the raising of livestock, but little industry. The agricultural production co-operatives once provided many with their livelihood. Since unification, Mecklenburg West-Pomerania has become Germany's poorest state with the highest unemployment rate (16%). Joblessness has affected people from all walks of life, including laid-off university researchers, teachers, day-care workers, and factory workers in plants which are considered unprofitable by free-market standards.

Until recently, in the former East German state (GDR), self-help and mutual aid programs resembling anything like those in the West were, at best, possible only in the relatively autonomous churches.

The concept was unknown to the public as a whole. Initiatives of this kind were undesirable to the government and even forbidden. Groups not fitting into the state or social scheme could be viewed as conspiring against the state. The problem was compounded by the fact that state-sponsored health services and guaranteed institutional services such as daycare, children's programs and employment, to name but a few, all left self-help with a more limited scope of activity than it otherwise would have had in a country with a free market economy.

It is paradoxical that a highly organized socialist state which hemmed people in, maintained intelligence files on individuals and dictated all that happened in public life should have been able to offer people a degree of security in social terms (on the provision that they stayed within the established framework). This security is sorely missed by many people, including those whose protests resulted in the momentous changes of 1989 and 1990.

The health services monopoly which the state held and the cost-free comprehensive medical and social package it maintained for the public often led to reduced personal initiative, a lack of sense of responsible action and self-determination, and a basically indifferent attitude, all of which are tendencies dangerous in a free-market oriented society.

It must be borne in mind that the entire way of life that people had become used to changed dramatically in a very short period of time.

Fear of becoming unemployed now rules the day. One perceives colleagues and fellow workers as a threat and refuses to have anything to do with them, suspecting that they may retain their position while one is left empty-handed when unprofitable factories are shut down or privatized. These are fears which beset people and which give rise to seemingly unrelated physical illnesses which are nevertheless psychologically rooted. Women have been the hardest hit by unemployment. These are women who have always known work and who are being obliged to take early retirement or are simply being laid off. One participant in our self-help programs gave vent to a commonly held feeling when she said, "We cannot simply throw away 40 years of our lives!"

A loss of personal and political identity is what the people of the new German provinces are going through. Shedding a former identity is a phenomenon which one psychotherapist has said can be compared to a grieving process lasting for years. It may conceivably take up to seven years until a new identity can be adopted which will help stabilize the psyche of the people and help heal the sensitive, even hypersensitive conflicts that have arisen among the people of the once divided German nation.

Germany's unification took place in 1989-90. But there will be a long and very difficult process, one of transforming the socialist governmental organization to that of a self-organized society (von Appen, 1992). Poldrack (1992) adds that this transformation process will be accompanied to a greater extent by dangerous crises and destructive forces in society than it will be by productive impulses to modernize.

In the midst of their difficulties–which the people in the new provinces sometimes like to enumerate in self-pitying tones–one thing is clear; most of them do not want to live under socialism again. They recognize that the private sphere has grown and that there is more room for self-determination. They are still getting the feel for this concept and must learn to use it and to see its opportunities even while acknowledging certain boundaries which cannot be overstepped. To convey the value of self-determination and to help people in their development on this new terrain without fostering overt one-upmanship are the important tasks facing self-help programs in the new German provinces.

THE INTRODUCTION OF SELF-HELP IN SCHWERIN

An important principle of the health system in the GDR was that of the unity of prevention, diagnosis, therapy and rehabilitation. Health education was included under the heading of prevention. Education itself must be understood in a very wide sense. It concerned not only the teaching of subjects in schools, but also dealt with health consultation and health promotion for everyone. This specific work was organized by the "Kabinett für Gesundheitserziehung," together with the "Komitee für Gesundheitserziehung," a social institution whose members, coming from all fields of society, participated as non-professionals (von Appen, 1990).

During the transformation period, health education has become more and more centered on socio-psychological concerns. The rising lack of any sense of security among the population and the accompanying psychological symptoms prompted many members of the "Kabinett für Gesundheitserziehung" in the new German provinces to begin setting up self-help groups in Schwerin, Suhl and Erfurt. Expressive of the underlying civil discontent in the new provinces, the first self-help event in Schwerin was a demonstration by single mothers. They wanted to voice their fears about the anticipated elimination of social benefit programs–fears compounded by the spectre of losing their jobs, something which indeed has beset women in particular. The beginnings of self-help in the new provinces have taken on a quality similar to situations found in West Germany in the '60's. There is an expression of discontent with the status quo, one which reflects bitter first-hand experience with societal shortcomings.

The Process of Establishing the Contact-Center

In June, 1991 the Ministry for Families and the Elderly sought applicants for participation in a model program called "Special Measures Toward Social Self Help in the New German Provinces." Grants were allocated to fund the program's work and research for four and a half years. Well over 160 applications were submitted from the new provinces. Seventeen were then chosen for funding.

Before programs were selected for grants, regional information seminars and related events were held in Schwerin for those working in the social and health fields as well as for representatives from the Ministry for Social Affairs in Mecklenburg West-Pomerania. The information thus gathered and sent to the Ministry for Families and the Elderly, accompanied by an application for acceptance to the model program, led to the Schwerin program's being among the seventeen chosen for grants. Its acceptance created a middle-term perspective for four and a half years of funded activity for self-help in Schwerin and also for the contact-center, a registered society with 30 members. Early in March 1992, Frau Rönsch, Minister for Families and the Elderly, set the model program into motion.

The contact-center for self-help groups in Schwerin now employs three full-time staff. They are university graduates. Salaries for two of these employees are provided by an employment program sponsored by the job-office in Schwerin. Funds for the third are allocated by the Ministry for Families and the Elderly. It will be crucial for the continued existence of the contact-center to convince the job-office of the necessity to extend the employment program. For the moment, the local community is not able financially to support the contact-center nor pay the salaries.

The research institutes associated with the work of the contact-center during the term of the model program are: (1) The ISAB Institute (Institute for Social Science Analysis and Counselling/Institut für sozialwissenschaftliche Analysen und Beratung, Cologne/Leipzig), (2) GSD (Society for Systems Research and Services in Health Care/Gesellschaft für Systemforschung und Dienstleistungen im Gesundheitswesen, Berlin), and (3) NAKOS (National Information Center for Self-Help Group Support and Initiative/Nationale Informationsstelle zur Anregung und Unterstützung von Selbsthilfegruppen, Berlin) (source: ISAB, 1992b).

The goals of the work of these research institutes are: to help publicize the concept of self-help in the new German provinces; to support the further instruction of those who are ready to engage themselves in the area of self-help and mutual aid, such as professionals, workers in social and health fields, and also members of the various self-help groups; and to construct a model for the seventeen contact-centers in the new German provinces (ISAB, 1992a, 1993).

The Development of Self-Help in the New German Provinces and in Schwerin

Awareness of the concept of self-help has not risen spontaneously out of any expression of the needs of the lowest strata in society. Well-researched and established self-help programs are being offered to people in the new eastern provinces who at first knew nothing about the concept and could not imagine what it might entail. It is unthinkable for many suffering under physical or psychological hardship that something might be done in the way of self-help without the assistance of doctors, psychologists or the state health system.

But, that which established self-help networks in other countries would refuse to do–set up groups under the guidance of professionals who might be perceived as "dictating" what will happen–will indeed be necessary in the new provinces as long as the people living there are still tied to their earlier habits of thought and do not know enough about the philosophy of self-help and mutual aid, or about the possibilities inherent in supporting each other and using their collective strength to change their individual and common social situations.

Such have been the developments of self-help in Schwerin since the fateful events of 1989. There have been qualitative changes in the ways groups establish themselves and evolve, ranging from the first professionally initiated self-help groups to groups started by those themselves in need of help.

The following developments have been noted:

1. Professionals, in this case workers from the contact center, found a self-help group based on a perceived need after a period of public relations work. The groups take a distinct form as a rule, but are dependent on an organizer who suggests topics and leads the group. Three variants here have been recorded: despite considerable efforts to keep things going, some groups disband after a short period, due to lack of participation or lack of a perceived agenda; some groups continue meeting but require constant guidance for lack of initiative from within the groups; or some groups, after a few meetings and initial guidance, take on a life of their own, becoming self-supporting. These last groups continue to call on the services of the contact-center for the use of rooms or help in making an event public through the local press, but are otherwise self-reliant.

2. The group is established by professionals from outside the contact-center, for example, a nurse or social worker. Members of the group develop a strong attachment to their contact person whom they have come to know well through hospital care or other treatment. Becoming self-supporting is quite an obstacle for a group like this. A great deal of organizational help is needed on the part of the contact-center to support the group. For the moment, this type of group appears to be helpful to participants, owing to the changes which have been made to the health care system in the new provinces.

3. The group is established by an existing group from western Germany which offers exchanges and information about a certain ailment or illness, and reports on its experience in its part of the country. The contact-center tries, through the media, to attract participants who then get in touch with the existing group individually or form a group locally if larger numbers are present. This is a good way to become acquainted with self-supporting groups, and is particularly fitting for people with less common problems which occur infrequently within their community.

4. Self-help programs, well-known elsewhere but previously unknown in the GDR, have found their way to us by way of the former western German states. Members of two groups from Hamburg–Alcoholics Anonymous and Gamblers Anonymous–visited Schwerin. Lengthy discussions with these visitors impressed the local groups a great deal. The reports of extreme suffering on the long road to abstinence as well as evidence of an admirable commitment to the cause were part of these exchanges. They noticed that we were still caught up in a helping syndrome, which we had to admit was correct. One painful learning experience that we gained from the contact was stressed repeatedly by people in Alcoholics Anonymous: the alcoholic has to have reached absolute bottom before any offer of help is effective. This observation may be correct, but it runs counter to our desire to take preventive action immediately. It is particularly important in these difficult times to give support to self-help and enablement programs for the addicted at all stages of the rehabilitative process.

5. The concept of self-help is apparently becoming more familiar to the general public. This becomes evident when we note that women, and men as well, inquire about joining existing groups or forming new ones. The contact-center puts these people in touch with existing groups or establishes a new group with the help of those interested and provides help when desired at the initial stage. Everyone is impressed by how openly and, in fact, how professionally the participants speak of their situation, their problems and their illnesses. Women seem to be more active than men in setting up self-help groups. Since the establishment of the contact-center, only one group has been set up by a man. This man, a veterinary surgeon, jobless after unification, was a single father with a handicapped son.

He quickly found five men with similar problems. But the group dissolved when they found work again.

Women, on the contrary, have founded very stable groups, with agendas including violence against women, "Women who love too much," bulimia, sexual abuse, etc.

6. One change that groups go through, which cannot be helped but which is also understandable, is their being quickly assigned status as a society with a juridical existence, shortly after being constituted, and then being adopted by a state-wide or national association which provides professional as well as occasional financial support. The hierarchical structure which results from this cannot be avoided. Efforts to set one society off from another and competition for members between societies are two unseemly results of this development.

7. Another noticeable tendency was found in Schwerin at the inception of self-help/mutual aid. Physicians and psychologists did not understand fully the meaning of these concepts. They occasionally referred patients to the contact-center with the remark that their joining a group would be good for them. (In most cases, the group was AA or another addictions group.) But the patients were also instructed to report to their doctor whether or not they had joined a group, and if so, tell what group they had joined. The doctor possibly wished to control the patient, and perhaps also to exert an influence over the contact-center. This form of cooperation must be strictly avoided because the contact-center cannot be perceived as the "longer arm" of professionals. One of these doctors expressed his understanding of cooperation with this comment: "You know, it is nice that these groups exist. We do not have all that much time to talk to our patients."

Has self-help become a last ditch measure for some physicians to provide assistance where medical and health care institutions no longer find it possible to help, or do doctors perhaps even feel they cannot help, given the new health services system which also demands that doctors think and act in terms of a free-market economy?

On the other hand, opportunities for collaboration and reciprocal support have developed. During the initial phase of the introduction of self-help to Schwerin, professionals often refused to participate in the self-help movement. The possibility for collaboration and interaction was regarded with skepticism. Now, two years later, health professionals, psychologists and health insurers see many possibilities for and even the necessity of collaboration. But this collaboration implies a danger, namely that "the group could move in the direction of traditional professional standards, thereby losing its unique qualities of self-reliance and empowerment and may even become no more than an appendage of the traditional structure" (Pape, (N.D.), p. 4).

SPECIFIC GROUPS HELPED BY THE CONTACT-CENTER

People who turn to the contact-center have a variety of concerns. An atmosphere of trust enables a majority to speak openly about their problems. Staff members give advice and support in a variety of ways. They refer clients to existing groups with similar problems, or to groups in other regions. They give support in setting up new groups, and help to find space for meetings, either in the contact-center or elsewhere. They also help clients in contacting the news media, politicians, and other professionals, including health insurers.

Here is an attempt to give a breakdown of the most common concerns brought to the contact-center (Table 1):

1. Social problems. The jobless or those finding themselves in early retirement, whether male or female, suffer a great deal when they realize they are no longer needed. "It can't be without consequences for the state if experience, knowledge, competition, that is, the biographical resources of a whole generation are allowed to lie fallow, or are ignored. It will be dangerous if a premature, officially sanctioned creation of this group of people leads to their social limitation and lack of self-respect" (Poldrack, 1992, p. 66).

Given the critical nature of the situation now at hand in the new German provinces, the promotion of self-help groups is also to be viewed in a political perspective.

In another development, we note that when the program was first introduced, group members spoke specifically about their problems of being laid-off or dismissed, or given early retirement. The diffi-

TABLE 1. List of Groups by Types, Numbers of Members, Frequency of Leader's Contacts with the Self-Help Center (Jan.-March 1993).

TARGET GROUP (illness, disease, etc.)	TYPE	NUMBER OF GROUPS	NUMBER OF MEMBERS	FREQUENCY
Morbus bechterew	association	1	30	1
Multiple sclerosis	shg	1	30	2
Spinal disease	shg	1	5	2
Rheumatism League	project assoc.	1	70	3
Hearing impaired	local assoc.	1	70	2
Heart troubled patients	shg	1	8	2
Scleroderma	shg	1	5	6
Retinitis pigmentosa	shg	1	12	3
Osteoporosis	shg	1	5	5
Food allergies	shg	1	5	5
Colitis ulcerosa	shg	1	12	3
Apoplectic	shg	1	4	6
Dialysis patients	shg assoc.	1	70	3
Bulimia	shg	1	5	2
Colon-cancer patients	shg	1	9	7
Throat-cancer patients	shg assoc.	1	20	3
Psychological problems	shg	5	40	14
Women who love too much	shg	1	8	4
Women and sex	shg	1	4	1
Parents groups:				
Children with heart disease	shg	1	3	1

TARGET GROUP (illness, disease, etc.)	TYPE	NUMBER OF GROUPS	NUMBER OF MEMBERS	FREQUENCY
Children with diabetes	shg	1	3	2
Handicapped children	shg	1	15	1
Hyperactive children	shg	1	12	1
Union for protection of children	association	1	?	1
AA	shg	1	12	4
Al-Anon	shg	1	?	3
Friendship group "Problems With Alcohol"	shg	1	5	1
Molli-chic (over eaters)	shg	1	6	3
Early retirement	shg	5	60	18
Creative work	shg	1	8	4
Creative dancing	shg	1	15	3
Painting for seniors	shg	1	14	1
Support for workers and seniors	assoc./ initative	1	60 60	1
Center for the unemployed	assoc.	1	?	1

Source: Kontaktstelle für Selbtshilfegruppen in Schwerin

culties of the transformation process were the most important concerns they discussed. Now that most of them have become friends, they have set up an ambitious cultural program, including visits to the theatre, expositions, and meetings with groups in other provinces. Some have offered to work as volunteer members of the contact-center's executive board. (The contact-center is a nonprofit organization.) Other groups, founded by and for the elderly, are given to activities such as painting, creative dance and other arts. These groups are composed largely of former white-collar workers such as civil servants, institutional staff, teachers, child care workers, office workers and others. Four groups were formed in a very short time; they meet once a week, often in the contact-center.

2. Psychological problems. Four such groups were quickly formed. Participants have usually received therapy, and are able successfully to find help in preventing both relapses and the recurrence of depression and fear. These groups are highly self-sufficient and require only materials from the contact center. Members often acknowledge that talking in the group is more helpful than the therapy they receive in the psychiatric clinic. For some, the self-help group gives the only kind of therapy they need.

3. Addiction problems. While the new German provinces can consider themselves lucky to have so few people with drug addictions, there is a high rate of alcoholism which is rising even higher. Also, the increase in the number of gambling addicts is alarming. Here is one story–recently a young, religious father of three girls confided that he had fallen into a gambling addiction which was ruining his family financially and that he wanted nothing more than to commit suicide. It must be admitted that counselling sessions of this kind can have a disturbing and troubling effect. Gambling halls were not a part of life before unification.

4. Chronic illnesses. These include groups for people suffering from rheumatism, Bechterew spinal disease, and osteoporosis, among others. In the summer of 1992 the contact-center recorded that 28 groups in this category had been formed since 1990 (von Appen, & Schwarz, 1992).

5. Cancer groups. A high frequency of cancers is to be observed in the area. Before 1990, physicians, surgeons and psychologists continued to care for their patients after these patients had been discharged from the clinic following operations or treatment. The situation in which it was possible for out-patients to receive medical advice from clinic doctors who knew them and their illnesses well no longer exists. They must now consult a family doctor. Patients regard this lack of dispensary walk-in treatment as a painful loss.

Knowing this situation, the contact-center suspected there was a strong need for cancer self-help groups. But it proved difficult to put interested people in touch with one another and to set up and run groups, even with the help of the contact-center. Members prefer therapeutic groups under the guidance of a psychologist. There are three groups at the moment for: throat cancer patients; colon cancer patients (stoma); and mastectomy patients. The groups are dependent on an organizer and require constant guidance.

6. Health-related problems. Two examples typify the formation of groups in this category at the contact-center. A young woman who came to the centre explained that she was suffering from bulimia. She said that, at first, she had not known what her illness was. After studying medical journals, she believes she now knows more about her illness than a physician does and wants to help other women by starting a self-help group.

Another woman had been suffering from a food allergy for a long time, and wanted to share with other women what she had experienced. She arranged public lectures for patients and doctors which were well attended. These examples show that self-help is becoming more familiar to the public and also to the physicians who are willing to support self-help groups.

7. Parent groups. These are formed by mothers and fathers of sick children who want to provide support in the context of self-help and mutual aid. Groups include one very small group for parents of children with heart disease, and a large one for parents whose children are suffering from leukemia. The contact-center brought this second group into contact with a well established group in western Germany that had a great deal of experience in organizing social support and mutual aid for leukemic children. Other groups are for parents of autistic children, hyperactive children, or children with other illnesses, including celiac disease.

8. Disabilities. There are a great many people with various disabilities or handicaps who are organized into local groups or associations that were formed after unification. (Only associations for the blind and deaf were permitted in the former German Democratic Republic.) But these local groups, owing to their affiliation with national organizations, often lose the unique character of a truly self-reliant group, and are subject to the hierarchical structure of the national group or organization. In such circumstances, they

can no longer be called self-help groups. Nevertheless, they often maintain limited contact with the contact-center.

SOME REMARKS CONCERNING THE CATEGORIZATION OF SELF-HELP ACTIVITIES

The present model program providing for social self-help in the new German provinces was set up very much along the lines of a similar program which was conducted from 1987 to 1991 under the auspices of the Ministry for Families and the Elderly in the states of the former Federal Republic. Research findings from this earlier program were made public in 1992 and 1993 (Braun and Opielka, 1992; ISAB, 1993). As in these reports, a similar categorization of self-help activities in Schwerin is useful in describing the groups.

Type 1–Small groups bringing together people suffering from common problems in order to talk about them, thereby giving support to themselves and each other. These meet the criteria of a genuine self-help group; they do not turn to the public for help nor do they have a lobby. One example here is a group dealing with psychological problems.

Type 2–Self-help groups, interested in helping themselves and others, seek to make their concerns public and also to address these concerns to the local authorities. Their structure requires delegation of tasks to different group members. Members work on a volunteer basis and receive no professional guidance. An example here is that of a group for those in early retirement.

Type 3–Self-help groups concerned not only with their members' concerns but with educating and counselling families and individuals similarly affected. Such groups have at least one full-time professional worker often made available through a job program. Examples include parent and health education groups or initiatives.

Type 4–Groups which are commonly self-help projects that have professional staff with funds coming from job programs. Members affected by a certain disability or problem find a common cause in helping one another and others suffering from the same problem. They make their concerns and demands known to the public. Groups for the mentally handicapped are an example of this type.

Type 5–Self-help projects offering alternative employment to young people, in health and cultural affairs. The large majority of projects are accomplished with the help of professional staff. These projects seek to change social conditions and may be referred to as social work projects. One example is the project "Work for Women."

Contact-centers work with all forms of self-help groups, but most are directly concerned with the first three types discussed above. This is the case for the contact-center in Schwerin. Table 2 reports the activities of the Schwerin Contact-Center from January to March, 1993.

DISCUSSION

Self-help as it has been practised for decades in the former West German state and in other western countries was almost totally unheard of and hardly likely to be implemented in the former German Democratic Republic before unification, given the then prevailing restrictive state policy and monopoly on all matters concerning health. It was possible to form self-help groups only within the protected sphere of the church.

Despite this, much social initiative, albeit subject to state control, was put into the hands of certain registered associations–for the most part collectives, unions and solidarity groups, company health care groups, and some therapeutic groups under professional guidance.

After unification, swift and radical changes to the health care system as people had known it, accompanied by massive unemployment and early retirement schemes, all led to a severe loss of identity among the older population, to uncertainty within many classes of workers, and to an increase in aggressiveness among the youth.

This new socio-psychological situation which at first led to introversion among the people also inculcated incipient, unconscious needs, ones that might be met only by self-help. Such a condition was therefore a precondition for the successful development of self-help.

The booklet "What is Where?" (von Appen & Schwarz, 1992) groups all institutions with social commitment established after unification, excluding those formed by the local authorities. There are 34 different kinds of self-help groups and associations, 16 advisory organizations (Beratungsstellen), and 19 societies, all having a

TABLE 2. Activities of the Schwerin Contact-Center (January-March 1993)

Number of calls or contacts (distribution by sex)	
Women	69
Men	25
Age	
30 or younger	30
30-50	43
50 or older	29
Employment Status	
Unemployed	34
Not working (early retirement, old age pensioners, people with social assistance benefits)	33
Employed	27
Contact with the center made	
by phone	42
by letter	- -
in person	52
Reason for contact	
General information	24
Information not concerning self-help	11
Information concerning self-help	61
Source of referral	
Media	59
Friends and aquaintances	15
Professional	20
Reason for seeking information on self-help	
What is self-help, what are self-help groups?	71
How do they work?	64
How to enter self-help groups?	25
How to run a self-help group?	21
Municipal and professional services	21
Joblessness, legal consultation	21
Socio-psychological help	34

variety of social concerns. All of these organizations operate with the help of volunteers; some employ social workers whose salaries are funded by the employment program of the job office in Schwerin, but only for a period of 1 to 3 years. It goes without saying that all are struggling for an extension of the job program.

A tendency to network with, and mutually support and consult each other has become noticeable among self-help groups, initiatives, projects, clubs, organizations and professionals in Schwerin. Contacts are also being made with groups in western Germany. Rivalry among groups and clubs has also been observed. Viewed in its entirety, the self-help experience in eastern Germany is one of initial hesitance being offset by positive developments.

These developments were supported by the model program "Special Measures Toward Social Self Help in Eastern Germany," sponsored by the Federal Ministry for Families and the Elderly. With the help of this program, it became possible to:

- promote the awareness of self-help among wide segments of the population
- enhance the awareness, acceptance and support of self-help among professionals, politicians and institutional workers
- enable 17 contact-centers to act temporarily as a central clearing house for self-help activities (with research and other forms of support from the Ministry)

CONCLUSIONS

Self-help is gaining more and more acceptance among the citizens of the new German provinces.

Self-help and mutual aid are necessary and viable alternatives to the health and social services systems that have not yet found their final form in the new provinces.

The idea of self-help and mutual aid must be further propagated to draw people out of their isolation, and to help those who are struggling to overcome problems resulting from the difficult transition period.

The contact-centers play an important role by bringing people with the same experience together and helping them to find appropriate groups, by expanding existing networks of groups, and by promoting self-help among professionals and local authorities.

There is a great deal of concern for the fate of the contact-centers once the model program has ended. The Schwerin Contact-Center still lacks any organizational structure that might allow it to secure the funding necessary for the continuation of its work and the maintenance of the existing job program positions.

REFERENCES

Braun, J., & Opielka, M. (1992). Selbsthilfeförderung durchSelbsthilfekontaktstellen, Abschlußbereicht der Begleitforschung zum Modellprogramm "Informations- und Unterstützungsstellen für Selbsthilfegruppen" des Bundesministeriums für Familie und Senioren (Clearing Houses and the Promotion of Self-help). *Schriftenreihe des Bundesministeriums für Familie und Senioren*, Vol. 14. Köln: Kohlhammer.

ISAB, (Ed.) (1992a). Förderung der sozialen Selbsthilfe in den neuen Bundesländern. Ausgangslage und Ziele des Modellprogrammes des Bundesministeriums für Familie und Senioren (The Advancement of Self-help in the New German Provinces). *ISAB Schriftenreihe* No. 14. Köln: ISAB Verlag, 1992.

ISAB, (Ed.) (1992b). Soziale Selbsthilfe in den neuen Bundesländern. (Social Self-help in the New German Provinces). *ISAB Schriftenreihe*, No. 15. Köln : ISAB Verlag.

ISAB, (Ed.) (1993). Selbsthilfekontaakstellen–eine Investition in die Zukunft (Self-help Contact Centers–An Investment for the Future.) *ISAB Schriftenreihe Berichte aus Forschung und Praxis*, No. 16. Koln: ISAB Verlag.

Olk, T. (1992a). Empfehlunggen zur Förderung von Selbsthilfezusammenschlüssen in den neuen Bundesländern (Recommendations for the Advancement of Self-help in the New Provinces of Germany). In Selbsthilfe in den neuen Bundesländern–Stand und Fördermöglichkeiten Schriftenreihe des BMFuS (ed.) Vol. 11, pp. 58-87. Köln: Kohlhammer.

Olk, Th. (1992b). Selbsthilfe und Selbsthilfeorganisation–sind die Erfahrungen aus dem Westen Rezepte für den Osten? (Self-help and Organization of Self-help: the Experiences of the "West"–Are They Prescriptions for the "East?") In *NAKOS Extra*, No. 15, Berlin 1992, pp. 14-25.

Pape, B. (N.D.). An Introduction to Self-Help/Mutual Aid. Canadian Mental Health Association. In Self-Help Canada Series.

Schulz, R. (1990). Der Aufbruch der Selbsthilfebewegung in der DDR (The Origins of the Self-help Movement in the GDR). In NAKOS Extra No. 8, Berlin: pp. 7-11.

von Appen, U. (1990). Theoretisches Konzept und gesellschaftliche Wirklichkeit der Gesundheitserziehung des Kreiskabinetts für Gesundheitserziehung Schwerin (Theoretical Concepts and Social Reality in Health Education: Experiences of the Regional Health Committee, Schwerin). In W. Thiele (ed.), *Das Gesundheitswesen der DDR: Aufbruch oder Einbruch?*, pp. 265-269, Schriftenreihe Forum Sozial-und Gesundheitspolitik, Vol. 1, St. Augustin : Asgard.

von Appen, U. (1992). *Von der staatlichen Organisation zur selbst organissierten Gesellschaft?* (From governmental Organization to a Self-organized Society?). In *NAKOS Extra Berlin*, 1992, pp. 3-133.

von Appen, U., and Schwarz, U. (eds.) (1992). *Was ist wo?* (What is Where?). Schwerin.

Chapter 5

Advocacy on Self-Help for Patients with Chronic Illness: The Hong Kong Experience

Donna Wong
Cecilia Chan

University of Hong Kong

SUMMARY. While in Western countries, the development of the self-help movement is flourishing in the social service and health-care scene, there is a lack of such parallel development in Hong Kong. This may be due to the different cultural orientations as well as the lack of deliberate effort on the part of the government and related professionals. The present establishment and service delivery system of the healthcare institutions in Hong Kong has few provisions to cater to the social adjustment and quality of life for chronic patients. Although Chinese families and kinship networks are invaluable assets in providing support to patients and caregivers, the cultural stigmatization against illness and the strong sense of paternalistic professional domination in the present medical system are obstacles to the development of self-help among patients in Hong Kong. Witnessing the gross hardship and neglect of chronic patients, the authors took on an action research project to advocate for gov-

Address correspondence to Donna Wong, Department of Social Work and Social Administration, The University of Hong Kong. Pokfulam Road, Hong Kong.

[Haworth co-indexing entry note]: "Advocacy on Self-Help for Patients with Chronic Illness: The Hong Kong Experience." Wong, Donna and Cecilia Chan. Co-published simultaneously in *Prevention in Human Services* (The Haworth Press, Inc.) Vol. 11, No. 1, 1994, pp. 117-139; and: *Self-Help and Mutual Aid Groups: International and Multicultural Perspectives* (ed: Francine Lavoie, Thomasina Borkman, and Benjamin Gidron) The Haworth Press, Inc., 1994, pp. 117-139. Multiple copies of this article/chapter may be purchased from The Haworth Document Delivery Center [1-800-3-HAWORTH; 9:00 a.m. - 5:00 p.m. (EST)].

ernment support to self-help groups and policy changes on the scope and models of rehabilitation services to chronic patients. Based on the action research project and the organizing experiences in advocacy for government recognition and provisions for their needs, this paper attempts to describe the social dimensions of coping with illness and the potentiality and benefits of the development of the self-help movement in the Chinese culture of Hong Kong.

INTRODUCTION

Hong Kong is a congested metropolitan city with 5.9 million people residing on 1,045 square kilometres of land. Being one of the "Four Little Dragons" in Asia, Hong Kong has witnessed a very prosperous economical growth over the previous decade and still has a very promising economic future as the "southern window" to Mainland China. Having been under the British colonial administration for over one hundred years, many of Hong Kong's social policies and social service provisions are planned on an incremental basis. The Hong Kong government often attributes the present prosperity and success to its "positive non-interventionist policy," which implies that the government would intervene as little as possible and only when necessary. Therefore, in tackling the population's increasingly complicated social and health problems, many of its existing policies and provisions are often criticized as incomprehensive and lacking in vision and foresight. Hong Kong is also said to be a place where the East meets the West. While an overwhelming majority of its population are Chinese and many of the traditional customs and beliefs are still preserved, the Hong Kong way of life is predominantly a mixture of Western and Eastern culture. As opposed to Western countries where the flourishing development of the self-help movement is conspicuous in the social service and healthcare scene, there is lack of such a parallel development in Hong Kong. This may be due to the different cultural orientations as well as the lack of deliberate and conscious effort on the part of government and related professionals to adopt the self-help strategies in models and structure of service and help. The interest, readiness and ability of Chinese patients to participate in self-help activities may be different from their counterparts in the West. This paper will describe the social dimensions of coping with illness as well as the development of the self-help movement with respect to the process of an action research on members of self-help groups for chronic patients.

PROBLEMS OF CHRONIC PATIENTS AND HEALTHCARE IN HONG KONG

According to the Social Welfare White Paper on "Social Welfare Into the 1990s and Beyond," published in March 1991, life expectancy in Hong Kong is expected to rise to 76.6 for males and 82.3 for females by the year 2000. The proportion of the elderly population is expected to rise from 13% in 1990 to 15.4% in 2000 (Hong Kong Government 1991: 6). With the advancement in medical treatment and an increasing proportion of the aging population, the number of chronic patients is growing. There were 233,000 hospital admissions related to illness with chronic consequences in Hong Kong in 1992 (Hospital Authority, 1993). The care for elderly persons and chronic patients will constitute a great psychological and emotional stress, and a financial burden on the individuals, families and society at large. It will also create considerable demand for support services such as home help and family aide. Unfortunately, the capacity of family care will decrease as family size is projected to fall from 3.4 persons in 1990 to 3.0 by 2000. Alternative self-help and community support will be essential in order to strengthen the deteriorating self-care capacity of individuals and families.

However, the present establishment and service delivery system of healthcare institutions in Hong Kong has few provisions to cater to the social adjustment and quality of life for chronic patients. Under the present service categorization and segregation between social services and medical care, services for chronic patients are mostly confined purely to medication. The whole spectrum of psychosocial needs and difficulties brought about by illness is largely undermined by the present social service sector. In the existing social service provisions, the scope of rehabilitation service is quite narrowly defined by the government. Rehabilitation services are restricted to the physically and mentally disabled, while chronic patients are excluded from the list. Under the present rehabilitation policy, visceral disability and other disabilities brought about by chronic illness are not included as target groups for rehabilitation services. Therefore, there are no support services to relieve patients of their psychosocial stress and assist them in coping with their chronic burden and difficulties.

CHINESE CULTURE AND SELF-HELP IN COPING WITH CHRONIC ILLNESS

Cultural Stigmatization Against Illness

There are a lot of myths among the Chinese population concerning illness. A sick person is considered to carry bad luck and is excluded or rejected by others because of superstitious beliefs. In Chinese culture, being ill is often regarded as a fatalistic punishment for evil deeds of the patient or his/her ancestors, or because he/she must have offended some evil spirits from hell. Chronic patients often feel a strong social stigma, isolation and loss of their 'healthy' friends who are mostly uncomfortable socializing with them after the illness. There are family members who see chronic illness as being contagious and avoid eating with them at the same table. The patient's sex life may also be affected and very few Chinese would seek help on sexual matters, as it is also a taboo. The stress, anxiety, emotional tension, sexual difficulties and financial burden associated with illness have led to the breakdown of marriages.

The family life, self-esteem, social network, and work of the chronic patient will all be affected. Chinese are expected to tolerate hardship, withstand sufferings quietly and not make demands on the system. Because of associated strong negative labels, chronic illness brings about social isolation and loneliness. Life philosophy of patients and family members may change. A significant number of patients have suicidal thoughts when faced with a chronic illness.

Living with a permanent disability is humiliating. Disabled or chronically ill persons are seen as a burden to the family in the Chinese culture. The patient's capacity to cope is severely hindered by the lack of psychological preparation and social recognition for individual rights and the dignity to live a decent life. It is especially true when patients know very little about their diagnosis, treatment, prognosis and rehabilitation. There is a very strong sense of helplessness among the disabled or chronically ill population.

Social Support and Family Cohesion

As stated in the Social Welfare White Paper on "Social Welfare Into the 1990s and Beyond": "Social networks are part of Chinese culture and tradition and have always existed in Hong Kong. They are most clearly demonstrated in the role of the family as the primary providers of care and welfare and by the contributions of clansmen associations, neighbourhood organizations and volunteers" (Hong Kong Government, 1991).

The family is still a very strong social unit in Chinese societies. Chinese families are important caring and social support units that have a high utilitarian value and social integrative functions. Chinese are willing to make personal sacrifices for the sake of other family members, and they are expected to do so. Filial piety and parental reciprocity are highly valued in Chinese families. Parents are expected to be unconditionally supportive of their children and the children, in turn, are expected to do the same when the parents are in need. The familial responsibility network involves relatives and kin. Women are often expected to perform the caregiver's role to the sick or the old. The capacity of the family to mobilize resources and manpower in the provision of concrete care is usually high. Relatives and friends are willing to contribute towards the care of sick persons if necessary. The extensive family networks and close kinship ties are a strong asset for Chinese patients. However, the strength of family and kinship ties is gradually reducing with decreasing family size and the changing role of women in Hong Kong (Ngan, 1990).

Chinese are trained to be modest, cautious, self-contained, and to operate within an obligation network. Chinese have a strong collectivistic orientation in protecting and safeguarding the interest and well-being of the whole family (Yang, 1986). They would greatly hesitate to disclose family and private matters to non-relatives, social workers, etc. Chinese are expected to tolerate hardship and sufferings quietly and are socialized to restrain from revealing strong emotions and personal feelings. The concept of self-help outside the family and kinship network is alien and foreign to Chinese people as they think in terms of the family as a unit and not the individual. Seeking help beyond the family and kinship system on personal and private matters would be seen as a last resort and is not a common practice. Thus, it would be difficult to develop self-help activities among the patients themselves without some initiation from professionals, doctors and social workers.

Traditional Culture in Folk and Herbal Medication

Two distinctive cultural systems and practices regarding health care and treatment co-exist in Hong Kong. Alongside the officially institutionalized health care system that is based on western medical science and technology, there is the Chinese folk and herbal medical tradition that penetrates deeply into ordinary people's way of life. Chinese believe in the total well-being and homeostasis of the 'five materials' (metal, wood, water, fire and earth), as well as 'the hot and cold' (yin-yan) components in the body. Eating nutritious food, practicing tai-chi and chi-gong, and taking herbal medicine and tonic regularly are ways of keeping the body in good balance. The body, the mind and the interaction with the environment is seen as an integral part of homeostasis.

With the strong emphasis on food and tonic, Chinese have very elaborate practices concerning diet and use of herbal materials in maintaining the fitness of the body and preventing disease. There is also the popularity of alternative medicine like acupuncture, acupressure and chi-gong which are treasured as traditional wisdom in health care. Actually, the folklore practices can be regarded as forms of self-help among Chinese people that supplement the formal healthcare system in upkeeping fitness of the body and health conditions. Various forms of tai-chi classes, chi-gong classes and diet training are popular among healthy individuals as well as patients.

Patients are keen to exchange among themselves the use of herbs and diets in enhancing body functions. However, such practices, although culturally acceptable and popular, can also be controversial as to whether they should be properly recognized by health professionals and social workers in their roles and functions in patient groups. These practices provide a less personal and threatening focus of exchange and coping for the patients, as opposed to group activities that require verbal and emotional sharing, which are rather demanding to the reserved and less articulate Chinese patients. However, while traditional practices have the merit of emphasizing self-responsibility and preventive orientations in sustaining the wellness of the body and the mind, the healing effects in chronic illness of many folklore practices are sometimes exaggerated and mystical. Alternative medicine is widely practiced and yet the standards and accreditation of practitioners are not monitored by government. Many chronic patients tend to turn to alternative medicine when they lose hope of recovery under western medication. They may hang on illusively to the hope of complete recovery instead of facing and coping with the reality of their chronic disability.

Self-Help Among Patients in Hong Kong

In the present healthcare system, there is a strong sense of professional paternalism in which doctors dominate the treatment process and patients are submissive to the professional authority. Patient involvement is minimal since patient-doctor interaction and communication is inadequate. For example, in an outpatient clinic, patients may have to wait for four hours to receive a three minute consultation and in specialized clinics, they may have to wait for months before getting an appointment. Doctors cannot spare the time to explain in detail the treatment process and implications. Chronic patients, in particular, have few channels to learn about their illness and related healthcare practices. Public health education and screening has not been given much emphasis and the general standard of medical and health knowledge is rather low. Respect for authority and fear of conflict among the Chinese often lead them to silence and compliance to the prescriptions of doctors and nurses. The notion of self-responsibility and mutual support among patients is largely undermined in the present healthcare system.

Patients can hardly come together and be acquainted with each other under the present medical delivery system. There is a great turnover of inpatients and the overloading of outpatient services hardly allows patients to have the chance to meet each other. Mutual help among chronic patients is rare as there are too few professionals, medical doctors, nurses and social workers who have taken on the leadership of organizing patients to help themselves. The existing manpower ratio of medical social workers is one to ninety beds, which is extremely inadequate. With limited manpower and resources, medical social workers can only deal with the more urgent and substantial patient needs like financial hardships, compassionate rehousing and caring for family members. They cannot spare the time and resources for patient counselling, organizing support groups, etc.

ACTION RESEARCH ON SELF-HELP GROUPS FOR PATIENTS WITH CHRONIC ILLNESS

Rationale and Background of the Action Research

In 1991, the government had decided to set up a working group to review the rehabilitation policy and to enlist suggestions and service recommendations in the form of a Rehabilitation Green Paper. The paper will act as a blueprint for the development of rehabilitation policy and services for persons with chronic illness in the decades to come. Seeing that it was timely to take this opportunity to alert the policy makers on needs and hardships of chronic patients and to introduce the notion of self-help in patient rehabilitation, the authors of this paper began to plan for an action research project on self-help groups for chronic patients. The authors are now teaching staff of The Department of Social Work and Social Administration of the University of Hong Kong. Witnessing the gross hardship and neglect of chronic patients in Hong Kong and given the strong community organizing expertise of the authors, the action research project was focused on advocacy and changes in the rehabilitation policy through patient participation. On the other hand, there is also the idea of advocacy for the recognition and promotion of self-help groups as a unique form of patient support.

The action research project's approach mainly utilized community organizing and advocacy strategies in parallel with the research process. According to Voth (1979), "Action research is research used as a tool or technique, . . . and has as its objectives the acquisition of valid information, action and the enhancement of the problem solving capabilities of the community or organization." The aim of the research project is to identify existing self-help groups for persons with chronic illness in Hong Kong, share with them their experience of organizing self-help groups, and discuss their hopes and aspirations for the Rehabilitation Green Paper. The distinctive feature of the research project is that the whole research process is an organization process, in which the groups and patients are mobilized through the interviews and forums to specify and act on their own needs. The research is committed to problem solving and community action. The findings, information on the needs of persons with chronic illness and the existing self-help conditions among these patients and their families, together with a series of recommendations, were supplied to the Health and Welfare Branch. The latter is working on the White Paper on Rehabilitation Policies and Services.

Phase One: Client Group Contact and Problem Identification

The research team identified 16 self-help groups for persons with chronic physical illness in Hong Kong by using a snowball method; with the help of professionals, the mass media and informants; and by asking doctors and social workers in major public hospitals. This number is very small compared to other cities in the world. The groups were mostly formed with the help of doctors, nurses and social workers. However, patients and their family members are fully autonomous in matters of daily operation, making all decisions concerning their group activities and programmes by themselves. The name of the 16 self-help groups for persons with chronic illness identified in the study and the type of illness or disability that they target are:

Name of Self-Help Group	Type of Illness/Disability
Hong Kong New Voice Club	Laryngectomees, speech loss
CanSurvive: H.K. Cancer Information and Support Group	Cancer
H.K. Stoma Association	Stoma
Hong Kong Lupus Association	Systemic Lupus Erythematosus (SLE)
Regeneration Society	SLE, arthritis and cancer
Cooley's Anaemia Parents Mutual Aid Society	Cooley's Anaemia
H.K. Haemophilia Association	Haemophilia
PHAB Ankylosing Spondylitis Club	Ankylosing Spondylitis
UCH Renal Dialysis Group	Kidney failure

Renal Companion Association	Kidney transplant
Pneumoconiosis Mutual Aid Association	Pneumoconiosis
H.K. Rheumatoid Arthritis Association	Rheumatoid Arthritis
Hong Kong Asthma Society	Asthma
Diabetic Mutual Aid Society of H.K.	Diabetes
Paraplegic & Quadriplegic Association	Paraplegia and Quadriplegia
Direction: Volunteer Service for the Handicapped	Paraplegia and Quadriplegia

During the initial phase of the research process, researchers made use of the data collection and interviewing process to contact the leaders and core members of the self-help groups and to engage them in active participation and involvement. This allowed leaders and members to understand the aims and objectives of the research and to be aware of the significance of the Rehabilitation Green Paper as well as the importance of reflecting their needs to government. The study consists of three parts: (1) a survey on the organizational structure of self-help groups for persons with chronic illness in Hong Kong; (2) a survey of the core group members of these self-help organizations; (3) a survey of professionals who are advisors to self-help groups for persons with chronic illness. Questionnaire surveys and long interviews were used in this research. Personal experiences of patients and their family members were recorded to illustrate their hardships and aspirations.

For the 16 self-help groups under study, their time of establishment varied; however nearly half of the groups were organized for a period of less than three years (from the time of the study). Most of them (50%) have a membership size of 100 to 300. As for their activities, most of them have social and recreational functions (14 groups); health talks (12 groups); community education (7 groups) and publications (9 groups); hospital visits (7 groups), etc. As regarding their goals and objectives, most of the groups emphasize mutual support and facilitation of patient understanding into their illness in their constitutions. They also share common difficulties, of which the most frequently mentioned were the lack of fixed venue for activities and meetings (13 groups); shortage of manpower resources (12 groups) and lack of stable financial support in programmes and other expenses (9 groups). On the other hand, very few of them (3 groups) have included the advocacy of patient rights and goals of policy or system changes into their group goals and objectives.

Respondents were asked to express their views on financial assistance, housing, community support services, transportation, social and emotional counselling, as well as government support for self-help groups for persons with chronic illness in Hong Kong. Respondents were very enthusiastic in expressing their views on possible improvements in social policy and service provisions to persons with chronic illness. They felt that they have long been suffering from neglect in government policy and have much firsthand experience of how difficult it is for patients to gain access to services that are situated in gaps between social and medical service provisions. The data collection process served important functions in facilitating core members' articulation of their needs and arousing their awareness of the importance of voicing their problems and concerns during the policy formulation and consultation phase of the Rehabilitation Green Paper.

Phase Two: Mobilization and Consensus on Action Goals and Strategies

Besides data collection and interviews, the research team had organized frequent sessions and forums to facilitate the mutual sharing among self-help groups on their needs, difficulties and expectations towards government on relevant rehabilitation policies. In these meetings, patient representatives began to realize the importance of grouping themselves together and voicing out their needs and concerns to government during the consultative period of the Rehabilitation Green Paper issued by the Health and Welfare Branch in March, 1991. Their critique of existing services and provisions to chronic patients and their overall recommendations to the government were organized into a position paper. Specifically, they had built up a consensus on several areas of concern and pushed for prompt action and serious consideration by government as follows:

1. To include visceral disability in the classification of disability in the White Paper on Rehabilitation Policy and Services;
2. To set up an interdepartmental working group under the Health and Welfare Branch to examine the needs of chronic patients and develop appropriate policy and service guidelines in meeting these needs;
3. To set up patient resource centres in hospitals, clinics and in the community to provide patients with health knowledge, enquiry services, community nursing, self-help groups and a whole range of community-based rehabilitation programs to patients;
4. To strengthen supportive services in home-help, housing arrangements, counselling services, transportation arrangements, occupational placement and training; as well as recognizing chronic patients' special needs for financial assistance.

The 16 self-help groups thus organized themselves into an ad-hoc group called "The Concern Group of Chronic Patients" and launched a series of actions to plead for their needs and services.

Phase Three: Action and Public Appeal

The Rehabilitation Green Paper was publicly announced in March, 1991 and there was a three month consultation period. The Concern Group used the consultation period to enlist public appeal and attention of policy makers. In order to arouse attention in a short time, the Concern Group decided to organize a march to plead for support through a wider coverage of press and mass media reports. Each self-help group sent representatives to the march and petitions to the Office of Members of Legislative Council. Case interviews conducted earlier were presented to legislative councillors and the mass media by the patients themselves in the petition. Basic organizational information such as a brief preface on each type of chronic illness and related disabilities, a general introduction to each self-help group and the Concern Group's position paper on the Rehabilitation Green Paper were organized into an information kit for distribution to the press and legislative councillors. The research materials were fully utilized in the action process and were very useful in helping the reporters and councillors to understand the background of chronic illness within the short petition time span. Much public sympathy and attention was gained through the mass media and many of the summary recommendations received consideration from legislative councillors and government officials.

After the petition, newspapers and television reporters made use of the hot issue to have press features and case interviews that showed some of the hardships of chronic patients, policy gaps that neglect patient needs and the function of self-help groups in patients' coping. Officials of concerned government departments, professional bodies of doctors and medical social workers and political groups began to pay attention to patient needs as well as the role and function of self-help groups in rehabilitation. The research findings on patient difficulties and functions of self-help groups were organized into a report in which the systematic presentation of research findings helped different parties concerned to grasp the existing situations of the 16 self-help groups. The research data, in its organized and concise format, was a useful tool for advocacy and political lobbying. Several aspects of the research findings were highlighted in the advocacy process: (1) hardships and needs of patients: patients express difficulties in finance, social participation, housing, transportation, etc.; (2) functions of self-help: respondents highly regard the benefits of participation in self-help groups; (3) organizational and operational difficulties of self-help groups.

Phase Four: Formal Organization

On the other hand, the government was reviewing its medical fee charging policy and the Concern Group also raised its standpoints and concerns to appropriate bodies regarding the issue. After a series of actions, patient self-help groups began to realize the need for patient empowerment; they also began to see the need for a long term platform for chronic patients in advocacy of their rights and communication with professional bodies and government on medical and rehabilitation issues.

With the formal drafting of the constitution and registration under the Society Registration Office, the self-help groups involved in the research became the backbone of the Alliance of Patients'

Self-Help Groups which had its inauguration ceremony on February 27, 1993. The formation of the Alliance signified the potentiality and emergence of a more prosperous development of the self-help movement in Hong Kong. It is the first of its kind in Hong Kong. Although it is newly formed and has very little resources and formal recognition, it has aroused concern among health professionals and social workers regarding the importance and contribution of self-help groups. There are positive gestures by government in allocating resources for furthering the development of self-help groups for patients.

Intervention Approaches

The researchers took on the role of community organizers in the whole process and worked with the patients in their advocacy and actions. Altrichter et al. (1991) identified the following principles as the working definition of action research:

1. People reflect and improve their own situations by tightly interlinking their reflection and also making their experience public, not only to other participants but also to other persons interested in and concerned about the work and the situation;
2. Data-gathering by participants themselves (or with the help of others) in relation to their own questions;
3. Participation in decision-making;
4. Power-sharing and the relative suspension of hierarchical ways of working towards industrial democracy;
5. Collaboration among members of the group as a "critical community";
6. Self-reflection, self-evaluation and self-management by autonomous and responsible persons and groups;
7. Learning progressively (and publicly) by doing and by making mistakes in a "self-reflective spiral" of planning, acting, observing, reflecting, replanning, etc.

The principles resemble the participatory and empowerment process in community development. The present action research project with patients also has all the following features: actively involving the patients in the process of identifying their problems, building up consensus on action goals, planning for actions and expressing their needs and demands to public and related government officials. Throughout the whole organizing process, the research team adopts a wide range of community action strategies mainly concerned with empowerment, policy advocacy and public appeal to help patients to solve their problems.

Strategies in Patient Empowerment

The essence of empowerment is to enable clients to help themselves. Patients with low self-esteem must be revitalized to develop a sense of confidence, dignity and pride in order to assert their rights regarding rehabilitation services and fair treatment and attention to their needs. Organizers help them in re-establishing a positive self-image and self-acceptance by support and empathy. On the other hand, organizers help patients to build up an assertive attitude when presenting their needs and claims. They were encouraged to see clearly that they are suffering from difficult life circumstances that they may or may not be able to revolt against. However, they can definitely bring about change to cope with the situation positively. With the seminars, sharing sessions and forums, patients were supplied with information regarding government's rehabilitation policy, the comparison of the range of services for chronic patients to those of their disabled counterparts and the structure of decision making in government. Clients therefore began to be aware of the need to organize themselves together as a united front and to advocate their needs. A process of training and coaching through rehearsal and role play, as well as policy analysis and consolidation were employed to increase the assertiveness of patients and to bolster their confidence when pleading for their rights before legislative council members and government officials.

Strategies in Public Advocacy

In the various actions launched by the chronic patients, a conscious effort was made to promote public awareness of hidden hardship and human sufferings which the public is not aware of. Detailed policy analysis and proposal of alternatives are useful to government officials and political groups so as to improve public policies and increase relevance of these policies to tackle hard core problems in society. Groups for chronic patients were originally less vocal and articulate in voicing their needs. The research findings and studies on individual cases helped to present their sufferings and problems more systematically in order to gain public and legislative council members' sympathy. Case histories were presented as vivid illustrations of the research and statistical data. With objective research data, subjective experiences and case histories of patients, the issue obtained favourable coverage in the mass media, which serves an important function in arousing the public and government in public advocacy.

Strategies in Extensive and Inter-Disciplinary Lobbying

Once the social actions were staged publicly by the chronic patients, they immediately received wide public attention and concern. The Concern Group then began to launch a series of lobbying initiatives to seek support from various disciplines and decision making bodies. Having the position paper as a blueprint for their policy recommendations and service reforms, the patients made contacts with different government departments, advisory committee members, political groups, professional bodies and social service agencies. It was most impressive that an alliance composed of doctors, social service agencies, individual academics and medical bodies joined hands to support one of the patients' requests for the setting up of a community based patient resource centre. The mobilization of patients as well as professionals and political groups in the advocacy process has proved to be a success as shown by the promising responsiveness of government in the resource centre.

SIGNIFICANCE OF THE ALLIANCE ON FUTURE DEVELOPMENT OF PATIENT SELF-HELP IN HONG KONG

Self-Help in Supplementing the Formal Medical Service Delivery System

Traditionally, patients are merely powerless recipients in the bureaucratic system of medical service. They are submissive to doctors' authority and expertise and have no say in policy planning and monitoring of service quality. In the formal medical system, doctors cannot spare enough time during the consultation to explain the details of the disease and the treatment process. Patients do not have enough knowledge about their own illness and many care givers are helpless because of ignorance in the basic understanding of the patients' situation and the technical mastery of patients' care. Many patients turn to self-help groups for guidance and assistance. For example, The Stoma Association helps new patients and caregivers on stoma care and periodically organizes talks by medical specialists on related topics for patients and family members. Their mutual support and encouragement supplement the inadequacies of existing formal medical service delivery systems. Many chronic patients would need a high level of knowledge and understanding of the illness in order to cope and prevent further deterioration. For example, the diabetic patients would need to know how to calculate calories and restrain themselves in diet control to prevent deterioration of their health. If such health education is neglected, society may have to bear an increasing cost in medical care when the patients develop complications and require more intensive and costly institutional care. The Alliance of Patients' Self-Help Groups advocates on the importance of health education for patients and the contribution of self-help groups that enhance the quality of life for chronic patients. This aspect of psychosocial care bridges the gap between medical and social service in Hong Kong and the cost-saving potential is appealing to policy makers and professionals.

Empowerment of Patients in Policy Planning and Implementation

With the establishment of patient self-help groups and the Alliance, dialogue and communication channels have been established among policy makers, professional bodies, hospital executives and patients. Patients have their platform to reflect their views and opinions on issues pertinent to their well-being. Most active members of the Alliance enjoyed taking part in the lobbying activities as the process increased their sense of confidence and self-esteem. Although the Alliance is still in its infancy stage, it functions as a catalyst for patients' knowledge and awareness of policy matters and mobilizes patients to participate actively in policy planning and priorities in resource allocation. Patients' involvement is important in monitoring service quality and increasing the responsiveness and sensitivity of bureaucracies in catering to their needs. However, it would be up to government and professional bodies to answer to the rising expectations of patients in the medical system. How well policy-makers and doctors can be receptive and open to public monitoring is still in question. Nevertheless, with the formation of the Alliance and an increasing number of self-help groups, the medical system would have to adjust itself to face the changing demands and hopefully effect greater democratization in addressing patients' needs.

Partnership Between Professionals and Patients

With more patients organizing themselves into self-help groups, it can be envisaged that cooperation and partnership between health professionals and patients would be enhanced. Owing to the strong compliance of patients to authority, doctors in Hong Kong should be actively involved in acting as catalysts to the formation of new groups of patients. Patients can easily be mobilized by doctors' invitations and suggestions for group participation. Many doctors serve as honourary consultants or volunteers to the self-help groups and assist the groups in their activities. Doctors often refer patients to the self-help groups for pre-operational support and sharing. Patients with prior experiences serve as sources of peer counselling and modelling to new patients. Patients are actually important resources in the medical system. Self-help groups and health professionals also have many co-operative ventures in public health education. For example, kidney transplant patient groups and doctors join hands in the promotion of organ donations. With cooperation and partnership between health professionals and self-help groups, medical care can be more humanitarian and comprehensive. With the advocacy of the Alliance, which pleads for government support in facilitating the self-help movement in patients' care, two major hospitals in Hong Kong have begun to experiment with this approach by setting up patient resource centres in their hospitals. Many doctors are aware of the need for patients to support and play an active role in the formation of self-help groups. These are encouraging signs for the self-help movement in the medical scene and hopefully, patients and doctors can work hand in hand for the benefit of all.

CONCLUSION: SELF-HELP MOVEMENT IN HONG KONG'S CULTURAL CONTEXT

For Chinese people, coping with illness and misfortune is largely a private and family business. Effort has to be made to persuade them to seek help from people and systems outside their immediate family. On the other hand, the self-help movement would also expand and enhance the family's coping ability. While Chinese families in Hong Kong are still an important and cohesive social unit in supporting patients in times of crises and illness, self-help groups can strengthen the family's resources and give support to patients and caregivers. With rapid urbanization and the increasing trend of small families, the self-help movement should be a timely strategy to support Hong Kong families in their caregiving capacity as well as their ability to cope with the stress of chronic illness.

As Chinese people tend to be inarticulate and reserved in revealing their feelings, most of the activities organized by the existing mutual help groups are social and educational in nature. It would require more professional social work input to help the patients to open up and make full use of the group by sharing their feelings and personal problem solving techniques. With social work support, the existing self-help groups can actually expand their existing functions and include more types and varieties of programs like stress management training, therapeutic groups and sharing sessions that can be organized to enhance patients' capacity to cope with the chronic illness and related difficulties. Hospitals and clinics can institutionalize peer counselling sessions and new patient orientation programs through the patient resource centre so that social workers can reach out to patients in the hospitals. All patients will be involved so that they will not be stigmatised as someone with a personal problem. Once patients participate in mutual help activities, they usually report great satisfaction in finding persons who have similar experiences and who understand. Despite the reserved cultural norms regarding sharing of personal problems and feelings among Chinese, such barriers can have breakthroughs with the gradual group work intervention process.

Cohesion and support in self-help groups for chronic patients and their family members counteracts the cultural stigmatization and negative labelling of being ill. Many patients suffer from rejection, shame and distancing from close relatives and even family members because of their misconception about illness. They may develop a sense of guilt in being unable to fulfil their family obligations and responsibilities, as well as increasing the burden to family members. They often feel relieved and supported when they find other patients in self-help groups who share similar problems. It is only in such patient' groups that they can build up their self-esteem and encourage each other to counteract and face social discrimination and rejection squarely.

Public education on health and illness would rectify some of the irrational cultural myths and misconceptions. For example, to people in Hong Kong, cancer is still a taboo subject, which they associate immediately with a death sentence. It is painstaking for cancer patients and their family members to learn about the disease and the way to cope with it. With more patient groups and public health education, they can learn that many cancer patients can have a good prognosis and increase their sense of mastery while avoiding unnecessary despair. Integration of the sick into the community would be a gradual process that would favor modification and demystification in cultural beliefs. Such a process can be facilitated with the emergence of more self-help groups and their continuous effort in patients' education.

REFERENCES

Altrichter, H. Kemmis, S., McTaggart, R. & Zuber-Skerritt, O. (1991) "Defining, Confining or Refining Action Research." In Zuber-Skerritt, O. (ed.), *Action Research for Change and Development.* England: Avebury, Gower Publishing Company Limited.

Chan, C., Wong, D., Ho, P., Ip, F., Tong, H. (1992) *Report of a Survey of the Members of Self-Help Groups for Persons with Chronic Illness in Hong Kong.* Department of Social Work and Social Administration, University of Hong Kong.

Chan, Cecilia (1991) The Contribution of Medical Social Services to Hospitals:

The Model of Social Work Practice in Hospitals. Paper presented in the *Symposium on "In the Hospital Authority, is Medical Social Service Necessary?"* 24th January, 1991, Hong Kong Council of Social Service.
Cheung, K.J. (1988) "Awareness and Organization of Parents." In the *Seminar on the Promotion of Parents' Organization*, Joint Council of Physically & Mentally Disabled, Hong Kong Council of Social Service.
Gottlieb, Benjamin (ed.) (1988) *Marshalling Social Support: Formats, Processes and Effects*. London: SAGE.
Humble, Stephen & Unell, Judith (1989) *Self Help in Health and Social Welfare*. England and West Germany, London: Routledge.
Hong Kong Government (1991) *Social Welfare White Paper: Social Welfare into the 1990s and beyond*. Hong Kong: Hong Kong Government Printer.
Hospital Authority (1993) *Hospital Authority Statistical Report*. Hong Kong: Hospital Authority.
Koo, Linda (1987) Concepts of Disease Causation, Treatment and Prevention Among Hong Kong Chinese: Diversity and Eclecticism. *Social Science and Medicine*, Vol. 25, No. 4, pp. 405-417.
Koo, Linda (1989) Ethnonutrition in Hong Kong: Traditional Dietary Methods of Treatment and Prevention Disease. *Hong Kong Practitioners*, Vol. 11, No. 5, May 1989, pp. 221-231.
Lieberman, M.A., Borman, L.D., & Associates (1979) *Self-Help Groups for Coping with Crisis: Origin, Members, Processes & Impact*. London: Jossey-Bass Publications.
Ngan, M. H. (1990) *The Informal Caring Networks among Chinese Families in Hong Kong*. Unpublished Doctoral Dissertation, The University of Hong Kong.
Richardson, Ann & Goodman, Meg (1983) *Self-Help and Social Care: Mutual Aid Organizations in Practice*. London: Policy Studies Institute.
Robinson, David & Henry, Stuart (1977) *Self-Help and Health: Mutual aid and modern problems*. London: Martin Robertson.
Self-help Clearinghouse of Metro-Toronto (1991) *Directory of Self-Help Groups of Metro-Toronto*. Toronto: Self-Help Clearinghouse of Metro-Toronto.
Topley, M. (1975) "Chinese and Western Medicine in Hong Kong." In Kleinman, A. (ed.), *Culture and Health in Asian Society*. Schenkman.
Voth D. E. (1979) "Social Action Research in Community Development." In Blakely E. J. (ed.), *Community Development Research: Concepts, Issues and Strategies*. New York: Human Sciences Press.
Wong, J.W. (1988) "Importance of Parents' Organization." In the *Seminar on the Promotion of Parents' Organization, Joint Council of Physically & Mentally Disabled*. Hong Kong Council of Social Service (mimeograph).
Yang, K.S. (1986) "Chinese Personality and Its Change." In Bond, M.H. (ed.), *The Psychology of the Chinese People*. Hong Kong: Oxford University Press.

APPENDIX 1. Schedule of Actions and Events of the Alliance of Patients' Self-Help Groups.

Date	Events
July, 91	Formation of the Research Team on Self-Help Groups for Persons with Chronic Illness, collect names of patient self-help groups
July-Nov., 91	Visits to self-help groups and data collection
Oct., 91	Sharing meeting for the Self-Help groups: At the meeting, representatives of the self-help groups introduced their scope of services and the difficulties encountered. They also raised concerns towards government policies and needs of chronic patients. The idea of building up a common platform to reflect their views was agreed upon.
Mar. 92	Forum on Rehabilitation Green Paper: The groups commented on the Green Paper and the Concern Group for Persons with Chronic Illness was formed to be responsible for reflecting their collective views and press for government concern towards their needs.
April, 92	Petition "Who cares about ill people?": A procession was organized to plead for support to the Office of Members of Legislative Council. The action had received good coverage by the press and TV. Much public support was enlisted in this action.
April, 92	Seminar on "Chronically Ill Persons and Medical Fee Charging": Presentation of survey findings and discussion on different alternatives of medical fee charging.
April, 92	Meeting with Commissioner on Rehabilitation: Representatives of Concern Group met the Commissioner to discuss the suggestions and opinions of patients towards the Green Paper.

Date	Events
May, 92	Presentation of Views in Fees and Waivers Working Group under the Health & Welfare Branch: Representatives of Concern Group met the working group members and presented their views and concerns regarding the fee charging policy that would be reviewed and revised by the working group.
June-Aug., 92	Survey on Medical Expenses of Chronic Patients
Sept., 92	Press Conference: Public announcement of the setting up of the Preparatory Committee for the Alliance of Patient Self-Help Groups & Announcement of Position Paper on Rehabilitation Policies for Chronic Patients
Sept.,92-Feb.,93	Regular meetings among patient self-help groups, lobbying of political parties, drafting of constitution of the Alliance, encouraging other patients to form new groups
Feb., 93	Inauguration Ceremony of the Alliance of Patients' Self-Help Groups cum Seminaron Comprehensive Patient Care

Chapter 6

Mexican American and Anglo American Parents of the Mentally Ill: Attitudes and Participation in Family Support Groups

Louis J. Medvene

Wichita State University

Keh-Ming Lin
Agnes Wu
Ricardo Mendoza
Norma Harris
Milton Miller

Harbor-UCLA Medical Center

This study was supported by funding from the Research and Education Institute at Harbor-UCLA Medical Center, The Fletcher Jones Foundation, and the Center for Self-Help Research and Knowledge Dissemination at the University of Michigan, Ann Arbor. The authors wish to thank executives Alfredo Larrios, of El Centro Human Services Corporation, Rose Massa, of La Puente Valley Mental Health Center, and Delores Encinas, of the Los Angeles County AMI for their guidance and support. Additionally, the authors thank research interviewers and assistants Olivia Valdepena, Enriquetta Chipana, Raquel Pizano, Ingrid Bustamente and Eric Kaneshiro.

Correspondence may be addressed to Louis J. Medvene, Psychology Department, Box 34, Wichita State University, Wichita, KS 67260-0034.

[Haworth co-indexing entry note]: "Mexican American and Anglo American Parents of the Mentally Ill: Attitudes and Participation in Family Support Groups." Medvene et al. Co-published simultaneously in *Prevention in Human Services* (The Haworth Press, Inc.) Vol. 11, No. 1, 1994, pp. 141- 163; and: *Self-Help and Mutual Aid Groups: International and Multicultural Perspectives* (ed: Francine Lavoie, Thomasina Borkman, and Benjamin Gidron) The Haworth Press, Inc., 1994, pp. 141-163. Multiple copies of this article/chapter may be purchased from The Haworth Document Delivery Center [1-800-3-HAWORTH; 9:00 a.m. - 5:00 p.m. (EST)].

SUMMARY. Mexican American parents (N = 32) and Ango American parents (N = 34) of an adult son/daughter with serious mental illness were interviewed in order to identify factors related to their interest in attending a family support group. Parents were interviewed regarding their caregiving burden (level of distress), their causal attributions regarding their son/daughter's problems, and level of satisfaction with their social support network. Additionally, Mexican American parents were invited to participate in one of two Spanish-speaking support groups facilitated by a bilingual Hispanic mental health professional. There was some support for the hypotheses that interest in attending a meeting would be greater among parents who attributed their son/daughter's problems to an illness rather than to a moral weakness, and that interest would be greater among parents who were less satisfied with their social support networks. Additionally, 44% of the Mexican American parents attended at least one group meeting. Parents who attended a meeting experienced more caregiving burden than non-attenders, and were more likely than non-attenders to believe their son/daughter's problems were due to an illness.

Researchers, self-help participants, and policy makers have noted and expressed a desire to increase the low rates of participation in self-help groups by members of culturally diverse groups (the Surgeon General's Workshop on Self-Help and Public Health, 1988). The desire to increase the participation of Latino Americans, African Americans, and Asian Americans (among others) in self-help groups is felt to be especially important given that members of such culturally diverse groups often have few economic resources, and frequently underutilize formal sources of help (Lin, 1982; Sue, 1992).

However, there is a lack of agreement regarding the causes of low rates of participation. For example, suggested reasons for the low rates include culturally based preferences for alternative sources of help, as well as the organizational characteristics of self-help groups and organizations themselves. Guiterrez, Ortega and Suarez (1990) have suggested a strategy of developing special local chapters of national self-help organizations which match participants' cultural, linguistic and organizational preferences, e.g., conducting meetings in Spanish, and linking them to indigenous institutions and leaders.

Despite the importance of these issues there is little empirical data regarding the level of interest in participation in self-help groups by members of culturally diverse groups, or factors related to their actual participation. The present study is a response to this deficit and is concerned with both the level of interest expressed by Mexican Americans in family support groups, and with their participation in specially created local chapters of the National Alliance for the Mentally Ill (NAMI). NAMI is a self-help organization for caregivers of seriously psychiatrically disabled family members, most of whom are diagnosed as schizophrenic (Medvene & Krauss, 1989; Sommer, Williams & Williams, 1984).

Nationally, only six percent of NAMI's 120,000 family members are Hispanic (Jensen, 1991), and in Los Angeles only four percent are Mexican American (Medvene, 1990). Higher rates of participation would be expected in Los Angeles given that 29% of the population is Mexican American (Summary Tape: File 1, 1990), and 19% of the individual cases treated for schizophrenia by the Department of Mental Health in Los Angeles County in 1990 were Mexican American (Clinical Information Service, 1990).

CONCEPTUAL FRAMEWORK

The conceptual framework for this study was derived from the help-seeking literature. This literature was developed with reference to use of professional services, and the present study explores its relevance to participation in family support and self-help groups. The help-seeking literature indicates that people typically seek help first and most frequently from informal sources, such as friends and family, and only secondarily and much less frequently, from formal sources such as mental health services (Gourash, 1978; Veroff, Kulka & Douvan, 1981). The help-seeking literature also suggests that people are most likely to seek help from mental health professionals when levels of distress are high, and when the stressful situation is defined as a psychological problem (Veroff, Kulka & Douvan, 1981; Wills, 1983).

Additionally, the help-seeking literature suggests that people are more likely to seek help from more formal sources when their friends and family members are unable to help them with the focal problem, and when they refer them to mental health professionals (Wills, 1983).

The literature on the underutilization of medical and mental health facilities by Latinos is consistent with the more general help-seeking literature, and indicates that cultural factors as well as organizational barriers, are related to underutilization (Anderson, Lewis, Giachello et al., 1981; Rogler, Malgady & Rodriguez, 1989; Wells, Golding, Hough, Burnam & Karno, 1988). Cultural factors can include alternate beliefs about the "somatic" nature of mental and physical illness that may predispose people to avoid seeking help from mental health or health professionals (Rogler, Malgady & Rodriguez, 1989), and encourage them to utilize alternate helping systems–such as members of the extended family, folk healers or priests (Keefe, 1979).

This conceptual framework is useful in integrating the findings from the few studies that have been carried out which distinguish participants from non-participants in family support groups and self-help groups. For example, in a study of Anglo American mothers' use of community-based family support programs, Telleen (1990) reported that, in comparison to a control group of demographically similar mothers, program participants were: (a) more stressed by their children's behaviors; (b) more likely to attribute to themselves responsibility for their child's behavior problems; and (c) more socially isolated.

Simoni (1992) reported similar findings in a study of the factors which distinguished participants from non-participants in "school-based mutual support groups for Latino parents." Mothers who participated reported greater parenting stress, and less satisfaction with social support. Levy and Derby (1992) reported that widows who joined Bereavement Support Groups were significantly more depressed than non-participants.

In summary, if self-help groups are considered to be a relatively formal source of help, the help-seeking literature suggests that parents of a mentally ill son/daughter, both Anglo American and Mexican American, will be most interested in participating in a family support group when: (a) they are distressed; (b) they label their son/daughter's problem as involving a psychological disorder; and (c) they are dissatisfied with their social support.

LITERATURE ON FAMILIES' RESPONSES TO MENTAL ILLNESS

The literature on families' responses to severe mental illness includes measures of parental distress, mental health beliefs and level of satisfaction with social support.

Family burden. Family burden has frequently been used to measure the level of distress experienced by caregivers of people with a diagnosis of schizophrenia. Measures of family burden include both: (a) "objective burden," such as the general disruption of the life of at least one other family member (Noh & Turner, 1987), and (b) "subjective burden," which is associated with the emotional stressors related to family interaction (Anderson, Reiss & Hogarty, 1986). Recent research with Latino Americans indicates similar caregiving burdens (Guarnaccia et al. 1992; Jenkins, 1988a, b). Additionally, parents express concerns about future caregiving arrangements, and who will take responsibility when they are no longer able to provide care (Wu, 1992).

Explanatory beliefs. Parents' beliefs about the nature and causes of their son/daughters' psychiatric problems have been studied by measuring their endorsement of several mental health beliefs. Medvene and Krauss (1989; Krauss, 1989) developed a Mental Health Beliefs scale to measure the extent to which parents endorsed four specific beliefs: (a) psychogenic, problems caused by problems in parent-child interaction; (b) organic, problems caused by an underlying biochemical disease or illness; (c) stress, problems caused by external circumstances and events; and (d) "moral," that family members were not ill, but were malingering and manipulative.

Recent studies of Latino populations report that the term "nervios" (weak nerves) is used as a descriptive and explanatory concept for schizophrenia, as well as other psychiatric problems for Mexican Americans (Jenkins, 1988a, b), and for other Latino populations (Guarnaccia, Parra, Deschamps, Milstein & Argiles, 1992; Rogler, Malgady and Rodriguez, 1989).

Social support. The members of families in which someone is suffering from serious mental illness often experience high levels of stigmatization and lack of support from family and friends (Kreisman & Joy, 1975; Hatfield, 1979). Research indicates that Latino

Americans experiencing mental health problems frequently get help from family members (Guarnaccia et al., 1992; Gutierrez, Ortega & Suarez, 1990; Rogler, Malgady & Rodriguez, 1989). However, there is little data about the level of satisfaction with help from family and friends.

RESEARCH HYPOTHESES

The present study tested the extent to which level of distress, causal attributions, and satisfaction with social support were related to the interest which Anglo American and Mexican American parents expressed in attending a family support group, and in having contact with other helpers. Additionally, these same variables were related to the participation of the Mexican American parents in specially created family support groups. The study tested several hypotheses, based on the help-seeking literature. Across both cultures it was hypothesized that:

1. There would be a positive relationship between level of family burden and interest in participating in a family support group, as well as in having contact with another parent with similar problems, and in having contact with a mental health professional;
2. There would be a positive relationship between endorsing an illness attribution (organic, psychogenic, or stress) and interest in participating in a family support group, as well as in having contact with another parent with similar problems, and in having contact with a mental health professional;
3. There would be a negative relationship between both size and satisfaction with social support network and interest in participating in a family support group, as well as in having contact with another parent with similar problems, and in having contact with a mental health professional.

Additionally, the study was intended to explore the nature of the differences between Mexican American and Anglo American parents regarding their experience of family burden, their mental health beliefs, their use of social support networks, and their help-seeking preferences.

METHOD

Procedures

Only parents were recruited to participate in the study because most NAMI members are parents, and because it was assumed that the questionnaire items would have a different meaning for siblings or spouses. Parents were invited to participate in the study if they had a son or daughter who was currently in treatment on an outpatient basis at a publicly funded mental health facility in Los Angeles. Patients had to meet the following criteria: (a) between 18 and 58 years of age; (b) diagnosed as having a schizophrenic, schizo-affective, or major affective disorder; and (c) have at least 4 hours of contact per week with parents, or living with the caregiver during, at least, a total of six months in the last twelve months.

The process of recruiting involved: (a) requesting the therapist's permission to contact patients; (b) requesting patients' permission to contact their parents; and (c) inviting parents to participate in the study.

Anglo American parents. All participants were selected with the assistance of the Center for the Study of the Psychobiology of Ethnicity at Harbor-UCLA Medical Center, which is under the direction of the second author. Of the 59 parents contacted, 39 agreed to participate and 34 completed the process. Reasons for not completing the process included: inability to contact (79%), lack of interest (20%), and inconvenience (10%).

Mexican American parents. Participants were recruited by staff from two mental health agencies that served primarily Mexican American patients in and around east Los Angeles. Of the 55 cases that met study criteria (most cases failed to meet criteria because of diagnosis, and ethnicity), 58% of the parents participated. The major reasons for not participating were: therapist refusals (35%), patient refusals (26%) and parent refusals (48%).

Data was collected from Mexican American and Anglo American parents through in-person interviews. Interviews lasted approximately two hours and in each case the interviewer read the questions to the parents and recorded their responses. All of the Anglo American parents were interviewed by the third author. All of the Mexican American parents were interviewed by one of four bilingual Hispanic clinical staff members from one of the two community mental health agencies.

Interview Schedule

For Mexican Americans the interview began with nine items selected from Cuellar's 20-item Acculturation Scale (Cuellar, Harris & Jasso, 1980). The selected items concerned preferences regarding language and socialization. Responses to these nine items were summed and averaged so that they yielded a five-point scale, such that the higher the number the higher the level of acculturation to American culture. Cronbach's alpha for the nine items was .95. This scale was used to determine whether the interview should be conducted in Spanish or English.

Cross-cultural validity. Several techniques were used to maximize the cross-cultural validity of the Mexican American version of the personal interview (Brislin, 1980; Flaherty, Gaviria, Pathak, Mitchell, Wintrob, Richman & Birz, 1988): (a) back-translation from English to Spanish to English; (b) critical review of the Spanish by two translators who worked with Mexican Americans in Los Angeles in medical settings; and (c) two pilot interviews with Mexican American caregivers.

Level of distress. This variable was assessed using three subscales selected from Pai and Kapur's (1981) family burden interview schedule. The three subscales were: (a) the "disruption of family interaction" subscale, which consisted of five items; (b) the "impact on physical health of other family members" subscale which included two items; and (c) the "impact on emotional health of other family members" subscale which included two items. In addition, two items were added to assess parents' concerns regarding the future care of the family member (Wu, 1992).

Interviewers scored each item on a four point scale ranging from "no burden" to "severe burden." Interviewers were instructed to use their clinical judgement in scoring the items. Cronbach's alpha for these 11 items was .82.

Parents' mental health beliefs. Information about parents' causal attributions was collected through a 33-item, closed-ended questionnaire which was a modification of an earlier instrument–the "Mental Health Beliefs" scale (Medvene and Krauss, 1989; Krauss,

1989). The Mental Health Beliefs scale measured the strength of parents' endorsements of the psychogenic, organic, stress, and moral causal attributions. Each item required a response on a seven-point Likert-type scale ranging from "strongly disagree" to "strongly agree."

Five items were used to measure parents' endorsement of the organic attribution. That is, the belief that their son/daughter's problems were caused by some organic or biochemical problems. The Cronbach's alpha for Mexican Americans was .32; for Anglo Americans it was .59.

One item was included in the organic sub-scale to measure parents' endorsement of the idea of "nervios":

> La conducta, pensamientos, o sentimientos problematicos de mi hijo/a son causados por algo erroneo en su cerebro o sistema nervioso;
> My son/daughter's problematic behaviors, thoughts or feelings are caused by something wrong with his/her brain or nervous system.

A seven-item index was used to measure the strength of parents' endorsement of the psychogenic attribution. That is, the belief that the problem was caused by disturbances in the parent-child or family interactions. Cronbach's alpha for Mexican Americans was .80; for Anglo-Americans it was .92.

A three-item index was used to measure strength of endorsement of the stress attribution. That is, the belief that the problem was caused by life stress. Cronbach's alpha for Mexican Americans was .59; for Anglo-Americans it was .52.

A seven-item index was used to measure the strength of endorsement of the moral attribution. That is, the belief that the problem is malingering or laziness rather than an illness. Cronbach's alpha for Mexican Americans was .66; for Anglo-Americans it was .74.

Satisfaction with social support and stigmatization. The short form of Sarason's Social Support Questionnaire (Sarason, Levine, Basham & Sarason, 1983) was used to compute summary measures of the number of sources of social support, and satisfaction with social support.

Parents' help-seeking preferences. Parents were asked about their interest in attending a meeting of a local chapter of NAMI. The organization was described in the following way:

> The NAMI is an organization which was organized by and for families who have a mentally ill member. The members are mostly parents who have a son or daughter who is mentally ill, and participate in local groups.
> The purposes of the local groups are:
> a. to educate parents about mental illness;
> b. to provide emotional support for parents; and
> c. to advocate for more services for persons with mental illness.

Parents were asked to express their interest in attending a meeting on a five-point scale that ranged from "not at all" to "very interested." Parents were also asked about their preferences regarding how the support group should function: (a) whether the group facilitator should be another parent, or a mental health professional; and (b) whether the group should be a small support group, or a larger educational group. Additionally, parents were asked about their interest in having contact, on an individual basis, with another parent who knew more about how to deal with the problems of mental illness than they did, and with a mental health professional.

The final section of the interview included demographic questions about the parents and their son/daughter, as well as some questions about illness severity. The Brief Psychiatric Rating Scale (BPRS, Overall and Gorham, 1962) was included as a measure of the severity of patients' symptomatology. Patients' therapists completed the 18-item BPRS; each item involved a seven-point scale which ranged from "not present" to "very severe."

Participation in family support groups. All Mexican American parents were referred to one of two specially created family support groups and their attendance was tracked over a one year period (see Medvene, Mendoza, Lin, Harris & Miller, 1993 for details). Lack of resources prevented the creation of comparable groups for Anglo American parents.

Characteristics of Research Participants

All parents were of a similar age (60 and 61 years of age for the two cultural groups), gender (84% of Mexican Americans, and 85% of Anglo-Americans were female), and marital status (47% of the Mexican Americans and 44% of the Anglo-Americans were married). However, the Anglo American parents had achieved higher levels of socioeconomic status. For example, only 33% of the Mexican Americans had completed high school versus 91% of the Anglo American parents; and almost 50% of the Mexican Americans reported earning $10,000 or less per year versus three percent of the Anglo American parents.

The Mexican-American parents were primarily monolingual Spanish-speakers, with a level of acculturation of 1.2 on the 5 point scale. This level of acculturation indicated a preference for speaking Spanish, and for associating primarily with Mexican Americans.

The mentally ill son/daughter of both Anglo American and Mexican American parents was most likely to be male (61% and 69%, respectively), and to be 33 years of age. There were several significant differences between the Anglo American and Mexican American patients in terms of: (a) level of educational achievement–only 49% of the Mexican Americans had a high school level of education or higher versus 66% for the Anglo Americans; (b) living arrangements–89% of the Mexican Americans lived at home versus 74% of the Anglo Americans; (c) number of hospitalizations–an average of two for Mexican Americans versus five for Anglo Americans; and (d) symptom severity–Mexican Americans averaged 29 on the BPRS versus 45 for the Anglo Americans.

During the interviews it was discovered that 44% (N = 15) of the Anglo American parents were already members of local chapters of NAMI. Only the data from the 56% of the Anglo American parents (N = 19) who were not members of NAMI was included in the hypothesis testing. Data from all of the Anglo American parents were included when cultural differences between Mexican American and Anglo American parents were explored. Data from all of the 34 Anglo American parents were included only after chi-square and t-tests revealed no differences between NAMI members versus non-members on the variables of interest.

RESULTS

With regard to help-seeking preferences, both Mexican American and Anglo American parents expressed relatively strong interest in attending a local NAMI meeting: $M = 3.71$ for Mexican Americans, and $M = 3.87$ for Anglo Americans, on a five-point scale. Regarding their preferences for the characteristics of NAMI groups, both Mexican American and Anglo American parents preferred professional leadership to parent leadership: 68% of Mexican-American parents, and 62% of Anglo parents expressed such preferences. And, all parents preferred small groups to large groups.

With regard to participation in the specially created family support groups, 44% (14 of 32) of the Mexican American parents attended at least one support group meeting over a one year period.

Both Mexican American and Anglo American parents preferred contact with a mental health professional to contact with another parent ($M = 3.9$ versus $M = 3$ for Mexican Americans, and $M = 4$ versus $M = 3.3$ for Anglo Americans). This difference was statistically significant for both cultural groups ($t\ [31] = -4.12, p < .0001$, and $t\ [11] = -2.19, p < .05$, for Mexican and Anglo American parents, respectively).

Research Hypotheses

The research hypotheses were tested separately for Mexican American and Anglo American parents.

Family burden and social support. There was no support for the first hypothesis that caregiver burden would be positively related to interest in attending a NAMI meeting. As Tables 1 and 2 indicate, measures of family burden were not correlated with interest in having contact with another parent or with a professional.

However, the behavioral data of Mexican American parents was consistent with the first hypothesis. Parents who attended a meeting were rated as experiencing more total burden than non-attenders ($M = 1.6$ versus $M = 1.2$; $t\ (18, 13) = -1.96, p < .06$). With regard to the family burden sub-scales, attenders were rated as more burdened than non-attenders by concerns about the future care of their son/daughter, and by emotional health issues ($M = 2.4$ versus $M = 1.7$ regarding future care, and $M = 1.4$ versus $M = .7$ regarding

TABLE 1. Correlations of Help-Seeking Preferences with Attributions, Family Burden and Social Support: Mexican American Parents.

	Help Seeking Preferences		
	Contact with Another Parent	Contact with Professional	Interest in AMI
BURDEN			
Total	.12b	−.05b	−.23b
Interaction	.09b	−.17b	−.28b
Future Care	−.03a	−.02a	−.03a
Physical Health	.22	.07	−.02
Emotional Health	.06	.08	−.23
ATTRIBUTION			
Psychogenic	.10	−.09	−.04a
Moral	.01a	−.15a	.10a
Organic	.29b	.29b	.35*b
Stress	.58**b	.46**b	.37*b
SOCIAL SUPPORT			
Mean Number	−.17a	.02a	−.41*a
Mean Satisfaction	−.31+c	−.12c	−.18c

N = 32; a: n = 31; b: n = 30; c: n = 29.

+ $p < .10$

* $p < .05$

** $p < .01$

emotional health). These differences were statistically significant: t [18, 14] = −2.50, $p < .02$, and t [18, 13] = −2.04, $p < .05$, respectively.

Causal attributions. Both Mexican American and Anglo American parents endorsed the organic and stress attributions most strongly ($M = 4.53$ and $M = 4.51$ for Mexican Americans, and $M = 5.01$ and $M = 4.64$ for Anglo Americans, respectively). Endorse-

TABLE 2. Correlations of Help-Seeking Preferences with Attributions, Family Burden and Social Support: Anglo-American Parents +.

	Help Seeking Preferences		
	Contact with Another Parent	Contact with Professional	Interest in NAMI$_A$
BURDEN			
Total	.26	.00	.22
Interaction	.20	−.01	.26
Future Care	.43	−.03	.29
Physical Health	−.07	−.29	−.09
Emotional Health	.27	.29	.20
ATTRIBUTION			
Psychogenic	.63***	.50*	.29
Moral	.57**	.37	.19
Organic	−.63***	−.43	−.38
Stress	.28	.47	−.06
SOCIAL SUPPORT			
Mean Number	−.25	−.17	−.53*
Mean Satisfaction	−.29	−.14	−.47*

+ Includes only parents who are not members of NAMI

N = 12; $_A$n = 13

*$p < .10$; **$p < .05$; ***$p < .03$.

ment of the "nervios" questionnaire item by Mexican Americans was $M = 6.4$; for Anglo Americans it was $M = 6.0$.

The second hypothesis was that endorsement of any one of the three illness attributions–psychogenic, organic and/or stress–would be correlated with interest in attending a NAMI meeting, and with interest in contacting another parent and a mental health professional.

There was some support for this hypothesis among Mexican

American parents, as Table 1 indicates. The more strongly Mexican American parents endorsed the stress attribution, the more interest they expressed in attending a NAMI meeting, as well as in having contact with both another parent and a mental health professional. Additionally, the more strongly Mexican American parents endorsed the organic attribution, the more interest they expressed in attending a NAMI meeting.

There was less support for these hypotheses among Anglo American parents. Parents' endorsements of the attributions were not related to their interest in attending a NAMI meeting. However, as Table 2 indicates, the more Anglo American parents attributed their son/daughter's problems to psychogenic causes (faulty parent-child relationships), the more interest they expressed in having contact with another parent, and with a mental health professional.

The behavioral data was consistent with the second hypothesis. Mexican American parents who attended a family support group meeting endorsed the moral attribution (not a disease) less strongly than parents who did not attend ($M = 2.8$ versus $M = 3.9$; t [18, 14] = 2.45, $p < .02$).

Cultural differences in mental health beliefs. A comparison of Cronbach alphas for the organic attribution (.17 for Mexican American parents versus .59 for Anglo American parents) indicated a difference in the structure of Mexican American and Anglo American parents' beliefs about the organic causes of their son/daughter's problems. Analyses of the intercorrelations of the five items of which the organic subscale consisted indicated that for Mexican American parents, the idea that their son/daughter's problems were caused by something wrong with their his/her "brain or nervous system" was not correlated with the idea that their son/daughter's problems were caused by a biochemical disorder (r [30] = − .04, $p <$ .81). In contrast, for Anglo Americans the idea that their son/daughter's problems were caused by "something wrong with his/her brain or nervous system" was highly correlated with the idea that their son/daughter was suffering from a biochemically based disorder (r [34] = .79, $p < .0001$).

A second cultural difference was indicated by the finding that Mexican American parents endorsed the moral attribution more strongly than Anglo American parents ($M = 3.52$ versus $M = 1.76$, respectively). This difference was significant based on post-hoc Scheffe contrasts following a MANOVA test of differences between and within subjects (F [189, 3] = 52.02, $p < .0001$).

Social support. There was some support for the third hypothesis that interest in helping sources would be negatively related to size and satisfaction with the network. For Mexican American parents, the smaller the size of their social network, the more interest they expressed in attending a NAMI meeting, as shown in Table 1.

Similarly, the smaller the size of the social network of Anglo American parents, the more interest they expressed in participating in a NAMI chapter, as shown in Table 2. Anglo American parents' level of satisfaction with their support network, was marginally related to their interest in a NAMI chapter.

Behaviorally, Mexican American parents' attendance of a family support group meeting was not related to either the size of their support network or their satisfaction with the network.

There were no differences between Mexican American and Anglo American parents in terms of the average size of their support networks, or their level of satisfaction with support. However, there were differences regarding the frequency of use of specific network sources: Mexican Americans were more likely to rely on neighbors and religious sources than Anglos (M = 41% and 22% versus 11% and 5%, respectively), while Anglo Americans were more likely to rely on friends than were Mexican Americans (M = 74% versus 8%, respectively).

DISCUSSION

The findings provide some support for the idea that variables from the help-seeking literature can differentiate parents who are interested in participating in family support groups from those who are not. With regard to level of distress, although family burden was not related to the interest parents expressed in attending a NAMI meeting, Mexican American parents who attended support group meetings had higher levels of caregiving burden. This behavioral data is consistent with findings from other studies of participation in family support groups and self-help groups which reports that people with higher levels of distress are more likely to participate (Levy & Derby, 1992; Simoni, 1992; Telleen, 1990).

The inconsistency between the behavior of Mexican American parents and the attitudes they expressed may have been due to the wording of the attitudinal question. The attitudinal question to which parents responded, expressing their interest in attending a support group meeting, described a NAMI meeting in generic terms. However, the meetings which parents were invited to attend had a number of specific features: they were meetings of a Spanish-speaking family support group that met weekly at La Puente Valley Mental Health Center, which was facilitated by an Hispanic mental health professional, and which their son/daughter's therapist had invited them to attend. Fishbein's theory of reasoned action suggests (1979) that there might have been more consistency between the behavioral and attitudinal responses of the Mexican American parents if the NAMI meeting had been described in such specific detail in the questionnaire.

Causal Attributions

Despite the generic way in which the NAMI group was described in the attitudinal question, the interest parents expressed in attending a meeting was related to their beliefs about the causes of their son/daughter's problems. And, behaviorally, Mexican American parents were less likely to attend a meeting if they believed their son/daughter's problems were due to moral defects–i.e., laziness or manipulativeness–rather than to an illness.

It is possible that more support for the relationship between parents' causal attributions and their interest in attending a NAMI meeting would have been found if additional attributional items had been asked. Other studies suggest that parents' beliefs about their ability to influence the future course of their son/daughter's problems would have been relevant. For example, Telleen (1990) reported that family support group participants were more likely than non-participants to take responsibility for their pre-school childrens' problems, and to feel responsible for solving them. Future studies of potential NAMI participants should include questions regarding parents' beliefs about their ability to influence the course of their son/daughter's treatment. For example, parents who feel a great deal of responsibility regarding future care arrangements might be more likely to participate. Such parents might be especially interested in NAMI because of its advocacy efforts to create more professional services.

As hypothesized, the size of parents' support networks was negatively related to the interests parents expressed in attending a NAMI meeting. However, neither size, nor satisfaction with social support were related to the actual participation of Mexican American parents. It is possible that satisfaction with social support was measured in too general a way here. For example, both Simoni (1992) and Telleen (1990) measured satisfaction with social support with items that were problem-specific. Future research should measure satisfaction with support with reference to the focal problem.

Cultural Differences

The findings indicated a structural difference in the beliefs of Mexican Americans and Anglo American parents with regard to the organic bases of severe mental illness. The data suggested that the Mexican American idea of "nervios" concerned a constitutional weakness which was not believed to be related to an underlying biochemical disease process. In contrast, the findings indicated that these two ideas were closely related in the minds of Anglo American parents.

Secondly, the data indicated that Mexican American parents endorsed the moral attribution more strongly than Anglo American parents. These preliminary findings need to be followed up in future research.

Implications for Increasing Participation in NAMI

The strategy of modifying mainstream self-help organizations to conform to the specific preferences of members of culturally diverse groups (Gutierrez, Ortega & Suarez, 1990) seems promising given the high attendance rates of Mexican Americans reported in this study. Conducting groups in Spanish was helpful. Additionally, responding to parental preferences for professional involvement was important. Both Mexican American and Anglo American parents preferred contact with mental health professionals to contact with other parents. It may be that recruitment efforts will have more success if mental health professionals are involved. Parents who are unfamiliar with self-help groups may be unclear about how they can be helped by other parents; they may have clearer, although unrealistically high expectations about how they can be helped by professionals.

At the same time, questions need to be raised about whether extensive professional involvement undermines self-help processes such as empowerment. We consider it an empirical question as to whether professional leadership and involvement necessarily undermines lay leadership, and empowerment. Ultimately we believe that it is the behavior of the mental health professional and the values he/she promotes which are crucial, rather than the presence or absence of a professional.

The general implications for recruiting for other types of self-help groups are that formative research studies ought to be carried out to collect information from potential participants regarding: (a) issues that are most distressing to them, (b) beliefs about the causes of their problems and their ability to influence the course and outcome of their problems, and (c) their desire that the group be linked to a treatment agency which has a specific ethnic identity.

LIMITATIONS OF THE STUDY

One limitation of this study is that cultural differences were confounded with socioeconomic differences. Caution needs to be exercised in deciding how much of the cultural differences discussed above should be attributed to cultural factors and how much to socioeconomic differences between the Mexican American and Anglo American parents. The Mexican Americans in this study had significantly lower levels of educational achievement and income, which are often associated with lower levels of acculturation. In future research it would be most desirable to include participants of comparable socioeconomic backgrounds. An additional note of caution about cultural differences concerns the fact that the Anglo

American patients exhibited more severe symptoms than the Mexican American patients. It is possible that the different beliefs expressed by Anglo American and Mexican American parents were due, in part, to the different levels of severity of symptomatology exhibited by their family member. Ideally such differences will be reduced in future research.

A second note of caution is necessary regarding the generalizability of the findings to other Mexican Americans and to other Latinos. Caution needs to be exercised in generalizing the findings to Latinos who are more acculturated into American culture and have achieved higher levels of socioeconomic status. Additionally, the findings may not be generalizable to parents whose son/daughter has not received treatment from the mental health system. Such parents may have different beliefs and help-seeking preferences.

In conclusion, the findings provide some encouragement that the variables of level of distress, causal attributions, and satisfaction with social support promise to increase our understanding of the differences between parents who are likely to participate in family support groups and those who are not. Secondly, the data suggest that the likelihood of Mexican American participation in NAMI groups will be increased when local chapters are organized in ways which match parents' culturally specific linguistic and organizational preferences.

REFERENCES

Anderson, R., Lewis, S. Z., Giachello, A. L. et al. (1981). Access of medical care among the Hispanic population in the Southwestern United States. *Journal of Health and Social Behavior*, 22, 78-89.

Anderson, C. M., Reiss, D. J. & Hogarty, G. E. (1986). *Schizophrenia and the family: The practitioner's guide to psychoeducation and management*. New York: The Guilford Press.

Brislin, R. W. (1980). Translation and content analysis of oral and written materials. In H. C. Triandis and J. W. Berry (eds.), *Handbook of cross-cultural psychology: Methodology*, Volume 2, (389-444). Boston: Allyn and Bacon, Inc.

Clinical Information Service (1990). Special report of unique clients in fiscal year 1990/91: Age, ethnicity, primary diagnosis, living arrangement and employment status. County of Los Angeles Department of Mental Health Administration Services, Information Systems Support Bureau.

Cuellar, I., Harris, L. C., & Jasso, R. (1980). An acculturation scale for Mexican American normal and clinical populations. *Hispanic Journal of Behavioral Science*, *2*, 199-217.

Fishbein, M. (1979). A theory of reasoned action: Some applications and implications. In J. J. Page (ed.), *Nebraska symposium on motivation*. Lincoln, NE: University of Nebraska Press.

Flaherty, J. A., Gaviria, M. F., Pathak, D., Mitchell, T., Wintrob, R., Richman, J. A., & Birz, S. (1988). Developing instruments for cross cultural psychiatric research. *Journal of Nervous and Mental Diseases*, *176*, 257-263.

Gourash, N. (1978). Help-seeking: A review of the literature. *American Journal of Community Psychology*, *6*, 413-423.

Guarnaccia, P. J., Parra, P., Deschamps, A., Milstein, G., & Argiles, N. (1992). Si Dios quiere: Hispanic families' experiences of caring for seriously mentally ill family members. *Culture, Medicine & Psychiatry*, *16*, 187-215.

Gutierrez, L., Ortega, R. M. & Suarez, Z. (1990). Self-help and the Latino community. In T. Powell (ed.), *Working with self-help* (pp. 218-236). Silver Spring, MD: National Association of Social Work Press.

Hatfield, A. B. (1979). Help-seeking behavior of families of schizophrenics. *Journal of Community Psychology*, *7*, 563-469.

Jenkins, J. H. (1988a). Ethnopsychiatric interpretations of schizophrenic illness: The problem of *nervios* within Mexican-American families. *Culture, Medicine, and Psychiatry*, *12*, 301-329.

Jenkins, J. H. (1988b). Conceptions of schizophrenia as a problem of nerves: A cross-cultural comparison of Mexican-Americans and Anglo-Americans. *Social Science and Medicine*, 26, 1233-1243.

Jensen, A. (1991). Analysis of NAMI mail-in survey conducted in 1991. Available from Center for Health Policy Research, 2101 K. St., N.W., Suite 800, Washington, D.C. 20006.

Keefe, S. E. (1979). Mexican-American's underutilization of mental health clinics: An evaluation of suggested explanations. *Hispanic Journal of Behavioral Science*, 1, 93-115.

Kreisman, D. E., & Joy, V. D. (1975). The family as reactor to the mental illness of a relative. In M. Guttentag & E.L. Struening (eds.), *Handbook of evaluation research* (Vol. 2, pp. 483-516). Beverly Hills: Sage Publications.

Krauss, D. H. (1989). Cognitive, emotional and behavioral change in self-help groups for families of the psychiatrically disabled. Unpublished doctoral dissertation, Yale University.

Levy, L. H. & Derby, J. F. (1992). Bereavement support groups: Who joins; who does not and why. *Journal of Community Psychology*, *20*, 649-662.

Lin, K. M. (1982). Social cultural determinates of the helpseeking behavior of patients with mental illness. *Journal of Nervous and Mental Disease*, *170*, 78-85.

Medvene, L. J. (1990). Survey of membership of NAMI members in Los Angeles County. Unpublished manuscript.

Medvene, L. J., & Krauss, D. (1989). Causal attributions and parent-child relationships in a self-help group for families of the mentally ill. *Journal of Applied Social Psychology*, 19, 1413-1430.

Medvene, L. J., Mendoza, R., Lin, K. M., Harris, N., & Miller, M. (1993). Mexican-American participation in family support groups: Psychological, cultural and organizational factors. Unpublished manuscript available from Louis Medvene, Wichita State University, Department of Psychology, Box 34, Wichita, KS 67260-0034.

Noh, S., & Turner, J. (1987). Living with psychiatric patients: Implications for the mental health of family members. *Social Science and Medicine*, *25*, 263-271.

Overall, J. E., & Gorham, D. R. (1962). Brief Psychiatric Rating Scale. *Psychological Reports*, *10*, 799-812.

Pai, S., & Kapur, R. L. (1981). Burden on the family of a psychiatric patient: Development of an interview schedule. *British Journal of Psychiatry*, *138*, 332-335.

Rogler, L. H., Malgady, R. G., & Rodriguez, O. (1989). *Hispanics and mental health: A framework for research.* Malabar, Florida: Robert E. Krieger Publishing Company.

Sarason, I. G., Levine, H. M., Basham, R. B., & Sarason, B. R.(1983). Assessing social support: The social support questionnaire. *Journal of Personality and Social Psychology*, *44*, 127-139.

Simoni, (1992). School-based mutual support groups for Latino Parents: Who participates? Poster presented at the 100th meeting of the American Psychological Association, Washington, D.C.

Sommer, R., Williams, P. & Williams, W. A. (1984). Self-survey of family organization. *Psychiatric Quarterly*, *55*, 236-241.

Sue, S. (1992). Ethnicity and mental health: Research and policy issues. *Journal of Social Issues*, *48*, 187-205.

Summary Tape: file 1. (1990). *1990 Census of population and housing*. Available from State of California State Census Data Center, (916) 323-2201.

Surgeon General's Workshop On Self-Help and Public Health (1988). U.S. Department of Health & Human Services. Public Health Service, Health Resources and Services Administration, 224-250-88-1.

Telleen, S. (1990). Parental beliefs and help-seeking in mothers' use of a community-based family support program. *Journal of Community Psychology*, *18*, 264-276.

Veroff, J., Kulka, R. A., & Douvan, E. (1981). *Mental health in America: Patterns of help-seeking from 1957 to 1976*. New York: Basic Books.

Wells, K. B., Golding, J. M., Hough, R. L., Burnam, A. & Karno, J. (1988). Factors affecting the probability of use of general and medical health and social/community services for Mexican Americans and non-Hispanic whites. *Medical Care*, *26*, 441-452.

Wills, T. A. (1983). Social comparison in coping and help-seeking. In B.M. DePaulo, A. Nadler & J. D. Fisher (eds.), *New directions in helping* (Vol. 2, pp. 109-142). New York: Academic Press.

Wu, A. C. C. (1992). A cross-cultural, cross-national study of the family caregiver burden of a severely mentally ill family member. Doctoral dissertation, Graduate School of Social Work, University of Southern California.

Chapter 7

Are Twelve Step Programs Appropriate for Disenfranchised Groups? Evidence from a Study of Posttreatment Mutual Help Involvement

Keith Humphreys

University of Illinois at Urbana-Champaign

Brian E. Mavis
Bertram E. Stöffelmayr

Michigan State University

SUMMARY. Conventional wisdom about 12 step mutual help programs for substance abusers holds that these organizations appeal primarily to white, middle class men. To investigate the validity of this claim, a sample of 558 persons who were followed up one year after their intake to substance abuse treatment was studied. Contrary to conventional wisdom, the 178 persons who were attending mutual help after treatment were not significantly different from the 380 who

---

Address correspondence to Keith Humphreys, Center for Health Care Evaluation, VA Medical Center, 795 Willow Road (152), Menlo Park, CA 94025

[Haworth co-indexing entry note]: "Are Twelve Step Programs Appropriate for Disenfranchised Groups? Evidence from a Study of Posttreatment Mutual Help Involvement." Humphreys, Keith, Brian E. Mavis, and Bertram E. Stöffelmayr. Co-published simultaneously in *Prevention in Human Services* (The Haworth Press, Inc.) Vol. 11, No. 1, 1994, pp. 165-179; and: *Self-Help and Mutual Aid Groups: International and Multicultural Perspectives* (ed: Francine Lavoie, Thomasina Borkman, and Benjamin Gidron) The Haworth Press, Inc., 1994, pp. 165-179. Multiple copies of this article/chapter may be purchased from The Haworth Document Delivery Center [1-800-3-HAWORTH; 9:00 a.m. - 5:00 p.m. (EST)].

were not, on race, gender, education, employment pattern, or marital status. Supplemental analyses of the data suggested that women are more likely to drop out of 12 step groups than are men and that African Americans who attend self-help after treatment have better outcomes on clinical and social measures than do African Americans who do not attend self-help groups. Overall the findings suggest that 12 step programs both appeal to and benefit disenfranchised groups.

Substance abuse mutual help groups that are based on the "twelve steps" approach to recovery are an important influence on the professional treatment system in the United States. The philosophy and methods of Alcoholics Anonymous (AA) and Narcotics Anonymous (NA) are part of the standard package of care in many treatment programs. These mutual help groups are also frequently used as a form of aftercare.

While there is great enthusiasm for 12 step programs within some segments of the substance abuse treatment field, other researchers and clinicians have reservations about the value of 12 step programs to all substance abusers. Because the founders of these mutual help organizations were white, middle class men, some helping professionals and academics fear that AA and NA may be biased in their materials, philosophy, and approach in ways that deleteriously affect women, racial minorities, and persons of lower social class (Powell, 1987). For example, some have expressed concern that the emphasis 12 step programs place on individual responsibility for problems is inappropriate for members of disenfranchised groups (e.g., African Americans), whose problems result primarily from systematic social inequities (for a review of this debate, see Neighbors, Elliot, & Gant, 1990). From such a perspective, one could argue that participation in 12 step groups is damaging to African Americans and other racial minorities.

If 12 step programs are indeed biased against members of disenfranchised groups, one would expect that women, racial minorities, and persons of low social class would be less likely to affiliate with and derive benefit from these mutual help groups, and would be more likely to drop out of them after attending a few meetings. Although some evidence has emerged that AA members are disproportionately socially stable, white men (Ogbourne & Glaser, 1981), other studies have shown no such association (see Emrick, 1987, for a review). The question of whether 12 step programs are appropriate for disenfranchised groups must be viewed as one open to debate not only because of the mixed evidence but also because most investigations of AA and NA attendance are cross sectional studies with no comparison groups. Such studies cannot determine if the characteristics of the members of the mutual help group studied are due to some feature of the AA/NA organization as a whole, or are merely a reflection of the base fates of those characteristics in the substance abusing population and/or the community in which the study is done.

Conventional wisdom about AA and NA does not always stand up under the scrutiny afforded by more powerful research design strategies. Our study of 290 treated substance abusers, which included a comparison group and used a longitudinal design, showed that African Americans were *more* likely than whites to attend AA and NA six months after their intake to treatment. The same study also showed that women were more likely to be involved in AA/NA than were men and that measures of social stability had no impact on attendance (Humphreys, Mavis, & Stöffelmayr, 1991a). In the present investigation, we extend that earlier study by using a longer follow-up window and an expanded sample. In doing so, we hope to address three questions about disenfranchised groups and 12 step programs. They are:

1. Do twelve step programs for substance abusers attract members of disenfranchised groups, such as racial minorities, women, and persons of lower social class?
2. Do members of disenfranchised groups tend to drop out of AA and NA?
3. In our third question, we narrow our focus to a disenfranchised group that has been little studied in mutual help research: Do African Americans attend and benefit from 12 step programs?

METHOD

Participants

Participants in this study were 558 persons who were interviewed at the time of their admission to one of 32 public substance abuse treatment agencies in the state of Michigan and who were followed up 12 months later. These 558 clients were a subset (71.5%) of an original sample of 781 consecutive admissions, the remainder of whom were not located at follow-up. Comparisons on race, gender, education, age, and intake level severity of drug/alcohol use did not reveal any significant differences between those participants who were found at follow-up and those who were not.

A demographic breakdown of the sample of 558 treated substance abusers is presented in Table 1. As can be seen from the Table, the sample was young, moderately educated, mostly male and mostly unmarried. The sample was also culturally diverse.[1] Table 1 also shows how the study participants responded when they were asked what they considered their primary problem substance. Of the 558 clients, 302(54%) received outpatient care and 256(46%) received residential treatment.

Procedure

The Addiction Severity Index (ASI; McLellan, Luborsky, Woody, & O'Brien, 1980) was administered to all clients at intake by a trained assessor. The ASI determines need for treatment (or "prob-

TABLE 1. Demographic and Problem Information on 558 Treated Substance Abusers Who Were Followed-Up One Year After Intake

Race	Gender
288 White (52%)	401 Men (72%)
253 African American (45%)	157 Women (28%)
7 Native American (1%)	
10 Mexican American (2%)	
Employment Pattern, Last 3 Years	Marital Status
280 Full Time (50%)	77 Married (14%)
87 Part Time (16%)	159 Separated/Divorced (28%)
131 Unemployed (23%)	322 Single (58%)
60 Other (10%)	
Years of Education	Primary Problem Substance
Mean = 11.9 Standard Deviation = 1.9	220 Alcohol and Drugs (39.4%)
	176 Alcohol (31.5%)
Age	105 Cocaine (18.9%)
Mean = 31.0 Standard Deviation = 8.0	25 Polydrug (4.5%)
	32 Other (5.7%)

lem severity") in seven domains: medical, employment/support, alcohol, drug, legal, family/social and psychological problems. Problem severity scores range from 0-9, with a score of 4 or greater being a strong indication that treatment is needed in a particular domain. The ASI has excellent concurrent reliability (average concordance = .89) and has also been shown to have discriminant and concurrent validity across a variety of substance abusing populations (McLellan, Luborsky, Cacciola, Griffith, Evans, Barr, & O'Brien, 1985).

Most of the assessors were native to the areas in which they worked. As the assessment team was racially diverse, most study participants were interviewed by an assessor of their own race. All of these assessors had experience as substance abuse counselors or program managers and had at least a baccalaureate education.

Six and twelve months after the intake interview, the assessor recontacted (where possible) the client and readministered the ASI. At these interviews the client also reported on his or her involvement in mutual help groups, if any. Results of the six month follow-up have been reported elsewhere (Humphreys, Mavis, & Stöffelmayr, 1991a, 1991b).

RESULTS

Question 1: Do 12 step programs for substance abusers attract members of disenfranchised groups, such as racial minorities, women, and persons of lower social stability/class?

One year after they entered treatment, 222(39.8%) of those substance abusers who were followed-up reported that they had gone to at least one meeting of a self-help group in the past six months. However, not all of these clients were currently attending a group (i.e., some had dropped out). Approximately one third (31.8%, n = 178) of the sample reported that they were currently involved in a mutual help group one year after their admission to treatment. In order to be considered "currently involved" in a group, a participant had to report attending his or her self-help group in the month prior to the follow-up interview. Of these 178 self-help attenders, 78 (44%) were attending AA only, 66 (37%) were attending NA only, and 34 (19%) were attending both AA and NA.

The 178 treated substance abusers who were actively involved in a 12 step program one year after treatment intake were compared on demographic variables to the 380 who were not (see Table 2). There was no significant difference between groups on gender. Because of the small number of Mexican Americans and Native Americans in the sample, the comparison on race was dichotomous (White vs. racial minority) and did not approach significance. Employment pattern over the past three years, marital status, and educational level were used as operationalizations of social ability/class. None of these variables differentiated the attenders from the non-attenders.

Contrary to what some have argued, twelve step groups do not

TABLE 2. Demographic Comparison of Self-Help Attenders and Non-Attenders

		Total Sample (N = 558)	Non-Attenders (n = 380)	Attenders (n = 178)	H^2 Statistic
Race	White	51.6%	50.8%	53.4%	
	Minority	48.4%	49.2%	46.6%	0.32
Gender	Male	71.9%	73.1%	69.1%	
	Female	28.1%	26.8%	30.9%	0.99
Marital Status	Married	13.8%	14.2%	12.9%	
	Sep/Wid/Div	28.5%	25.8%	34.2%	
	Single	57.7%	60.0%	52.8%	4.29
Employment	Full-Time	50.2%	48.2%	54.5%	
	Part-Time	15.6%	16.6%	13.5%	
	Unemployed	23.5%	24.7%	20.8%	
	Other	10.8%	10.5%	11.2%	2.58
Education	Less than HS	30.5%	32.6%	25.8%	
	HS	43.9%	45.0%	41.6%	
	Some College	21.5%	18.9%	27.0%	
	4 Year Degree	4.1%	3.4%	5.6%	7.20

Note. Sep/Wid/IDiv = Separated, Widowed or Divorced HS = High School
All findings nonsignificant ($p > .05$)

seem to be particularly appealing to privileged substance abusers (e.g., middle class, white, men). One year after intake to substance abuse treatment, women are just as likely to be actively involved in NA/AA as are men, and racial minorities are as likely to be involved as are whites. Mutual help group attenders and non-attenders have similar marital statuses, employment histories, and educational levels, which argues against the notion that 12 step programs are only for the middle class, socially stable client. Thus the answer to the first question of interest seems to be yes, at least when one is discussing those substance abusers who come to mutual help after being treated by professionals. However, as the six month investigation of a portion of the current sample found that African Americans and women were more likely to be attending mutual help than were whites and men, It is surprising that the same finding did not emerge here. Members of disenfranchised groups may be more likely to give 12 step self-help programs a try and also more likely to drop out of these organizations. This issue is addressed in the next section.

Question 2: Do members of disenfranchised groups tend to drop out of AA and NA?

The six month follow-up data of the 380 persons who were not involved in mutual help one year after treatment were examined to see how many had been attending at the earlier follow-up. A small (n = 75) number of substance abusers were thus classified as self-help dropouts because they had been actively involved at the time of the six month follow-up interview but were no longer attending meetings one year after treatment. Demographic information on the dropouts is presented in Table 3.

The 75 persons who dropped out of mutual help were compared to those who stayed involved throughout the follow-up period. Although a somewhat greater proportion (54.7% vs. 46.6% of stay-ins) of the dropouts were racial minorities, this difference did not attain statistical significance (X^2 (1, N = 253) = 1.36, $p > .05$). A significantly greater proportion of the dropouts were women (44% vs. 30.9%, X^2 (1, N = 253) = 3.99, $p < .05$). The groups were similar with respect to employment history and educational level (12.1 vs. 11.9 years).

TABLE 3. Comparative data and relapse rates for 75 substance abusers who were attending self-help six months after treatment intake but had dropped out 12 months after intake

		Dropout (n = 75)	Attender (n = 178)	H^2 Statistic
Race	White	45.3%	53.4%	
	Minority	54.7%	46.6%	1.36
Gender	Male	56.0%	69.1%	
	Female	44.0%	30.9%	3.99*
Employment	Full-Time	48.0%	54.5%	
	Part-Time	20.0%	13.5%	
	Unemployed	25.3%	20.8%	
	Other	6.7%	11.2%	3.17

*$p < .05$

Relapse Rates of Dropouts at 12 months

14 (19%) with alcohol severity score > = 4 — Mean for all 75 dropouts = 1.64
9 (12%) with drug severity score > = 4 — Mean for all 75 dropouts = 1.31
3 (4%) with both drug and alcohol severity score > = 4

It is reasonable to wonder if these persons dropped out of self-help because they were doing well and felt they needed no more help or if they dropped out because they had relapsed. As shown in Table 3, most of the dropouts had not relapsed. An ASI severity score of 4 is usually considered as the cutoff where treatment for a problem is necessary, and the mean alcohol severity score for the dropouts was only 1.64. The mean drug severity score of the dropouts was even lower (1.31). Only 14 of the dropouts reported clinically significant alcohol problems 12 months after intake, 9 reported clinically significant drug problems, and 3 reported severe problems with both alcohol and other drugs. In other words, about three fourths of the dropout sample did not report clinically significant substance abuse problems, even though they were no longer involved in a 12 step program.

While the amount of data available is not great, the results of this 12 month follow-up study in conjunction with our earlier six month report (Humphreys, Mavis, & Stöffelmayr, 1991a) suggest that women are both more likely to try and more likely to drop out of 12 step programs after treatment. At 12 months after treatment, gender differences in 12 step group attendance rates disappear. No literature exists on why women like or dislike mutual help groups, making the stability and meaning of our finding difficult to assess. What makes women's higher rates of both "trying" and ""not buying" 12 step self-help groups an even more tantalizing question for future research is that race and measures of social class do not seem to predict this pattern of self-help attendance.

At least three potential explanations for the findings on women's higher drop out rate can be offered. The first explanation is statistical: the disappearance of the previous (6 month follow-up) significant finding of women attending self-help groups at higher rates than men could be an example of regression to the mean. A second group of explanations concerns the differing life contexts of men and women in the sample. The women in the sample may have been more likely to drop out of the groups because they assume a greater responsibility for child care than men, and thus do not find it is easy to be a regular attender at a group. Another possibility is that features of self-help groups affect women and men differently. Clinical lore in the field of professional alcoholism treatment suggests that women clients are less likely to drop out of treatment if there are all female client services available (Margaret Willmore, Center for Substance Abuse Treatment, personal communication 7/18/93). Although findings from professional treatment do not always generalize to mutual help groups, this finding suggests that future studies in this area should gather information on the gender composition of AA and NA groups to see if this affects dropout.

What dropping out of a self-help group signifies is not entirely clear. Some of these dropouts may rejoin AA/NA again later. Others of these former self-helpers may have had a positive experience with AA/NA but left the organizations because they felt that substance abuse was no longer disrupting their lives (an assumption that appears to be valid for three fourths of the dropout sample). However, ignoring the possibility that something about 12 step programs may be uncomfortable or inappropriate for at least some women and racial minorities would be overly sanguine. In order to investigate this possibility, future investigations could conduct observations of the groups which include such persons, to determine if the group process or philosophy affects them adversely. Such observations could be supplemented with interviews of persons who drop out of the group.

Question 3: Do African Americans attend and benefit from 12 step programs?

African Americans have been woefully understudied in self-help research. Hence, we now give detailed attention to the 253 African American substance abusers who were followed up 12 months after their intake to treatment. Most of them (61.3%) received residential treatment. The proportion of African Americans who were attending self-help (32.8%) was similar to the proportion of attenders (31.8%) in the total sample. The mean age of the African American sample was 30.8 years and their mean level of education was 11.8 years. The sample included 161 men (64%) and 92 women (36%). Most (68%) of the sample were single, 8% were married, and the remaining 24% were separated, widowed, or divorced.

As mentioned in the introduction, some commentators have argued that African Americans may not derive benefit from 12 step programs. The impact of self-help as a sole intervention cannot be determined by this study because the initial interview was done at the client's admission to professional treatment. However, African Americans who received professional treatment alone can be compared with those who received professional treatment and were also involved in mutual help 12 months after intake. In interpreting such an analysis, two facts must be borne in mind: (1) "Professional" treatment at the agencies in this sample often involved many 12 step ideas and approaches and often was administered by "recovering" counselors, especially at residential agencies (Mavis & Stöffelmayr, 1989). Hence the difference between professional treatment and 12 step self-help programs may be less than those labels imply; (2) The African Americans who were involved in 12 step programs one year after treatment intake tended to have been treated for greater lengths of time than were those African Americans who were not participating in 12 step programs. The African American self-help attenders who were treated in an outpatient setting were in treatment for an average of 2.2 months, compared to 1.6 months for the African American non-attenders ($t = 1.47$, $p = .142$). The African American self-help attenders who were treated in a residential setting were treated for an average of 2.3 months, compared to an average of 1.1 months for the African American non-attenders ($t = 3.67$. $p = .000$).

Table 4 shows the results of repeated measures ANOVAs for each of the seven problem areas assessed by the ASI. The African Americans who were attending mutual help 12 months after intake had significantly different scores than those African Americans

TABLE 4. Comparison of 82 African Americans who were attending a mutual help group one year after treatment with 171 African American Non-Attenders on Mean ASI Problem Severity Scores

		Assessment		F Statistic		
Problem Area	Group	Intake	Follow-Up	Group	Time	Group x Time
Medical	TX Only	1.69	1.54	0.11	1.06	5.87*
	TX+SH	2.07	1.29			
Employment	TX Only	3.95	3.38	11.41***	13.55***	0.78
	TX+SH	3.44	2.65			
Alcohol	TX Only	2.88	1.67	5.66*	45.03***	9.62**
	TX+SH	2.87	0.69			
Drugs	TX Only	4.44	2.01	4.15*	162.03***	18.03***
	TX+SH	4.74	0.88			
Legal	TX Only	1.88	1.06	15.09***	40.69***	0.22
	TX+SH	1.18	0.48			
Family	TX Only	2.97	1.71	2.02	62.80***	0.09
	TX+SH	2.77	1.43			
Psychological	TX Only	3.17	1.67	2.41	68.84***	0.41
	TX+SH	2.98	0.69			

Note
*$p < .05$
**$p < .01$
***$p < .001$
ASI = Addiction Severity Index
TX = Treatment
SH = Self Help Attendance One year After Treatment

who were not in four areas: employment, alcohol, drug, and legal problems. With the exception of medical problems, all problem areas showed statistically significant improvements over time for African American self-help attenders and non-attenders. Three of the problem areas showed a significant self-help attendance-by-time interaction: those African Americans who attended a self-help group had significantly greater improvement over time in the areas of medical, alcohol, and drug problems than did those who were not participating in a self-help group one year after treatment.[2]

Social indices of adjustment provide a useful supplement to traditional clinical measures of self-help efficacy. One question on the ASI asked participants to report on the number of close friends they had at intake and at follow-up. The African American substance abusers who were not attending mutual help groups at follow-up reported that they had fewer friends than they had had a year earlier (Intake mean = 1.94, SD = 3.40, Follow-up mean = 1.59, SD = 1.61) while those attending mutual help groups at follow-up reported an identical number of close friends (mean = 2.45) at follow-up and intake. However, at follow-up the self-help attenders and non-attenders reported spending similar amounts of time alone and similar levels of difficulties in their relationships with other people.

These data on social functioning are hard to interpret. Loss of friends and conflicts with others can be good or bad for a substance abuser, depending on whether the friends are substance abusers themselves. Nonetheless, one may tentatively make the interpretation that mutual help groups may help African American substance abusers maintain close friendships as they go through the recovery process. Mutual help groups might also provide an opportunity for substance abusers to build new friendships.

As a whole, the data on African Americans support a tentative, but affirmative response to our third question of interest. One year after treatment, African Americans were attending mutual help groups at the same rate as white clients. While the repeated measures ANOVAs do not prove that self-help was of benefit to these African American substance abusers, they are consistent with such an interpretation. Even after taking into account the African American self-helpers' longer length of treatment, it is still striking that they showed greater improvement in most problem areas than did the non self-help attenders. Further, the absolute scores of the self-help attenders at follow-up are most impressive. A severity score of 0 or 1 in a problem area indicates that the individual clearly has no problem in that area. The African American self-help attenders had mean problem scores of less than 1 in the domains of alcohol, drugs, legal, and psychological problems. None of the mean problem scores for the non self-help attending African Americans were less than one.

DISCUSSION

In this concluding section we address the question that forms the title of this presentation and overarches the three analyses we have presented: are 12 step programs appropriate for members of disenfranchised groups? This question has been debated on theoretical, political, and clinical grounds by researchers and clinicians. While arguments among members of the helping professions and academia about what is good for members of disenfranchised groups can sometimes be informative, our view is that actually examining the choices and experiences of members of disenfranchised groups is a more fruitful line of inquiry. If one assumes that women, racial minorities and persons of lower social class are basically competent people who can look out for their own interests (an assumption that is consistent with the philosophy of the self-help movement), then their decision to involve themselves in 12 step programs may be taken as strong evidence that 12 step programs are appropriate for them in a way that truly matters.

There are good reasons, in addition to the data presented here, to believe that 12 step programs are appropriate for racial minorities. For example, the African American community has a long history of engaging in mutual help activities of various sorts (Neighbors, Elliot, & Gant, 1990). Further, the spiritual philosophy of 12 step programs is similar to that which is taught in many African American churches. Finally, because 12 step groups are not administered by a homogeneous professional class of helpers (as is psychotherapy), participants can make alterations in the program to make it more suitable to their culture (Rogan, 1986). Thus, while an AA meeting of African Americans or Mexican Americans is still an AA meeting, the group process, modes of behavior, and style of expression tend to be quite different than they are in AA meetings of, for example, white rural alcoholics.

As for the issue of gender, the fact that most members of 12 step substance abuse programs are men cannot be taken as evidence that the program is biased against women. Most substance abusers are men, so a large proportion of men in AA and NA is to be expected. In fact, Denzin (1987) has observed that women often have an easier time adjusting to 12 step programs than do men because these mutual help groups focus heavily on emotional awareness and communication of feelings, with which women often feel more comfortable.

Finally, with regard to social class, the implications of Lofland and Lejeune's (1960) finding that variance in social class is much greater between meetings than within them should be carefully considered. Thus, a researcher or helping professional who observes an open meeting in a suburban area may note that all in attendance are middle class and therefore falsely conclude that 12 step programs are exclusively middle class organizations. In the inner city, there are 12 step meetings where no one is a socially stable middle class person and few or no people are white. Yet these are not, unfortunately, the kinds of setting where one typically encounters helping professionals and university researchers. In fact, the assertion that 12 step programs for substance abusers are a white, middle class phenomenon may say more about where researchers and clinicians focus their attention than it does about biases within the AA or NA organizations.

NOTES

1. "Culturally diverse" is of course a relative term. Because Michigan is a northern U.S. state that does not border an ocean, our sample included no members of recent immigrations to the United States (e.g., Cubans, Haitians). All participants were U.S. citizens and spoke English as their first language.

2. A supplemental analysis showed that these interactions were significant for both African American men and women, suggesting no differential benefit by gender.

REFERENCES

Denzin, N. K. (1987). *The recovering alcoholic.* Newbury Park, CA: Sage.

Emrick, C. D. (1987). Alcoholics anonymous: Affiliation processes and effectiveness as treatment. *Alcoholism: Clinical and Experimental Research,* 11, 416-423.

Humphreys, K., Mavis, B. E., & Stöffelmayr, B. E. (1991a). Factors predicting attendance at self-help groups after substance abuse treatment. *Journal of Consulting and Clinical Psychology, 59,* 591-593.

Humphreys, K., Mavis, B., & Stöffelmayr, B. E. (1991b). *Substance abuse treatment agencies and self-help groups: Collaborators or competitors?* Paper presented at the 99th Annual Meeting of the American Psychological Association, San Francisco, CA. (Available from ERIC Document Reproduction Service No. ED 341 927.)

Lofland, J., & Lejeune, R. A. (1960). Initial interaction of newcomers in Alcoholics Anonymous: A field experiment in class symbols and socialization. *Social Problems, 8,* 102-111.

Mavis, B. E., & Stöffelmayr, B. E. (1989, August). *Paraprofessionals, staff recovery status, and client satisfaction in alcohol treatment.* Paper presented at the 97th Annual Meeting of the American Psychological Association, New Orleans, LA.

McLellan, A. T., Luborsky, L., Woody, G. E., & O'Brien, C. P. (1980). An improved diagnostic evaluation instrument for substance abuse patients: The addiction severity index. *Journal of Nervous and Mental Disease, 168,* 412-423.

McLellan, A. T., Luborsky, L., Cacciola, J., Griffith, J., Evans, F., Barr, H. L., & O'Brien, C. P. (1985). New data from the addiction severity index: Reliability and validity in three centers. *Journal of Nervous and Mental Disease, 173,* 412-423.

Neighbors, H. W., Elliot, K. A., & Gant, L. M. (1990). Self-help and Black Americans: A strategy for empowerment. In T. J. Powell (ed.), *Working with self help* (189-217). Silver Spring, Maryland: NASW Press.

Ogbourne, A. C., & Glaser, F. B. (1981). Characteristics of affiliates of alcoholics anonymous. *Journal of Studies on Alcohol,* 42, 661-675.

Powell, T. J. (1987). *Self-help organizations and professional practice.* Silver Spring, Maryland: NASW Press.

Rogan, A. (1986, Fall). Recovery from alcoholism: Issues for Black and Native Americans. *Alcohol Health and Research World,* 42-44.

Chapter 8

Understanding Worldview Transformation in Members of Mutual Help Groups

Mellen Kennedy
Keith Humphreys

University of Illinois at Urbana-Champaign

SUMMARY. Over the past 20 years a small number of researchers have advocated for the study of change in worldview among members of mutual help groups. Yet little research of this nature has been reported. Our purpose here is threefold: to reassert the importance of attending to worldview change in the study of mutual help groups; to discuss conceptual and methodological issues in the study of worldview including the use of naturalistic and narrative approaches; and to present a framework for exploring worldview change based on empirical studies. The proposed framework consists of four specific domains of belief: self, relationships with others, universal order and problem area. Examples from naturalistic studies of two 12 step mutual help groups are used to illustrate the four domains.

In order to be able to function, everyone must impose an order and regularity on the welter of experiences impinging upon him. To do this, he develops out of his personal experiences a

---

Address correspondence to Mellen Kennedy, Department of Educational Psychology, University of Illinois, Champaign, IL 61820 USA.

[Haworth co-indexing entry note]: "Understanding Worldview Transformation in Members of Mutual Help Groups." Kennedy, Mellen, and Keith Humphreys. Co-published simultaneously in *Prevention in Human Services* (The Haworth Press, Inc.) Vol. 11, No. 1, 1994, pp. 181-198; and: *Self-Help and Mutual Aid Groups: International and Multicultural Perspectives* (ed: Francine Lavoie, Thomasina Borkman, and Benjamin Gidron) The Haworth Press, Inc., 1994, pp. 181-198. Multiple copies of this article/chapter may be purchased from The Haworth Document Delivery Center [1-800-3-HAWORTH; 9:00 a.m. - 5:00 p.m. (EST)].

> set of more or less implicit assumptions about himself and the nature of the world. (Frank, 1973, p. 27)

In his classic work *Persuasion and Healing,* Jerome Frank (1973) argued that across contexts and cultures, psychological healing involves changes in the sufferer's "worldview" or "assumptive world." Mutual help groups are one example of a setting where this kind of change in worldview can occur.

Frank (1973) viewed the assumptive world as:

> a highly structured, complex, interacting set of values, expectations and images of oneself and others, which guide and are in turn guided by a person's perceptions and behavior and which are closely related to his emotional states and his feelings and well-being. (p. 27)

Frank's concept of assumptive world is similar to the notion of ideology which Antze (1976) and Suler (1984) have used to characterize mutual help groups. However, we prefer the term worldview or assumptive world and recommend it to others because it is more easily tied to earlier work on beliefs and healing, and because in our experience people misinterpret the term "mutual help ideology" to mean that mutual help groups are cult-like or somehow more ideological than are professionals or other groups.

Building on Frank's worldview concept, we assert that in order to understand the importance of mutual help groups in the lives of their members it is necessary to understand the role of worldview. We suggest three main reasons for the importance of studying worldview change among members of mutual help groups. First, a worldview is at the core of a mutual help group because, rather than being merely a program for treatment, recovery or coping, a mutual help group is a community of belief. As such it espouses a particular set of beliefs which constitute an approach to life. Each group has its own worldview, and a narrative which expresses it (Humphreys, 1992; Rappaport, 1993). Antze (1976) noted that the common view of mutual help groups (or self-help groups as they are also called):

> neglects the very feature of these groups that their members take most seriously. . . . Each claims a certain wisdom con-

> cerning the problem it treats. Each has a specialized system of teachings that members venerate as the secret of recovery. (p. 324)

Through this wisdom and teaching, the worldview of the group is passed on to its members.

The worldview of a mutual help group develops over time. The original members begin to record their experiences as a group. They record what has and has not worked for them and thus begin developing a set of principles or guidelines. Often catch phrases evolve in the group, such as Alcoholics Anonymous' (A.A.) "One day at a time." These phrases encapsulate pieces of the group's worldview and are recorded in the group's developing written materials.

Well-established mutual help organizations such as Alcoholics Anonymous (1976) and GROW (1982; Keogh, 1975) have developed extensive literatures which explain their "program" (as they call it). These are clear explications of the group's worldview, including sets of principles or beliefs and practical advice. They consist of the group's statement of the problem and steps or guides in recovery. Referring to the 12 Steps of the program of Alcoholics Anonymous, Denzin (1987) says "A.A.'s Steps may be understood as guidelines for self-transformation" (p. 180). Giving one's testimony, which is a well-established tradition in many 12 step groups, can be understood as telling a story of personal worldview transformation. The sum of the group's teachings, literature, stories and testimonies encapsulate and convey its worldview and is at the core of what is important to group members.

A second reason for studying the worldview of mutual help groups is that ample data suggest that worldview changes have a role in psychological healing. Within psychology, fields of inquiry such as schema theory (Bartlett, 1932) and personal construct psychotherapy (Kelly, 1955) recognize that human beings are active interpreters of their environments, and that the structure of an individual's interpretive worldview has a strong influence on his or her psychological functioning. This point has been most strongly made by psychologists who study reactions to traumatic events (e.g., Janoff-Bulman, 1985). These workers argue that stressful experiences have the power to change unconscious assumptions human beings make about the world (e.g., "The world is a meaningful place," "Life is fair," "I have worth"), and these assumptions frequently have to be consciously examined and changed for the person to find meaning in the traumatic event and therefore recover successfully from it.

One arena where such examination and reinterpretation of stressful/traumatic experiences takes place is mutual help groups. Suler (1984) emphasizes that worldview serves a therapeutic function in mutual help groups by addressing questions concerning meaning. He maintains that:

> The general therapeutic function of any belief system is its ability to alleviate the anxiety associated with ambiguity and uncertainty. For those people experiencing a problem for which no help or information is offered by formal institutions, a self-help group may provide a cognitive structure that creates meaning and purpose. The ideology will consist of beliefs that define the nature and causes of the problem, and values that specify goals to strive for and courses of action to obtain those goals. (p. 30)

A mutual help group's worldview can have the effect of decreasing anxiety and uncertainty for its members by offering them alternate interpretations of their experiences and guides in recovering and living. Committed members of mutual help groups go through transformations in their worldview. They report that changes in their beliefs are central to their experience of healing.

A third reason for studying worldview is that changes in beliefs are often accompanied by important behavioral changes (e.g., abstaining from drugs, becoming more honest). Research and theory in the area of cognitive change (e.g., Meichenbaum, 1977) suggest that changes in attitudes, perceptions, attributions and inference processes result in changes in emotions and behavior. Mutual-help researchers who are interested in the intrapsychic change processes which produce behavior change might find that worldview transformation is a productive avenue to pursue. Meichenbaum's work in combination with our own observations and the work of social scientists like Frank, Antze and Janoff-Bulman, persuade us that worldview transformation is an important process within mutual help.

CONCEPTUAL ISSUES IN STUDYING WORLDVIEW

Given that there are a number of compelling reasons for studying worldview among mutual help group members and that it has been almost two decades since attention was drawn to this topic (Antze, 1976), one must ask why it has yet to be seriously pursued. We propose that this is due at least in part to the limited conceptualizations of mutual help groups, the research process and worldview in mutual help groups. The currently dominant conceptualization of mutual help groups is as an alternative form of treatment or human services (rather than as a community). It follows from this metaphor that research on mutual help groups should focus on outcomes, methods and measures deemed appropriate for the study of a treatment. The over-reliance on the alternative treatment metaphor has led researchers to miss the important dimension of worldview change.

The dominant way of conceptualizing research, or paradigm, affects what is studied and studiable and this has had a limiting effect on the study of worldview in mutual help groups. Worldview in mutual help is more likely to be evident in research using the naturalistic paradigm rather than the traditional positivist paradigm. Yet researchers in some disciplines are unfamiliar with the naturalistic approach. The naturalistic approach and qualitative methods (Burgess, 1984; Charmaz, 1983; Denzin, 1990a; Glaser & Strauss, 1967; Goetz & LeCompte, 1984; Jacob, 1987; Lincoln & Guba, 1985; Spradley, 1979, 1980; Taylor & Bogdan, 1984) as well as narrative methods (Bruner, 1986; Colby, 1982; Howard, 1991; McAdams, 1990; Mumby, 1987; Nelson, 1993; Sarbin, 1986; Shank, 1990) have been explored and advocated by numerous researchers and are fruitful approaches to studying worldview. The tendency of some researchers to avoid such approaches has perhaps unwittingly steered them away from the study of worldview.

More specifically, the naturalistic approach is consonant with the setting of mutual help groups. An assumption of the naturalistic approach is that reality is complex and divergent and that within a given setting each member has a different experience and reality. Rather than a single, objective reality, there are different realities for each of the participants. As any social setting, mutual help groups are indeed complex. They are communities of interacting people with different experiences and realities. The naturalistic approach also assumes that the researcher and the respondent are interdependent and that a removed, objective stance is not possible. The experiential dimensions of mutual help cannot be understood from a distance. The strength of naturalistic research is that it represents a congruence of the characteristics of the phenomenon of interest and the research paradigm. As Bevan (1991) has noted, good science is the result not of a blind commitment to a standard research method, but of methods being selected on the basis of how well they map onto the phenomenon of interest.

In addition to the way of thinking about mutual help groups and the research process, perhaps the way of conceptualizing worldview in mutual help groups has also been a limiting factor in the conduct of research. Worldview in mutual help groups is a broad concept which lacks clarity and specificity. Possible components of worldview in mutual help have not been explored or proposed in detail. Suler (1984) did propose a scheme of major belief issues on which many mutual help group worldviews take a stand. However this has yet to be explored empirically. Although some attempts to study and measure worldview have been made (Ibrahim, 1991; Ibrahim & Kahn, 1987; Janoff-Bulman 1985, 1989; Kassera, 1989; Meyers, 1991; Schwartzberg & Janoff-Bulman, 1991) they have not been developed or grounded in mutual help groups. The lack of specificity of the concept of worldview along with the reliance on the traditional paradigm which requires operationalization has perhaps also unwittingly contributed to the dearth of research in this area. We will discuss the issue of the conceptualization of worldview in further detail in this paper.

A PROPOSED FRAMEWORK FOR STUDYING WORLDVIEW

In response to these conceptual issues of studying worldview in mutual help groups, particularly the last issue concerning the lack of specificity of the concept of worldview itself, we have conducted two studies of mutual help groups which we will discuss below. We propose that within the broad construct of worldview change, key domains of change need to be identified for the specific groups under study. As Frank (1973) indicated, people tend to take much of their assumptive world for granted until it creates a problem. Different life problems or transitions will call into question quite different domains of the assumptive world. For example, according to studies by Schwartzberg and Janoff-Bulman (1991) the life trauma of death of a parent for some respondents calls in to question the assumption of the benevolence of the world. Thus this assumption may be a key area of worldview change for bereavement mutual help groups, but perhaps not a critical domain in other types of mutual help groups. Thus the domains of worldview change need to be specific to the groups being studied.

In our investigations of these the two 12 step groups, we have developed a preliminary framework that specifies key domains of change in worldview for members of these groups. These four worldview domains concern beliefs about the self, relationships with others, the universal order and the problem area. Before discussing this framework, we will describe our studies and methods.

We have approached our studies viewing mutual help groups as communities and have attempted to understand the beliefs of those communities. We have conducted naturalistic studies of worldview change in mutual help groups. By using a naturalistic approach and qualitative methods, we were immersed in the setting of mutual help groups and in the stories of members. We listened to testimonies given in groups, engaged in conversations and interviews outside of groups and read the group literature. Members talked about often gradual and yet significant changes in how they viewed their world and about the behavioral changes that accompanied these belief changes. In conducting these studies, we have attempted to refine the concept of what a mutual help worldview is from the members' perspectives.

The two mutual help groups which we studied were Adult Children of Alcoholics (ACoA) and GROW. They both use a version of the 12 step philosophy which they adapted from Alcoholics Anonymous. Both organizations have been in existence since the 1950s, and both have seen considerable expansion in the past 15 years. GROW was founded in Australia by a group of people suffering from mental health problems. Recently, GROW has begun a highly successful expansion project in the United States (Zimmerman, Reischl, Seidman, Rappaport, Toro, & Salem, 1991). Meetings for children of alcoholics have existed within Al-Anon for many years (Ablon, 1982), but it was not until the 1980's that membership in the organization exploded. There are now three national organizations that are devoted to ACoAs, and any particular ACoA group may claim allegiance to any or none of them. GROW and ACoA also both employ extensive literature that outlines their body of teachings. In addition, members of both organizations get together socially both formally and informally and make a point of keeping in contact with each other regularly by phone.

Our research has been informed particularly by the work of ethnographers such as Cain (1991) and Denzin (1990b). The empirical materials presented in this paper are from two separate naturalistic studies of ACoA and GROW groups in a medium sized city in the midwestern United States. For each of the two groups, information was obtained from three sources: participant observation in meetings; the written materials of the group (including popular culture texts); and most importantly, from in-depth conversations and interviews with members. Each of us was a participant observer in a group over a period of two and a half years. In addition to our home groups where 90% of our observations took place, we each attended at least three other group meetings on occasion.

A total of 30 members were interviewed across the two groups. The focus of the interview was to obtain a narrative from the member's perspective on personal worldview changes since being in the group. We used a fairly open-ended rather than a highly structured interview format, an approach termed by Burgess (1984) as "conversations with a purpose" (p. 102), which utilizes a conversational style. A prerequisite of this approach is familiarity with the setting and with the people with whom the researcher is conversing. During our investigation, we each became well acquainted with the group we were studying, the organization, the meeting and its structure, and with a number of group members who were at varying stages in their tenure and involvement in the group. We have each attended over 100 meetings, participated in social gatherings both formal and informal and developed friendships with a number of group members. We now turn our discussion to the four domains of worldview change which we identified in our studies.

Domain Number 1: The Self

Change in beliefs about the self is the first domain of worldview which we discuss. Newcomers to 12 step groups often have a view of themselves as being morally and/or psychologically defective persons. In successful recovery, this view is replaced by a more positive experience of the self. To illustrate this change, one of the first principles of GROW is "Personal Value" which states that:

> No matter how bad my physical, mental or spiritual condition I am still a human person, loved by God and a connecting link between persons; I am still valuable, my life has a purpose, and I have my unique place and my unique part in God's work. (GROW, 1982, p. 7)

Here is part of a testimony from Anne, who was a member of GROW for more than fifteen years and was hospitalized numerous times for depression:

> In my life before GROW I didn't have special friends. Things like touching and hugs weren't that encouraged. So when I came to GROW that was amazing. It wasn't until then that the Principle of Personal Value fell into place because I thought everybody else was loving and caring for me, there must be something there. And then they went and told me "God doesn't make junk." So gradually I started to believe I must be worth something.

ACoA also assists members in changing their conception and experience of self, as shown in this reading from Rokelle Lerner's (1985) book, *Daily Affirmations for Adult Children of Alcoholics*:

> *I can honor myself without searching for approval*
>
> Today I no longer feel the desperate need to have everyone's approval. I will not submerge my real self to gain the approval

of all. As an adult, I do not need to blindly seek the "OK" stamp from everyone, for everything.

I grew up with a "criticizer" in my consciousness that demanded perfection. I grew up trying to please everyone to obtain love. I reject that script today. I challenge the old belief that I'll be rejected for being me.

Today I will relate to others with an inner conviction that I have worth.

In their stories, many ACoA's indicated that they had internalized negative beliefs about themselves from their abusive families, whereas many Growers indicated that they had internalized society's stigma of mental illness. The stories that they told typically included positive changes in these beliefs about themselves after joining the group. Members of ACoA and GROW who were well into the recovery process thus developed a worldview in which they saw themselves as valuable and worthwhile.

Domain Number 2: Relationships with Others

Change in beliefs about other people and relationships with others is the second domain of worldview which we found to be important in ACoA and GROW. In their stories, members told of having felt isolated and alone before the group and of having experienced friendship and mutual caring with others in the group. The emphasis in GROW on the transformation in beliefs about others is exemplified by the following quote from a conversation with a woman named Cindy who had been in GROW for over ten years.

> Before GROW I didn't have any friends to depend on or any support system. So when I was finally referred to GROW, GROW really answered a lot of those needs that I had. People say in GROW that "Friendship is the special key to mental health" and I certainly would testify to that. I think that, as another Grower so aptly put it, friendship reached me and reaches a lot of people where they're really knotted up and have stopped developing. It gets across the ideas about GROW without preaching. When I got involved in GROW there were

> two people who kept believing in me no matter what I did. In my family when I did something wrong, I was rejected. The message was "We don't love you anymore. You're not performing right, you're not pleasing us." In GROW I was challenged but not rejected. So those two people just kept being my friends–one person is still my friend. They gave me a lot of support.

Marcie, a 43 year old woman with 4 years of experience in ACoA describes her experience of changing perspective on relationships as follows:

> When problems came up in my intimate relationships, I always felt responsible, just as I had felt responsible for my dad's drinking. It took a lot of therapy and a lot of ACoA meetings before I could set limits with people and assert I wasn't to blame for everything that happened in a relationship.

The members we interviewed told of past difficulties in relating to others including beliefs that other people were dangerous or to be avoided. They spoke of changes in these beliefs since involvement in ACoA and GROW. They indicated they had become open to new avenues of social interaction and gratification and had learned that relationships can be rewarding.

Domain Number 3: The Universal Order

The third domain of belief change which we discuss is beliefs about a the universal order. In American 12 step groups, this domain typically deals with Christian-influenced concepts of a spiritual order and a Higher Power. Members of 12 step groups often go through transformations in their spiritual beliefs and experience. These changes are typically gradual, but sometimes have a drama that is reminiscent of accounts of spiritual conversion. This story was told by William, a 22 year old man about the night after his first ACoA meeting:

> During the meeting, I had wanted to say something but I couldn't let go. It was like I had a wall between my own

> feelings and everyone else's. It didn't break until I went home. I walked into my house, still thinking about the meeting and the feeling of love I had experienced there. I fell down on my knees and onto the floor. My chest got warm, like someone was pouring warm water into it. And then I cried like a baby. I felt very strongly that there was a loving presence in the room with me that loved me and understood how alone I felt. I have never doubted since then that my life, all life, has meaning.

The gradual transformation in beliefs about a Higher Power that can occur for members of GROW is conveyed in this passage from a conversation with Ben, a member of GROW for over ten years and an atheist since adolescence:

> I never talked about what I believed or about God as a problem in GROW. But, as another instance of the idea of the strength of the Program, that if you work conscientiously on a few things, other things begin to unravel, to unknot, to sort themselves out. One day the thought just came to me, I don't remember where I was. It was this release, a thought just came to me, "You don't have to think about God the way you did when you were a kid." That just put the whole thing in a different light. There I was, in '83, I would have been nearly fifty. I thought to myself "Here I am fifty years old, still essentially reacting as if I were fifteen. I don't have to do that. I am free to do what I choose." And one of the thing I chose was to start saying the Act of Surrender. That was an acknowledgement that whatever the mystery is, there was something about praying and acknowledging it that was more satisfying for me than denying it.

In the stories they told, some members came to view God or a Higher Power as a benevolent force. They were able to feel more security and less existential anxiety and to find richer meaning in life.

Domain Number 4: The Problem or Affliction

The final domain of transformation in worldview we will discuss is that of the group members' understanding of the problem or affliction that brought them to the group in the first place. This is an example from the testimony of a 40 year old woman named Fran who had been in GROW for about ten years, illustrating her changing beliefs about mental illness:

> After a number of years in GROW I realized that I was part of the remedy, that I wasn't going to be fixed by anybody else, there wasn't going to be any magic cure so to speak. All through my various types of treatment over the years, going through the whole system of mental health, I learned so much about mental illness and I learned that I was mentally ill in many ways, the depression and all this. I was told the depression was like this monster and when it came there wasn't anything I could do about it. I just kind of had to ride it out. No one ever really gave me the message of mental health and what it was about and that's what GROW has really given me. Finally this Program came along–it's kind of like someone handed me a map in this strange country that I'd been in before and I kind of knew the language, a real map to show me the way. I mean I had to do it, I had to choose that way and other people that were going that same way were giving me hope that it could be done and that it was something that was real. That's the main message that GROW has given me, that I can be a part of my own mental health. I was definitely a part of my own mental illness. But now I can really be a part of my own mental health and that's probably the most hopeful message that I've gotten from GROW.

Jay, a member of ACoA, related this gradual insight concerning his understanding of his family and their history of alcoholism:

> I guess I always felt that my family was the way it was because I didn't measure up. So I was always trying desperately to earn my place in the world, to redeem and fix my family. As I got into ACoA, I came more to see that generational stuff is why families get screwed up. My dad had problems because of the way his parents treated him, and I wasn't even alive then so it isn't my fault. Any more than it was my fault the way I was treated by my father.

In relating their stories, members of ACoA and GROW typically told about how their view of the problem that had prompted them to seek out the group had changed.

A Caveat: The Cognitive Antidote

Within a given domain of worldview, the nature of the change in beliefs may vary from group to group. In putting forward a general list of domains where worldview changes may take place, we do not intend to imply that members of every group undergo the same transformations in each domain. Antze (1976) has pointed out that each mutual help group develops a cognitive antidote that is particularly suited to the problem addressed. GROW believes that chronic mental patients too often experience themselves as having no control over themselves and their lives. In contrast, ACoA asserts that adult children of alcoholics (e.g., Marcie) exert *too much* control and feel unrealistically responsible for other people's behavior. Hence, although both organizations try to change their members' perception of the need for control over their problems, they do so in opposite ways: GROW tries to increase a sense of control and ACoA strives to lessen it.

CONCLUSIONS

One could ask about the generalizability of our concept of worldview transformation. We speculate that its utility will vary depending on the organization studied and the culture in which the research is conducted. For example, 12 step programs are primarily "ameliorator" groups (Steinman & Traunstein, 1976). They attempt to change members rather than society. However, other organizations (e.g., Alliance for the Mentally Ill) are "redefiner" groups that politicize members and help them fight against stigma and engage in political action. In order to give an adequate account of phenomenological change in such groups, a political domain of worldview change could be included.

In terms of cultural generalizability, we would not argue that identical changes in worldview will occur within domains across cultures. All cultures have a perspective on the universal order, but obviously not all cultures are Western, Judeo-Christian nations, Therefore, changes in the domain of universal order would not have the Christian overtones of most American 12 step groups in all cultures. Indeed, changes in this domain need not even involve conception of a deity, but could instead deal only with one's relationship to nature. For example, Ibrahim and Kahn (1987) have included beliefs about nature and the natural in the five dimensions measured in their assessment of worldview. This could be construed as part of the domain of beliefs about universal order.

Further, changes within the domain of self will look different across cultures because some cultures (e.g., The Unites States), view the individualistic self as very important (Sampson, 1988) whereas others view it as minimal importance next to the collective. In collectivist cultures, transformation in this domain may have less to do with increased agency and self-esteem and be more directed at increasing the inseparability of self from family, community and family relations.

We assert that worldview transformation is an important phenomenon in the stories and lives of mutual help group members. We contend that much research has underestimated and perhaps even overlooked the importance of worldview transformation in mutual help groups due to the dominant conceptualizations of mutual help groups and of the research process as well as the lack of specificity of the concept of worldview. Mutual help groups can be seen as communities rather than as alternative treatments. We suggest that by viewing mutual help groups as communities with their own teachings and narratives, researchers are more likely to attend to worldviews. We have suggested that over-reliance on the traditional research paradigm has precluded studying worldviews. We suggest the use of the naturalistic paradigm and its accompanying qualitative and narrative methods may enable researchers to attend to worldview in studying mutual help groups. We have also suggested that researchers attempt to identify domains of worldview that are salient for the particular group being studied. The specific worldview domains of concern are also likely to vary to an extent from group to group. Cultural sensitivity and cross-cultural work is needed to further develop the possible domains of concern in mutual help groups. We suggest that researchers endeavor to identify domains of change within the broad construct of worldview which are specific and appropriate to the group of interest, keeping in mind that the important domains as well as the nature of the change within domains is likely to vary across groups and cultural contexts. The four domains which we discussed exemplify this.

We conclude that to understand the power of the mutual help experience in people's lives, we need to pay attention to what mutual help group members are telling us about their lives, to the central role of worldview in mutual help groups, and to the phenomenon of worldview transformation.

REFERENCES

Ablon, J. (1982). Perspectives on Al-Anon family groups. In N. J. Estes & M. E. Heinemann (eds.), *Alcoholism: Development, consequences, and interventions* (pp. 319-328). St Louis: C. V. Mosby.

Alcoholics Anonymous World Service. (1976). *Alcoholics Anonymous.* NY: Author.

Antze, P. (1976). The role of ideologies in peer psychotherapy organizations: Some theoretical considerations and three case studies. *Journal of Applied Behavioral Science, 12,* 323-346.

Bartlett, F. C. (1932). *Remembering: A study in experimental and social psychology.* Cambridge, England: Cambridge University Press.

Bruner, J. (1986). *Actual minds, possible worlds.* Cambridge, MA: Harvard.

Bevan, W. (1991). Contemporary Psychology: A tour inside the onion. *American Psychologist, 46,* 475-483.

Burgess, R. G. (1984). *In the field: An introduction to field research,* London: George, Allen & Unwin.

Cain, C. (1991). Personal stories: Identity acquisition and self understanding in Alcoholics Anonymous. *Ethos, 19,* 210-253.

Charmaz, K. (1983). Grounded theory method: An explication and interpretation. In R. M. Emerson (ed.), *Contemporary field research: A collection of readings* (pp.109-126). Boston, MA: Little, Brown & Company.

Colby, B. N. (1982). Notes on the transmission and evolution of stories. *Journal of Pragmatics, 6,* 463-472.

Denzin, N.K. (1987). *The alcoholic self.* Newbury Park, CA: Sage Publications.

Denzin, N.K. (1990a). *Interpretive biography.* Newbury Park, CA: Sage Publications.

Denzin, N.K. (1990b). Researching alcoholics and alcoholism in American society. *Studies in Symbolic Interaction, 11,* 81-101.

Frank, J. D. (1973). *Persuasion and healing: A comparative study of psychotherapy.* Baltimore: Johns Hopkins University Press.

Glaser, B. & Strauss, A.L. (1967). *The discovery of grounded theory: Strategies for qualitative research.* NY: Aldine de Gruyter.

Goetz, J. P., & LeCompte, M. D. (1984). *Ethnography and qualitative design in educational research.* Orlando, FL: Academic Press.

GROW (1982). *GROW community mental health movement.* Sydney: GROW Publications.

Howard, G. S. (1991). Culture tales: A narrative approach to thinking, cross-cultural psychology and psychotherapy. *American Psychologist, 46*, 187-197.

Humphreys, K. (1992). *Stories and personal transformation in alcoholics anonymous.* Paper presented at the annual meeting of the Midwestern Psychological Association, Chicago.

Ibrahim, F. A. & Kahn, H. (1987). Assessment of worldviews. *Psychological Reports, 60*, 163-176.

Ibrahim, F. A. (1991). Contribution of cultural worldview to generic counseling and development. *Journal of Counseling and Development, 70*, 13-19.

Jacob, E. (1987). Qualitative research traditions: A review. *Review of Educational Research, 57*(1), 1-50.

Janoff-Bulman, R. (1985). The aftermath of victimization: rebuilding shattered assumptions. In C. R. Figley (ed.), *Trauma and its wake: The study and treatment of post-traumatic stress disorder* (pp. 15-35). New York: Bruner/Mazel.

Janoff-Bulman, R. (1989). Assumptive worlds and the stress of traumatic events: Applications of the schema construct. *Social Cognition, 7*, 113-136.

Kassera, W. (1989). Culture and conflict. *Journal of Humanistic Education and Development, 28*, 93-95.

Kelly, G. (1955). *The psychology of personal constructs.* New York: W. W. Norton.

Keogh, C. B. (ed.).(1975). *Readings for mental health.* Sydney: GROW Publications.

Lerner, R. (1985). *Daily Affirmations for Adult Children of Alcoholics.* Deerfield Beach, Florida: Health Communications.

Lincoln, Y. S., & Guba, E. G. (1985). *Naturalistic inquiry.* Newbury Park, CA: Sage Publications.

McAdams, D. P. (1990). Unity and purpose in human lives: The emergence of identity as a life story. In A. I. Rabin, R. A. Zucker, R. A. Emmons, & S. Frank (eds.), *Studying persons and lives* (pp. 148-200). NY: Springer.

Meichenbaum, D. H. (1977). *Cognitive behavior modification.* NY: Plenum.

Meyers, L. J. (1991). Identity development and worldview: Toward an optimal conceptualization. *Journal of Counseling and Development, 70*, 54-63.

Mumby, D. K. (1987). The political function of narrative in organizations. *Communication Monographs, 54*, 113-125.

Nelson, K. (1993). The psychological origins of autobiographical memory. *Psychological Science, 4*, 7-14.

Rappaport, J. (1993, February). *Narrative studies, personal stories and mutual help: A theory driven alternative to the treatment agency model.* Paper presented at the NIMH Workshop on Self-Help Research, Center for Self-Help Research, Ann Arbor, MI.

Sampson, F. E. (1988). The debate on individualism: Indigenous psychologies of the individual and their role in personal and societal functioning. *American Psychologist*, *43*, 15-22.

Sarbin, T. R. (1986). *Narrative psychology: The storied nature of human conduct.* NY: Praeger.

Schwartzberg, S. S. & Janoff-Bulman, R. (1991). Grief and the search for meaning: Exploring the assumptive worlds of bereaved college students. *Journal of Social and Clinical Psychology, 10*, 270-288.

Shank, R. C. (1990). *Tell me a story: A new look at real and artificial memory.* NY: McMillan.

Spradley, J. P. (1979). *The ethnographic interview.* NY: Holt Rinehart & Winston.

Spradley, J. P. (1980). *Participant observation.* NY: Holt Rinehart & Winston.

Steinman, R., & Traunstein, D. M. (1976). Redefining deviance: The self-help challenge to the human services. *Journal of Applied Behavioral Science, 12*, 347-361.

Suler, J. (1984). The role of ideology in self-help groups. *Social Policy, 14*, 29-36.

Taylor, S. J., & Bogdan, R. (1984). Introduction to qualitative research methods: The search for meaning. New York, NY: John Wiley & Sons.

Zimmerman, M. A., Reischl, T. M., Seidman, E., Rappaport, J., Toro, P. A., & Salem, D. A. (1991). Expansion strategies of a mutual help organization. *American Journal of Community Psychology, 19*, 251-279.

Chapter 9

Partnerships Between Health Professionals and Self-Help Groups: Meanings and Mechanisms

Miriam Stewart
Dalhousie University

Sheila Banks
Dalhousie University

Douglas Crossman
Nova Scotia Division of Canadian Mental Health Association

Dale Poel
Dalhousie University

This study was supported by a grant from the National Health Research Development Program (#6613-1477-61). The research team appreciates the contributions of the Project Coordinator, Marilyn Harris-Hart; the other two interviewers, Noreen Millar and Margaret Dorazie-Migliore; the two RA's, Allyson MacKillop and Joy Manual; and the Director of the Self-Help Connection, Linda Bayers. The astute advice of Dr. Benjamin Gottlieb, Professor of Psychology, University of Guelph and of Dr. James Coyne, Psychologist, University of Michigan is gratefully acknowledged.

Address correspondence to Miriam J. Stewart, School of Nursing, Dalhousie University, Forrest Building, 5869 University Avenue, Halifax, Nova Scotia, Canada B3 H 3J5.

[Haworth co-indexing entry note]: "Partnerships Between Health Professionals and Self-Help Groups: Meanings and Mechanisms." Stewart, M. et al. Co-published simultaneously in *Prevention in Human Services* (The Haworth Press, Inc.) Vol. 11, No. 2, 1994, pp. 199-240; and *Self-Help and Mutual Aid Groups: International and Multicultural Perspectives* (ed: Francine Lavoie, Thomasina Borkman, and Benjamin Gidron) The Haworth Press, Inc., 1994, pp. 199-240. Multiple copies of this article/chapter may be purchased from The Haworth Document Delivery Center [1-800-3-HAWORTH; 9:00 a.m. - 5:00 p.m. (EST)].

SUMMARY. The study aimed to identify the meanings and mechanisms of partnership between health professionals and self-help group members. The three project stages involved in-depth individual interviews of professionals (n = 47) and of members (n = 49) using a semistructured interview guide; separate group interviews of professionals and members to rank themes which emerged in Phase I, and a joint professional/member workshop. A Partnership Framework was developed. The predominant partnership characteristics identified by professionals were egalitarian, *flexible*, decreased professional control, *understanding* and *shared goals*; and by members were trusting, reciprocal, shared goals, flexible and understanding. The five critical obstacles to partnerships, from professionals' standpoint were *communication*, *attitudes*, role *ambiguity*, the *formal health care system* and *ideological conflicts*, and from self-help groups' perspectives were knowledge, the system, skills deficiency, attitudes and ideological conflicts. The foremost mechanisms for achieving partnership according to health professionals involved *education*, clearinghouses, and role and goal clarification; to self-help group members, they entailed trust building, communication building, and education. [Note: italics denote consensus by professionals and members.]

The growth of self-help groups, their impact on health service delivery, and their potential for health promotion necessitate the study of the relationship between self-help groups and health professionals. These relationships have been identified by Lavoie (1990) as an important area of study, because self-help groups complement traditional support resources. The professional's traditional direct service, "expert role" with individual patient/clients differs greatly from the collegial consultant role (Borkman, 1990; Maton, Leventhal, Madara & Julien, 1989; Reissman, 1990) called for in working with self-help groups. Moving from expert provider to equal partner will therefore require modification of roles and role preparation of professionals. It is important to determine the barriers that exist and the knowledge required to transform traditional professional-consumer roles into mutually acceptable partnership relationships.

This study aimed to identify the mechanisms and meanings of partnerships from the perspectives of health professionals and self-help group members. Individual interviews were conducted with 49 members and 47 professionals in Nova Scotia, Canada, followed by separate focus group interviews and by a joint workshop.

RESEARCH QUESTIONS

The key question guiding the study was: What are the meanings and mechanisms of an effective partnership between health professionals and self-help group members? More specifically, the study sought to elicit the experiences and perceptions of health professionals and self-help group members regarding:

1. the contribution that each makes to the self-help process,
2. the relationship between self-help groups and health professionals,
3. the characteristics of an effective partnership,
4. the tensions and barriers to effective partnerships, and
5. the best strategies for achieving partnership.

RELEVANT RESEARCH

Comparisons of Professional and Lay/Mutual Aid

Rogers (1987) indicates that any discussion of "fostering cooperation between professionals and mutual aid groups must first acknowledge their differences." Tensions have arisen because of the differences in their respective approaches and priorities. Some progress has been made in answering Katz's (1985) query "How does self-help differ from formalized professional helping?" Ten studies which compare self-help groups and professionals or professionally led groups along diverse dimensions (e.g., Toro, 1986; Marmar, Horowitz, Weiss, Wilner & Kaltreider, 1988; Galanter, 1988) were reviewed by Stewart (1990a). According to this review, the reported similarities between the professional and non-professional groups were skills, atmosphere, outcomes (physical, emotional, knowledge, behaviour), rated effectiveness and attendance. Professionals and professionally led groups value objectivity, education, science and traditional service models; have clientele/members who have experienced more stressful events; use open questions and reflection as helping-relationship skills; and believe that the self-help modality is effective for a few behavioural-control problems. In contrast members of non-professionally led self-help groups value mutuality, shared problem solving and responsibility, and informal structure; use support, role modelling, self-disclosure, warmth, information, rapport, social monitoring, and outreach; and consider that self-help can be useful for all problems.

Since this review, Toseland, Rossiter and Labrecque (1989) have found that groups led by professionals and those led by peers were equally supportive (Toseland, 1990) and effective in improving coping ability and feelings of self-efficacy (Toseland, Rossiter, Peak & Hills, 1990).Toseland's randomized intervention trials with female family caregivers revealed no significant differences between the two types of groups on short-term and long-term outcomes of psychological functioning or burden. Meissen, Gleason and Embree's (1991) cross-sectional investigation of one hundred randomly selected mutual aid groups found no significant difference between peer-led and professionally led self-help groups in identification of priority problems and needs. These studies are difficult to compare because of differences in design and outcome measures. Furthermore, the studies by Toseland and colleagues focused on support rather than mutual aid groups and Meissen, Gleasen and Embree (1991) studied the perceptions of leaders rather than members. The virtual absence of theoretical frameworks in these comparative studies is indeed regrettable. The function of lay members and professionals, however, do appear to be complementary, consistent with balance-theory premises (Miller, 1983).

Self-Help Group Member Perceptions of Professional Involvement

A comprehensive review of studies examining members' perspectives on relationships with professionals (e.g., Levy, 1983; Toro, Zimmerman, Seidman, Reischl, Rappaport, Luke & Roberts, 1988; Cherniss & Cherniss, 1987; Lotery, 1987) revealed a lay consensus on the desirability of the more indirect consultation and referral professional roles. There appears to be little support for professionals taking a direct "creator/initiator" role. Relationships and linkages with professionals were seen primarily in terms of individual members separately seeking professional help. In addition, self-help group collaboration with professionals, provision of service complementary to professional service, and mutual referral were suggested modes of interaction (Stewart, 1990a).

It would appear that, while members value certain unique features of self-help groups, they also think that self-help group interaction with professionals is desirable and that seeking professional help individually is acceptable. Although the World Health Organization [WHO] (1984) points to "partnership" as an ideal interface, this type of relationship is not investigated in these studies.

Professional Perceptions of Self-Help Groups

Studies of professional perceptions also emphasize the consultant role (Stewart, 1990a). Other professional roles identified as appropriate for work with self-help groups were referral resource, initiator, trainer, speaker, support provider, linking agent, facilitator, researcher, and member of advisory board. Most professionals stress referrals to self-help groups as the primary mode of linkage. Other forms of interaction acknowledged infrequently were attendance at meetings, informal collegial interaction, and mutual referrals. Although most of those sampled in these studies had a positive perception of interactions with self-help groups, there was little acknowledgement of the need for and value of "interdependence."

Interestingly, these studies (e.g., Black & Drachman, 1985; Stewart, 1989; Todres, 1982; Yoak & Chesler, 1985) do not reveal concerns about control and competition. Self-help group members, on the other hand, view professional-control issues as a primary obstacle to interaction. Regrettably, professionals' perceptions of other barriers to effective relationships, the desirability of partnerships, and strategies for achieving partnership have not been investigated.

Summary of Research Review

In sum, it is clear that the factors influencing and the ingredients and processes involved in partnership between professionals and self-help group members require explicit exploration, as this is a gap in the pertinent work conducted to date. Katz (1993) predicts that "a mutually respectful partnership, with acceptance of legitimacy and uniqueness on both sides, seems the desirable way ahead." (p. 81) In this context, the preliminary results of a study of professional competence for working with mutual aid/self-help groups identifies "attitudes" of partnership as a significant precondition of lay-professional helping relationships (Farquharson & Cardinal, 1990). Nevertheless, a "broad social consensus has not yet been reached on *mechanisms* for developing a new *partnership* between professionals and lay persons" (Rogers, 1987). This study therefore aimed to identify the mechanisms and meanings of partnership from the perspectives of both health professionals and self-help group members.

RESEARCH DESIGN

A qualitative research design (Morse, 1989) was used to study professional and lay experience in the working relationships between health professionals and self-help group members. Qualitative research, based on the premise that it is important to understand the meanings of people's experiences and the social context of human interaction, is particularly pertinent to mutual support studies (Tebes & Kraemer, 1991). As mechanisms and meanings of partnership–the ideal interface between self-help group members and health professionals–have not been conceptualized or empirically tested, an inductive approach was used. The three project stages involved (a) in-depth individual interviews; (b) separate group interviews of professionals and of members; and, (c) development of a Partnership Framework (based on analysis of the data from both individual interviews and group interviews) for presentation to a joint professional/member workshop. The study was conducted in Nova Scotia, one of Canada's four Atlantic Provinces. Nova Scotia's population is primarily rural–692,000 out of 900,000 (Census, 1991)–and its economic base is fishing, farming and mining.

Phase 1: Individual Interviews

The type of nonprobability sampling used was "theoretical" or "purposive," consistent with qualitative research methodology. As

Morse (1989) explained, informants are deliberatively selected according to the theoretical and research needs." Individual interviews were conducted with 47 health professionals with prior experience with self-help groups and with 49 self-help group members. Professionals and members were recruited through the Self-Help Connection–the provincial clearinghouse for Nova Scotia. In this study, negative cases were sought from self-help group members and professionals who reported that they had had negative or conflict-ridden interactions with the other in the past, had not established linkages, or had attempted and failed at such efforts. (Negative cases are more appropriate to qualitative methodology than are control groups.) These negative cases were added to the data.

Professionals were selected primarily from five health-related disciplines–clinical psychology, nursing, medicine, social work, and occupational therapy–identified in previous self-help group research reports (e.g., Black & Drachman, 1985; Meissen et al., 1991a). Health professionals included psychologists (n = 8), social workers (n = 10), nurses (n = 7), physicians (n = 8), occupational therapists (n = 7), and others, e.g., "counsellors" (n = 7). Professionals' experience in their field ranged from two to twenty-five years. Health professionals' involvement with self-help groups was on average seven years, ranging from two to twenty years. The types of self-help groups selected were guided by the five categories identified in Powell's (1988) typology and applied in Gottlieb and Peter's (1990) demographic portrait of mutual aid group participants in Canada, specifically: habit disturbance, general purpose, lifestyle, significant other, and physical handicap. These categories are consistent with other classifications proposed in self-help group research (Levy, 1983; Katz, 1981). The members represented diverse self-help groups: habit disturbance (n = 4), general purpose (n = 3), lifestyle (n = 12), significant other (n = 22), and physical handicap (n = 8). These participants were members of 42 different self-help mutual aid groups. Participants were recruited to represent both urban (n = 60) and rural (n = 36) sites in Nova Scotia. Six negative cases (3 professionals; 3 members) were included. Data from 5 interviews were not used, as three taped interviews could not be transcribed and consent was withdrawn after the interviews by two participants.

The semi-structured interview guide included 11 questions and pertinent probes about the following topics: reasons for involvement with self-help groups, actual roles that health professionals played with respect to self-help groups, actual roles of self-help group members, positive and negative interactions and relationships between health professionals and self-help group members, characteristics (meanings) and desirability of effective partnership, tensions or barriers to achieving partnership, and strategies (mechanisms) for promoting partnership between health professionals and self-help group members. These individual interviews were conducted to identify themes concerning the meanings and mechanisms of existing professional/self-help group working relationships and to explore the nature of the expectations that professionals and self-help group members had concerning their interaction and potential partnership. The primary purpose of these interview responses was to develop themes for potential validation by group interviews and secondary informants. The interviews were taped and transcribed and field notes were recorded.

Three masters-prepared interviewers, with background in qualitative-research methods, were briefed on the research objectives and given specific training through simulated interviews. Reliability of data was ensured by establishing interrater reliability between the two masters-prepared coders, by investigators rechecking coded data, and by checking information with secondary informants [as Morse (1989) recommends]. The coders and interviewers were different people. Validity was ensured by selecting exceptions or negative cases (Morse, 1989).

Phase 2: Focus Group Interviews

Six focus group interviews were conducted separately with health professionals and self-help group members previously interviewed in Phase 1 in both rural and urban areas. All of the professionals and types of self-help groups present in the individual interviews were represented. Focus group size ranged from 3 to 8 members, with an average of 4. A total of 13 health professionals and 16 self-help group members were interviewed. Separate group interviews are warranted in qualitative research examining sensitive issues, such as tensions and conflicts between professionals and laypersons. If professionals were members of focus group interviews in which laypersons also participated, they might dominate the discussion, assume or be given a role of authority, or, alternatively, participate in their service role as a professional caregiver or facilitator. These roles are inappropriate for the dynamics of the group strategy in which the moderator initiates and guides the direction of group response.

The focus group interview was used to: (1) identify areas of professional or self-help group member agreement concerning the meanings of health professional partnership with self-help group members, (2) challenge and clarify, with each group, areas where individual interviews (including negative cases) and the research literature suggest disagreement, tensions, or conflict between the two groups, and (3) press for consensus and ranking of optimum mechanisms and strategies for partnership. Specific focus-group procedures–interaction of the participants with each other, as well as with the interviewer/moderator, and the use of a discussion outline and stimulus materials (Goldman & McDonald, 1987; Greenbaum, 1988; Krueger, 1988) were incorporated. Participants were asked to rank each role, barrier, characteristic or strategy in order of importance on a Likert scale from 1 to 5, with 1 being least important and 5 being most important. One investigator facilitated the group discussion and one other investigator attended as a participant observer. Group discussions were recorded by the observer, and written rankings of themes were obtained from discussants.

Phase 3: Combined Workshop

During the final phase of this research, the preliminary findings of the individual and group interviews were relayed to a joint workshop of health professionals and self-help group members. Participation in the workshop was by invitation and included 6 health professionals and 6 self-help group members interviewed in Phase 1 and Phase 2, and 6 secondary informants (health professionals and self-help group members who were not interviewed as subjects but who would have met the inclusion criteria). Selected representatives from government, professional and volunteer agencies, and health professional schools were also invited. The total number of workshop participants was 24. A Partnership Model, which had been developed to depict the key themes identified in Phase 1 and ranked in Phase 2 and their interactions, was presented to participants for feedback. The workshop concluded by soliciting suggestions for strategies to promote partnership.

Data Analysis

Interviews with individual professionals and group members were tape recorded and transcribed, and field (assessment) notes were recorded. The transcripts were subjected to content analysis, using a category system of key concepts and themes that the investigators developed inductively from the data. The category system was validated by a consultant, Dr. Benjamin Gottlieb (an eminent contributor to social-support research). The majority of the coding was done by two research assistants. Content analysis is one type of qualitative research analytic technique used to describe a phenomenon from the perspective of the persons who are experiencing it. The process of content analysis involves the identification of the data elements to be examined, and developing the definitions of the categories to guide the coding, so that others who examine the same data would obtain the same or comparable results. The categories that are developed from the researchers' immersion in the data and used to code the data elements must meet several criteria: they must be inclusive (i.e., reflect the entire range of content that the respondents provide), useful (e.g., meaningfully connected to the data), mutually exclusive (e.g., separate and independent), and clear and specific (Berg, 1989).

Each category and subcategory was fully and clearly defined so that each coder could make a reliable and valid judgment about the correct category for each unit of analysis. Explicit coding rules were followed. To assure that the coding was as free from bias as possible and that it could be replicated by other researchers, the reliability of unitizing the data (selecting the data elements for coding) and of coding the units according to the category system was assessed by checking inter-rater agreement by two independent coders who had been trained in the system of analysis. Inter-rater reliability of 80% was selected as a minimum level. Inter-rated reliability was computed as a percent agreement score using the following formula: number of agreements divided by number of agreements plus disagreements (Green & Lewis, 1986). When there was low agreement on particular categories, they were eliminated (eg., deferential negative relationships). In some instances, categories were collapsed or combined and included in the definition of the dominant category (e.g., risk taking was subsumed within trusting as a characteristic of partnership.) Coders experienced initial difficulties distinguishing features of positive relationships from characteristics of partnership and attributes of negative relationships from tensions in relationships. In order to achieve appropriate levels of agreement coding rules were modified to ensure that all data were coded; double coding was avoided; data were coded according to the specific categories for specific questions; and sentences were not broken up for purposes of coding. The results of the content analysis for each group–health professionals and self-help group members–were compared.

Key themes were defined and then refined and validated through group interviews. We searched for negative cases that did not confirm the tentative partnership model and refined the model accordingly.

We then validated the model and modified it further through presentation to primary and secondary informants in the joint workshop. The literature was searched once more and the social-support expert was again consulted during this phase to validate the modified model.

RESULTS

Roles of Health Professionals and Self-Help Groups

Ten actual roles were identified for *health professionals*: educator, leader, legitimator, counsellor, referral source, consultant, member, empowerer, facilitator, and liaison. These roles are defined and numbers of health professionals and numbers of members who identified each role during individual interviews are delineated in Table 1. Interestingly, there was agreement between members and professionals during the individual interviews on the importance of

TABLE 1. Professional Roles Identified in Individual Interviews: Definitions and Frequency Counts

Health Professionals	Definitions	HP (N = 47)	M (N = 49)
– educator	informal teaching, formal teaching, training, speaking and role modeling; transmit, interpret or translate professional knowledge	26	30
– leader	initiate or create self-help groups, chair or direct meetings, and organize group structures and tasks	26	4
– facilitator	enable group start-up, group progress toward goals, and group process and interactions	25	7
– referral	encourage individual clients to seek help from a SHG, reach out to potential members or advise SHG of potential members	24	20
– empowerer	promote a sense of control and efficacy for members by fostering leadership, independence and advocacy	23	4
– helper	provide general assistance and encouragement; help by listening	23	19
– consultant	expertise, problem-solving, and change-agent activities focusing on group (not individual) capacity, organization and development; invited by group members	20	14
– liaison	encourage linkages among members, between SHGs, and from SHG to professional providers or agencies	17	5
– counsellor	professional guidance to individual members regarding alternative approaches to coping with personal problems	12	8
– legitimator	professional competencies which appear to lend credibility to SHG activities	11	8

[HP = Health Professional; M = Self-Help Group Member]

the educator, referral and helper roles. However, the leader, empowerer, and facilitator roles were identified by many more professionals than members in Phase 1.

The top five professional roles that were ranked in group interviews of health professionals were *referral source*, empowerer, *educator*, helper, and *facilitator*. The key roles identified as most important for professionals by self-help group members during

Phase 2 included educator, counsellor, referral source, facilitator, and consultant. [Those noted in italics indicate consensus among members and professionals.]

The individual interviews revealed that *self-help group members* participated in seventeen diverse roles/functions. These included sharing experiential knowledge; clarifying health professionals' knowledge; supplementing health professionals' support; supplementing natural network support; providing emotional support; providing appraisal support; collective advocacy; individual empowerment; destigmatization; reducing isolation; reciprocity; referral; outreach; organizational tasks; acting as "professional" (non-health) resources; learners; and engaging in social comparison. (Refer to Table 2 for definitions and frequencies.) During the Phase 1 interviews, professionals and members agreed on the importance of experiential knowledge and emotional support in particular. However, the significance of reduction of isolation and outreach were recognized as important functions of groups by more members than professionals.

The self-help group roles/functions most frequently identified by groups of health professionals included *reciprocity*, *destigmatization*, *emotional support*, isolation reduction, and *experiential knowledge*. Those ranked highest by self-help group members themselves during Phase 2 were emotional support, experiential knowledge, destigmatization, appraisal support, and reciprocity. [Roles in italics indicate consensus by members and professionals during group interviews.]

Relationships Between Professionals and Members

Relationships and interactions between health professionals and self-help groups were both positive and negative. *Positive* relationships were characterized by professionals and members as reciprocal, helpful, complementary, collaborative, understanding, and clear about the goals of the group and roles of each party. *Reciprocal* relationships necessitated give and take or bidirectional exchange of resources between members and professionals. A social worker illustrated the presence of reciprocity in a relationship with a self-help group:

TABLE 2. Member Roles Identified in Individual Interviews: Definitions and Frequency Counts

Self-Help Group	Definitions	M (N = 49)	HP (N = 47)
– organization	find speakers, obtain resources and chair meetings	39	19
– emotional support	caring, and understanding of the member's psychosocial or emotional needs	32	23
– experiential knowledge	role models, teachers or educators based on knowledge gained through their first-hand experience	29	27
– outreach	inform the public of the group's purpose, find new members	25	11
– learner	received information from a variety of sources to encourage new learning skill and/or growth	17	5
– reduce isolation	diminishing feelings of loneliness and of being apart from others	16	9
– supplement HP caring	complement or extend services provided by health professionals	12	15
– collective advocacy	speaking or writing on behalf of a SHG, lobbying and social action to bring about a desired result for the group	10	13

– destigmatization	reduces negative labelling and enhances a sense of normalcy	10	5
– referral	encourages members to seek help or advice from appropriate sources	9	6
– appraisal support	validate actions, give feedback, or build confidence	8	4
– empowerment	foster leadership and member's independence, sense of control and efficacy	8	5
– reciprocity	give and take in social exchanges between members of SHG or sharing ways of dealing with problems	8	4
– social comparison	members evaluate themselves through comparison with similar others (peers)	8	2
– professional resource	members use their specialized training and skills (e.g., teacher, lawyer) to contribute to the functioning of the group	6	2
– supplement natural network support	complement or extend the support provided by family, friends and colleagues	4	3
– clarify professional knowledge	explain, interpret, translate information conveyed by professionals	4	3

[HP = Health Professional; M = Self-Help Group Member]

> I think the fact that I share my skills, my knowledge, whatever knowledge I have of ways of coping with cancer that are more productive than other ways. My knowledge of relaxation techniques, so that I do a little bit of teaching along with the facilitating. They share the fact that they share themselves with me and with the rest of the group. Taking off their mask that we all wear, and showing this person that is underneath, this unique person. Being vulnerable in front of a group takes a lot of courage. And so, I see it as very much, I get and I give, it is very much a two-way street. (NGM 16, p. 22)

Complementary relationships involved activities or interactions which were consistent with and improved or supplemented the activities or contributions of the other party. A psychologist explained the complementary nature of good relationships:

> We are very much colleagues in the work that we do together. They are the experts on their own experience, I have a lot of knowledge and skills, and I have the abilities of the therapist to be objective. One of the major things that I offer is my ability to stand outside their situation and look at it relatively dispassionately. Which is an education in itself for most clients because they are not used to looking at things like that. I think that they know far more about themselves than I am ever going to know, and so I see the work that we do together as very much team work and collegial. (MLDM 11, p. 14)

Helpful relationships enabled the achievement of the goals of the group, as described by a member of a self-help group for spouse caregivers:

> If it is beneficial. As I said, I think in our case we would like to benefit from their expertise. And I think that is what you can get from professionals. So, depending on your group and what you want to know, or what you don't within your group, then it is really nice to get it from somewhere else. (NGM 37, p. 12)

Collaborative relationships were characterized by collective efforts directed toward the attainment of mutual goals. A psychologist observed:

> What I've valued about the relationship was that they were welcoming to the input that I was prepared to give. They worked very collaboratively with me. When they expressed an interest in having a course put on they really did a lot of work to get that going. Otherwise I might not have been as willing to devote that time. Because they did all the organizing all I had to do was come and present. I was really able to put something on that involved a lot of my professional time and I was able to do that for a token fee for those group members. So I felt that was a nice collaboration and we all got some good out of that. (NGM 02, p. 16)

Understanding relationships called for knowledge and awareness, as well as empathy and appreciation, of the concerns and interests of the other party. A social worker elucidated the importance of knowledgeable, empathetic interactions:

> I think maybe if they saw me as an expert and I was just going to do all the talking and it was going to be maybe more didactic teaching type of thing rather than sharing and that sort of thing. But fortunately we haven't had problems that way. I have been able to say to them that I don't live with someone who has Alzheimer's disease. I have worked with them but it is not like spending twenty-four hours a day with them, seven days a week. But you know, these other people in the group have that experience. So they have more knowledge about that part of it than I do. (NGM 46, p. 10)

Clarification of goals and roles elucidates the parts that each party plays in good relationships, as indicated by a psychiatrist:

> I would think a clear understanding of who does what. A clear agenda. Never a sense that somebody is up to something which is not up front. (MLDM 25, p. 11)

During individual interviews, both professionals and members frequently characterized good relationships as reciprocal and knowledgeable. More professionals thought that role clarification was necessary and members more frequently described such relationships as helpful (Table 3). The top four characteristics of a good relationship ranked in group interviews of professionals were complementary, *reciprocal*, *understanding*, and *clarified roles*, and of members were understanding, helpful, clarified roles, and reciprocal. [Italics indicate consensus.]

Negative relationships among professionals and group members were described as competitive, territorial, authoritarian/dominant, non-supportive, distant, and judgmental. These negative relations can involve role ambiguity and created dependence. A social worker exemplified *competitive* relationships in which each party was trying to get what the other sought:

> I think some colleagues see it as a competitive: if I can't do it, nobody can. And there is a danger in that. (MLDM 1, p. 23)

Territorial relationships entailed defensive responses which aimed to protect a domain of knowledge, expertise or skill. A member of a self-help group for agoraphobic persons explained:

> Professionals think that they are the experts in an area that they work in, but they're not. They don't live it; they do not, by any stretch of the imagination. Even just people with psoriasis or something like this that have started self-help groups. If you have had it long enough, you know every medication, you know how it works, you know its adverse effects, you know as you live with it day by day. The physician doesn't. You are still the expert in certain ways and can come to know the medical aspect of it as well as the physician. You are the expert from that position. (MHH 1, p. 16)

Non-supportive interactions reflected lack of understanding or concern and insensitivity. One social worker disclosed non-supportive feelings about a self-help group:

> I guess if you don't have an interest in something it does become frustrating. I guess maybe I learned that. I don't have an interest in alcoholics. I really don't. I find it difficult to deal with alcoholics in terms of treatment and clinical picture. So I have got involved with AA groups and I find it very frustrating. (MLDM 1, p. 23)

TABLE 3. Frequency Counts from Individual Interviews

RELATIONSHIPS/INTERACTIONS	Professional	Member
Positive		
– clarified roles	23	6
– collaborative	13	8
– complementary	24	11
– helpful	17	22
– understanding	30	23
– reciprocal	31	20
Negative		
– authoritarian/dominant	11	7
– competitive	4	0
– conflicted	11	4
– distant	14	15
– judgmental	13	9
– non-supportive	4	18
– territorial	7	6
CHARACTERISTICS OF EFFECTIVE PARTNERSHIP		
– clarification of roles	20	11
– collaboration	14	10
– diminishing professional control	7	1
– equality	13	10
– flexiblity	3	3
– reciprocity	16	10
– shared goals	12	3
– trust	3	7
– understanding	17	13
TENSIONS/BARRIERS TO PARTNERSHIP		
– attitudes	6	12
– communication	15	5
– competition	4	2
– created dependence	6	4
– ideological conflict	4	3
– language	10	2
– limited knowledge	2	5
– power struggle	5	7
– role ambiguity	10	3
– skills deficiency	5	3
– system	7	4
– time availability	9	6
STRATEGIES TO ACHIEVE PARTNERSHIP		
– clearinghouse	0	3
– communication building	13	9
– credibility	7	6
– education	10	9
– role and goal clarification	12	6
– trust building	13	13

Authoritarian, dominant interactions and relationships typically involved a health professional's perceived or actual power to control a specific activity or approach or a professional's control over a member of a SHG or over the group itself by virtue of ascribed status. These actions or views fostered group reliance on the professional for delivery of its program of self-help. A nurse was concerned about the assumed status of professionals:

> Yes, I am trying to think about when it is not a good relationship with them. I guess the same things that make them uncomfortable. Sometimes when they want you, they really want you to take over the group. They want to depend on you for organization, the content for, and there is this sort of tendency, oh, we can't do it so therefore you hand it to the professional to do. You are feeling helpless and unable and stuff like that, so there have been a couple of times with the singles group this fall that that is what they were trying to do; making it my responsibility to fill a gap or to identify what would be the best thing to do at this particular point in time. (NGM 14, p. 12)

Distant relationships were non-interactive, in that people did not rely upon or communicate with each other. These relationships were exclusive, parallel or independent. As a member of a group for sexual abuse survivors indicated:

> I think the support groups sort of stayed away from professionals pretty clearly. (NGM 52, p. 27)

Conflicted interactions involved conflict or were aimed at conflict avoidance and tension dissipation. A psychologist clarified how conflict can arise in relationships between professionals and groups:

> Now, if they are expecting you to provide direct answers for solving their problems, that can cause some tension. Because, there you are, you may be forced into the situation where you feel, oh, I have got to give an answer, I [have]got to give them a solution to this, otherwise they are not going to value me, sort of thing. That can cause tension. (NGM 13, p. 24)

Judgmental interactions involved negative evaluation or criticism of the other party. A physician explicated the problems of hostile criticism:

> In terms of self-help, I think perhaps the times that might have come closest to being negative, these have often been sort of small discussions . . . where there would be such a hostile feeling against the medical profession that I was simply there to be the kind of pin cushion for that. Where people's experiences of being dismissed or where their input had not been either heard or acknowledged or valued. And I was there kind of carrying the MD (label) and they wanted to have their say about the dreadful things that the doctors had done and said to them. (NGM 51, p. 16)

During Phase 1, professionals and members both acknowledged the problems associated with distant and judgmental relationships. Members described poor relationships as non-supportive more often than professionals, while professionals were more concerned about competitive relationships (Table 3). During Phase 2, the foremost features of a poor relationship were *authoritarian*, *territorial*, and competitive, role ambiguity, and nonsupportive, according to professionals; and, authoritarian, territorial, nonsupportive, judgmental and conflicted according to members. [Italics denote consensus.]

Characteristics of Effective Partnership

Eighty-three percent of all participants believed that partnerships between health professionals and self-help group members was desirable. Only 8% rejected the notion of partnership; the remainder were undecided. When asked whether a partnership was desirable, only 9% of professionals and 8% of members believed that a partnership was not advantageous. Effective partnerships between health professionals and self-help group members were depicted as understanding, reciprocal, collaborative, egalitarian, and trusting. Effective partnerships were also portrayed as necessitating clarification of roles, shared goals, risk taking, diminishing professional control and flexibility.

Understanding in partnerships required comprehension and appreciation of the other's experiences, thoughts, views and opinions. A social worker illustrated the importance of understanding.

> You know that we make our personnel, services available. That we are aware of what is happening in the SHG, and they are aware of what is happening here. (MLDM 4, p. 33)

Reciprocal partnerships called for a balance in the exchange of information and support between the professional and group members. A member of a mutual aid group for family caregivers delineated how reciprocity should be present in partnerships:

> I think mutual support. Their support for our group and our sharing our information back to them. I think it is that sharing of information. And I think that is where we see our group will go with this. I think we will want to tell them things that they need to know in dealing with their patients. They want to hear, I think, from us what those issues are and ways in which they can better meet their patients' needs. And for us, we know that one of the ways in which they can meet their patients' needs is to refer them to us. And they are doing that. So I think that is a partnership. (NGM 37, p. 22)

Collaborative partnerships necessitated a joint commitment to the functioning and outcomes of the relationships between the two parties. A mother who was a member of a group of parents of multiple births interpreted collaboration as follows:

> It would mean working together, working in conjunction for a better end . . . Symbiotic, is that the word? If you're working together to get the end result which is what you both want. (MHH5, p. 22)

Egalitarian partnerships involved a sense of similar status and non-hierarchial relationship despite differences in roles as a social worker clarified:

> Partnership sort of implies, you do something, I'll do something. And I think in order to really be responsible and to be

> involved in SHGs you have got to kind of be there as an equal member of the group. Not different. (NGM 15, p. 29)

A member of Friends of Schizophrenics further explained:

> I think of a partnership as being an equal sharing of responsibility and that you are equal in production. Now, I perhaps say that we are equally good, but different, in what we are doing. (MLDM 13, p. 16)

Trusting entailed assurance of the confidentiality of shared information, belief in abilities of another, unconditional acceptance of another, and willingness to take risks. A psychologist believed this was a particularly important characteristic of partnership.

> Well, based on those things that go into a partnership. Trust and respect for the other person's point of view. Not forcing your own particular points of view on them. Not allowing you to feel that you are being manipulated. I think that is important, and keeping the communication open and clear. That is the important thing. (NGM 13, p. 32)

Clarification of roles necessitates an ability to articulate different perspectives and functions of each partner, as explained by an occupational therapist:

> I think the characteristics would be acknowledgement of what each other's role is, and respect for each other's kind of involvement. (NGM 17, p. 30)

Shared goals or mutually acceptable aims for the relationship are essential in a partnership. A social worker clarified:

> You have a lot of the same goals but your roles might be a little bit different. (NGM 46, p. 13)

Diminishing professional control or the lessening of the professional's influence over the course of the relationship was an expectation of partnership by some professionals, illustrated by this nurse:

> There is at least shared leadership. If not, sometimes the leadership, need to support their leadership, and hopefully there is a gradual lessening of your need to do that. . . . being the expert or professional that is involved. Sometimes you may be involved in small ways in the beginning. (NGM 14, p. 22)

Flexible partnerships are able to change over time to suit individual needs of the professional, the group or its members. A psychologist illuminated the importance of flexibility:

> Some degree of flexibility and so that the professional is able to change over time and change to suit particular individuals. For example, to start looking at health care without looking at economics. If people do not have enough money to eat or feed their kids, well you can try and treat the aggression until you are blue in the face and you are not going to have much luck. So I think the issue of trying to take as broad a perspective and as comprehensive of a perspective as possible is important as well in terms of establishing an effective partnership. (MLDM 12, p. 13)

During Phase 1, members and health professionals concurred that understanding, equality, and reciprocity were key characteristics of partnership. More members than professionals identified the need for trust and more professionals contended that clarification of roles and goals was essential to partnership (Table 3). The most important characteristics or meanings of effective partnerships rated by professionals in group interviews were egalitarian, *flexible*, decreased professional control, *understanding* and *shared goals*; in group interviews of members they were trusting, reciprocal, shared goals, flexible and understanding. (Italics reveal consensus by members and professionals.)

Barriers to Partnership

Twelve barriers impede the development of effective partnerships between health professionals and self-help group members, according to respondents. Four of these impediments pertain to control and conflict; specifically power struggles, created dependence, competition, and ideological conflicts. *Power struggles* for professionals arose from the tension associated with lack of control over information, group decisions, and group criticisms of the health care system. For the member, this tension is reflected in professional controlling through language, organization of meetings or the group itself, and perceived differences in power/authority. One member of a group for survivors of sexual abuse explained:

> They tend to look down on support groups and support groups are already sensitive about their role in society. Because we are outcasts in a sense. Right? And so if we, say if it is a support group for women, I think we women would have a pretty hard time understanding if we had a professional come and start talking down to us. Because we've gotten if from the rest of society, why would we invite somebody who's going to? (NGM 52, p. 28)

Created dependence refers to limitations on the group's ability to exist or carry on without professional contributions or support. *Competition* implies that professionals and SHGs are "rivals" and represent alternative, as opposed to complementary, approaches to health care. A psychiatrist clarified how competition can be a barrier:

> Professionals . . . protecting their turf. Professionals being threatened by a sense that somebody is coming along and doing something that they think they should be doing. The fact the SHGs may be seen by professionals as challenging some of their imagined authority. I think there are still people in psychiatry or mental health, for example, who feel that they are the experts and that if you challenge or question what they are doing they get a little huffy about things. It still happens. (MLDM 25, p. 16)

Ideological conflicts give rise to differing beliefs about the formal positions within the health system, differing views about the nature of professional and lay relations, and differing claims about the direction, nature and values underlying the health care system. An occupational therapist illustrated these conflicts regarding responsibility for health care:

> I found it very difficult at times to separate myself from the health professional role. It was really hard at times to listen to the people complaining about what had happened in the hospital. Knowing from the other point of view that may not always have been accurate, but not realizing that that was not the place to deal with that. And that that would not help the person. So having to be quiet about it and let them just blow off steam. So I think that was the hardest part. (MHH 7, p. 4)

Six barriers pertain to the differences and deficiencies which impede the development of partnerships between professionals and self-help groups.These encompass language differences, inadequate communication, skills deficiencies, knowledge deficits, attitudinal differences, and role ambiguity. *Language differences* result from the distance between professional language (i.e., jargon, medical terminology) and common, everyday expression (i.e., lay terms), which leads to misunderstanding. A nurse illustrated the significance of language barriers:

> But there is also the other issue of I am not using complicated words as well with people who do not understand. Sometimes that is a little more difficult, partly because all of a sudden they are not complicated to you any more, and they are so much a part of language that you can't hardly find a substitute at times. And my clients are my best teachers about that. (NGM 14, p. 16)

Communication barriers beyond language differences may include inability to listen, poor channels for communication, inappropriate or infrequent communication, or misinformation, as one psychologist elucidated:

> The barrier to any effective partnership is a lack of communication. Whether it is two people or whether it has to do with you as group. The parameters, the dynamics are no different in communicating partnership with one other person than . . . with the group. Open communication. Trust, which involves respect for the person's point of view. (NGM 13, p. 33)

Skills deficiency can be perceived by both parties. Professionals perceive that SHG members do not have adequate resources (skills, knowledge, capacity) to participate in self-help. By contrast, members believe that professionals do not have sufficient training or awareness of self-help or that their practice itself is inadequate. A social worker acknowledged his lack of experience in facilitating mutual aid groups:

> I think if the group leader is as I was as a new group leader, then if the group leader is obviously tense, unsure of herself, I think that is a real barrier. People are already tense, they are already vulnerable. They're unsure of themselves because of the situation they are in. So that they need a calming influence. There is enough tension in the room to have a good group experience, if you will. But to add to that tension, to appear unsure, and I have appeared like that, and so I know what that is like, I know how the group reacts to me when I was a new group leader. People become more unsure, they become more, they do not, they feel that this person is not in control. That if somebody starts abusing them in the group, there is nobody in charge because it is obviously so shaky. So that is a barrier. (NGM 16, p. 24)

Knowledge barriers from the member's viewpoint assume that professionals lack information, lack "experiential" knowledge and/or have a limited problem-focused awareness. Professionals, in turn, perceive that SHG members are operating with limited knowledge of the illness/health context. One of the self-help group members who was interviewed illustrated the importance of experiential knowledge:

> I think that they have to see that if you don't walk in my shoes, you can't truly appreciate. So I think that in itself is the thing, and I think that is the case for a lot of health care professionals. I refer just to doctors, but that is only because they are always seen as the prime caregiver. . . . when they come into it (the group) they have to come into it on an even basis, not that that has to be a mutual thing, but you have to be open to the fact you are not coming in to tell us anything in a way that we don't already know. You are there to help in any way you can with

> whatever disorder it might be. But the people living it are the true experts. (MHH 1, p. 25)

Attitudinal barriers to partnership are based on negative predispositions towards or critical beliefs about the other (e.g., perception of the professional as authority figure), illuminated by a social worker:

> The major barrier I think of is history. And that is consumers, the SHG consumer, have already been through the system. Then there is a lot of history and there is going to be, usually, a lot of mistrust. So I think that the history of the client or the former clients, the SHG members, and the history of the professional. I know a lot of my contacts with SHGs, they have wanted to know a fair amount about me, like history. Where I've worked and what I've done is often very important. My sense has been that if I've worked in the wrong places with the wrong people that I would not have been trusted. So I think that can be a real barrier. Like what they have already been through. You know, in some cases I've known SHGs, people involved with them, they just have carte blanche, just will not deal with entire professional groups. Because they have just had such bad experiences, over and over and over again, that even if you were very good in that particular profession . . . you're branded. (MHH 4, p. 32)

Role ambiguity arises when there is confusion, lack of clarity, or misperceptions about the appropriate functions and responsibilities which health professionals or members may assume in their relationship. One physician illustrated the problems with role ambiguity:

> The barriers, I think, would be in my perception of what my role is. If they want someone to come in and give a presentation and I am not comfortable working in that style, then it would not be appropriate for me to accept the invitation. Or if their style of working is one that they are all paralysed at the presence of a resource person, and nobody wants any kind of experiential process, sharing, or telling of personal stories, or anything like that; then, if I couldn't adapt to that in that situation, then I shouldn't be there. So that would be a barrier. (NGM 51, p. 25)

Finally, practical constraints to partnership are imposed by both time and the system. *Time* availability poses problems within the context of professional duties when there is competition for time from other professional responsibilities, and SHG participation is viewed as an "add-on." The members' time in groups may compete with their family, recreational and work commitments. One psychologist exemplified this obstacle as follows:

> Time is a barrier. It is difficult in my particular practice, because I do everything, I do my own secretarial work, I do my own office work, just running the practice takes most of the time that I have got to keep the practice viable. And that does not leave much time for volunteer kind of work which I enjoy doing. (NGM 2, p. 26)

Limitations are also imposed by requirements of the formal *system*, organizational regulations regarding services, or personnel, the impact of health care facilities, and lack of financial resources. A psychologist contended:

> Well, money may be one . . . From a professional perspective, it is very difficult at this point. For example, in this area we are under staffed and the funding for manpower has a critical bite on it and there is not a lot of money out there to be had. So we are understaffed. We have ever increasing demands on service delivery. (MLDM 12, p. 13)

There seemed to be a common concern pertaining to control issues voiced by professionals and by members during the initial phase interviews. Professionals, however, were more troubled by language, communication, and role ambiguity and members were more distressed by attitudinal barriers (Table 3). The five most critical obstacles to partnerships, ranked in group interviews, from professionals' standpoint were *communication*, *attitudes*, role ambiguity, the *formal health care system* and *ideological conflicts*, and control, and from self-help groups' perspectives were knowledge, the system, skills deficiency, attitudes and ideological conflicts. [Italics indicate consensus.]

Strategies to Promote Partnership

Mechanisms for developing and maintaining partnership that were advocated by health professionals and self-help group members in individual interviews (Phase 1) included education, credibility enhancement, role and goal clarification, trust building, communication development, and clearinghouses.

Educational strategies help professionals and/or members to change attitudes, increase information or knowledge, and develop skills. A member of a mental health mutual aid group explicated the educational role of groups in building partnerships with professionals:

> Certainly SHGs, I think, are in the forefront of building these partnerships. And there are various organizations that, there's women's groups, Canadian Mental Health Association, there's SHGs that are going to sort of, I think they are going to educate the professionals that sort of aren't onside to at least illustrate to them a good reason why they should want to get involved in this partnership and why they should be making the effort to do that. (NGM 28, p. 21)

Credibility strategies portray health professionals and/or SHG members in more believable, convincing, visible or beneficial ways to each other. A member of a group for new parents illustrated this strategy:

> I think that the reason that we (the members) have such a good relationship is because we have shown that we are "professionals" and we are into this public relations part of it and we shall be as noticeable as possible. Like we go to a lot of, like we went to a Baby Fair, for example, which wasn't any big deal but there were other people that were there so we were able to be more visible, for example. And I think it is important for SHGs to be more visible. You know. And maybe if they're more visible and they can prove that they are serious about what they are doing, then I think the health professionals will embrace them a little bit more and maybe take advantage of them. (MHH 5, p. 24)

Role and goal clarification involves input from both parties which elucidates and negotiates respective roles and establishes aims that respect each other's interests. A psychologist elaborated:

> I would think that some strategies which focus on, become more focused in terms of specific areas; and how each side may contribute to the dealing with this sub-issue, if you will. I think some strategies of recognizing what each side is able to contribute. Having it is very clear as to what each side is capable of doing without compromising it in relation to the other is vital. (MLDM 18, p. 16)

Trust building activities develop belief in dependability, reliability and honesty of the partner; increase respect; and support confidentiality. Another psychologist explained how trust could be enhanced:

> Well, the encouragement of partnership, yes, I think sort of operating with other people in a way that you're open and honest in what you are seeing and saying and doing. This sort of building of trust and communication, I think, is really what affects a partnership. (NGM 13, p. 33)

Communication building strategies develop and improve exchanges of information and knowledge between health professionals and members such that each respects and understands the language of the other. A member of a mutual aid group for spouses of persons with health problems suggested mechanisms to enhance communication:

> We could formalize some meetings with health professionals on a regular basis. Providing them with, say, an annual report, or an update on what we are doing. (NGM 37, p. 23)

Although a few members mentioned *clearinghouses* or central self-help resources to facilitate or coordinate partnership between professionals and self-help groups, no professionals identified this strategy in Phase 1. Trust building was the preferred strategy of members. Individual professionals and members interviewed agreed that trust building, education, and communication were essential strategies. Professionals more frequently advocated role and goal clarification (Table 3). During the second phase, the foremost mechanisms for achieving partnership according to groups of health professionals involved *education*, clearinghouses, and role and goal clarification; to self-help group participants, they entailed trust building, communication building, and education. There was a consensus about education.

Partnership Framework

The Partnership Framework (Figure 1) illustrates that the diverse roles of health professionals and self-help group members, the reality of their relationships, and the barriers or impediments to productive relations must be identified when designing salient strategies which promote partnership. The model was inductively developed from the themes raised in the individual interviews, validated and ranked in the group interviews, and further validated and refined at the joint workshop for professionals and members. Participants at the workshop agreed that the dynamic evolution of relationships and the diversity and developmental level of self-help mutual aid groups must be acknowledged in appropriate applications of the partnership model.

DISCUSSION

The professional roles identified by respondents could be classified as indirect, "partner" roles rather than direct, expert, provider roles with one exception–counsellor. This role seems to acknowledge the personal needs of individual self-help group members, and the continuing needs of self-help group members for supplementary or "surrogate" professional support. Clearly referral, educator and facilitator roles were approved by both members and professionals in the group interviews, whereas leader roles were advocated by professionals more than by members in individual interviews. Leader roles can reduce group autonomy and egalitarianism (Borkman, 1990). The preferred professional roles vis-à-vis self-help groups identified in previous studies were consultant and referral resource (Stewart, 1989). Jacobs and Goodman (1989) predict that expanded professional consultation is an expected outgrowth of the legitimization of the self-help mutual aid model and of its empow-

FIGURE 1. Partnership Framework.

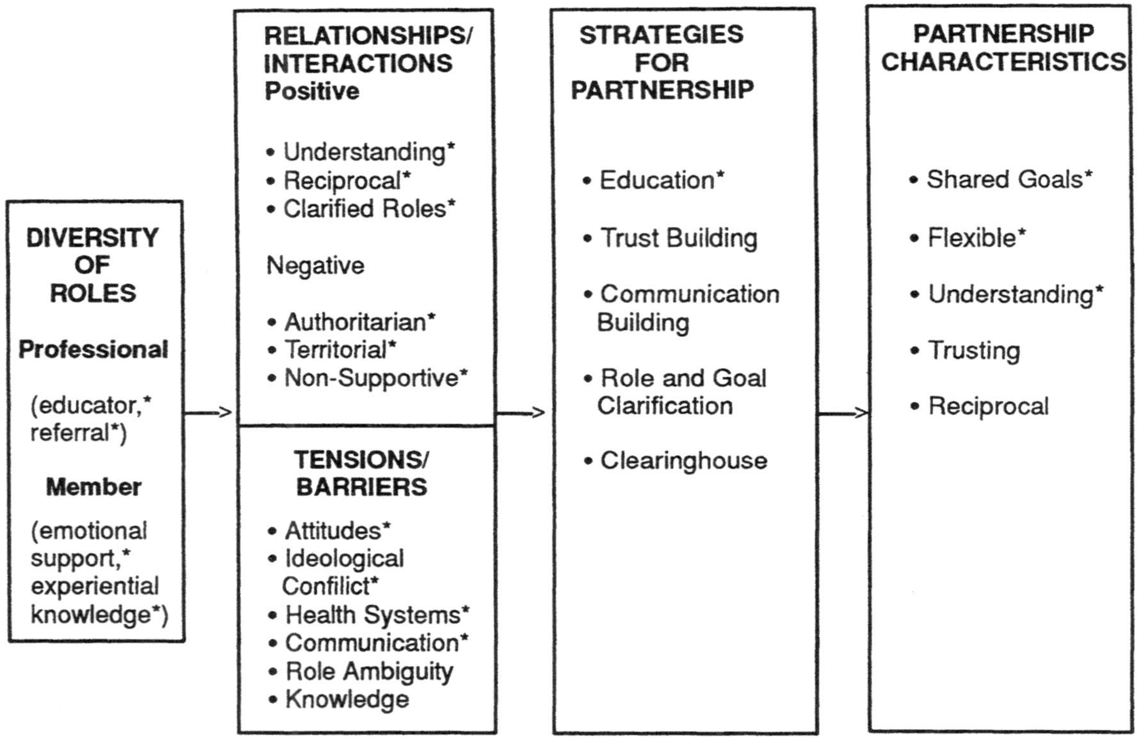

* Ranked high by both groups

erment by the health care system. Professionals typically play roles which involve referral, education, consultation, liaison, and facilitation (Chesler, 1991a; Katz, 1993; Meissen, Mason & Gleason, 1991). These roles reflect their professional knowledge base, distinguished by Borkman (1976, 1990) from the experiential knowledge base of mutual aid self-help groups.

Both professional and member participants endorsed sharing experiential knowledge as an important role for self-help groups. Participants in the joint workshop advocated treating experiential and "expert" knowledge equally. Self-help groups empower members by providing information and teaching coping skills (Chesler, 1991a). Our respondents also reported emotional support and reciprocity as key functions. The latter signifies another fundamental difference from relationships with professionals, which tend to be unidirectional, while bidirectionality is a significant feature of *mutual* aid. Emotional support and destigmatization are important functions, according to interviewees perhaps because they are viewed to be more effective or helpful from peers than from professionals. Dakof and Taylor (1990) contend that specific types of support are perceived to be helpful from specific network members. For example, emotional support is valued from spouses/partners and informational support from professionals. Our study suggests that peers are valued for both emotional and informational support. The predominant roles depicted for self-help groups reflected the essence of the mutual help process–help provision and advocacy. These two functions were considered challenging and rewarding in Revenson and Cassel's (1991) study of mutual help group leaders. Although organizational and outreach functions–comparable to the leader activities of systems maintenance, organizational growth, and building membership–were identified by many more members than professionals in Phase 1, neither ranked these highly in group interviews. These leader activities are not considered rewarding (Revenson & Cassel, 1991). More role conflicts between peers and professionals might have been observed if leaders only, rather than members and health professionals in diverse roles, had been interviewed. Professionals and peers are both valued for informational support, while peers are also valued for esteem emotional support (Dakof & Taylor, 1990). Desirable characteristics of professionals and of members have been identified in recent research conducted by Romeder (1990), Borkman (1990), Maton et al. (1989), Stewart (1989; 1990a, b) and Tracey and Toro (1989). Hence, the framework emphasizes the characteristics of relationships and of partnership.

Both professionals and members perceived relationships as positive if they entailed understanding of the other person in the relationship. Thus, knowledge is a critical feature of the different perspectives of professionals and groups are critical features of a successful relationship. Positive relationships with professionals were depicted as supportive, respectful and helpful, while negative relationships were described as distant and guarded in Warner's (1992) investigation. Relationships designated by participants in our study as negative typically were authoritarian and territorial–reflecting power struggles between professional and lay helpers. Chesler (1991a) reveals how traditional relations between health care providers and their clients can be conflicted and disempowering. Although some self-help groups do not want professional involvement (Emerick, 1990) it appears that increased interaction between groups and professionals is likely (Borkman, 1990; Bryant, 1990; Katz, 1993).

Clearly, partnerships were considered advantageous by both professionals and members. Partnerships were thought to be understanding, and flexible, and to entail shared goals. The characteristic "understanding" implies awareness and appreciation of the other partner's interests and issues. The notion of collaboratively developing shared goals recognizes the complementary roles that professionals and self-help groups can play in health care and in the support they provide to members. Coyne, Ellard and Smith (1990) contend that close relationships entail mutual responsiveness, caring, and shared or congruent goals. When goals are in conflict, there are tradeoffs and difficulties can emerge. Professionals identified egalitarian partnerships as important. Equality is needed for meaningful partnerships (Emerick, 1990). Workshop participants advocated equitable power distribution, yet professionals socialized according to the medical model believe in layperson dependence and nonegalitarian relationships (Barbarin & Chesler, 1986). Group members believed that reciprocity was a key characteristic of partnership. Some professionals may still be more comfortable with traditional, non-egalitarian, unidirectional relationships with laypersons, which tend to engender feelings of dependence and indebtedness (LaGaipa, 1990). Individuals are likely to seek support from both laypersons and professionals (Auslander & Litwin, 1990), as professionals are sources of surrogate support when natural networks are deficient or depleted. "Flexible" partnership implies a bending of boundaries and openness to shared control and co-leadership. The professional's role as leader rather than co-leader was identified by many more professionals than members in Phase 1, reflecting widely divergent views of the appropriateness of professional control. A coalition between self-help groups and professionals can result in a fundamental redefinition of the professional/client relationship (Chesler, 1991a). The partnership style of relationship differs from the conflictual/enmeshed and the autonomous style in that decision making is mutual, descriptions of past experiences are negotiated, and there is a mix of shared and independent activities (Coyne, personal communication, April, 1993).

Criteria used to assess the nature of the relationships between self-help group members and health professionals were based in part on Stewart's (1990a) review of this interface, Farquharson and Cardinal's (1990) prototype of professional-interaction styles, other recent references (Romeder, 1990; Borkman, 1990; Maton et al., 1989; Tracey & Toro, 1989) and Stewart's (1990b) proposed operational definition of partnership: "demonstrated by the frequency with which there is joint exchange of information and joint decision making followed by mutual working to achieve goals and joint evaluation of effectiveness of . . . outcomes. It is further demonstrated by the degree to which there is . . . perceived equality in levels of status control and responsibility with counterparts."

The key barriers to partnership recognized by both professionals and members were attitudes, ideological conflicts and formal systems. A national survey of self-help groups in the United States for former mental health patients (n = 104) revealed that group structures, group affiliation, and service models have a strong impact on level of interaction with mental health professionals. This reflects the broad range of ideological types of groups (Emerick, 1990). Attitudes are frequently ingrained and difficult to change and like ideologies may be inculcated through professionals' socialization.

The study goes beyond Farquharson and Cardinals' (1990) recommendation of attitudes of partnership by identifying the attitudinal shift required of self-help group members as well as of professionals. Students who enter professional programs typically come from a culture which socializes them to believe that expert solutions take precedence over experiential solutions (Gottlieb & Farquharson, 1985). Clearly, the socialization and professionalization of the health disciplines as expert providers poses an obstacle to collaboration. Consumer social movements, however, are challenging this professionalism. The struggle for control can be seen as a central tension in the conflicted relationships between professionals and members. Most self-help groups strive for social and system change (Katz, 1993). Thus, the first two barriers–attitudes and ideological conflicts–are amenable to alternation by educational strategies. However, system hindrances even to education are more difficult to remove (Schon, 1987). Any educational model of change must contain an understanding of the reproductive dimensions in a society (Popkewitz, 1984) that make orientations resistant to change. Organizational structures can also act as barriers to relationships (Stewart, 1991). Changes in the health care system may lead to change in points of conflict between professionals and members (Coyne, 1993, personal communication).

It is indeed noteworthy that the knowledge and skills deficiencies of professionals in particular–which along with attitudes can be addressed in educational programs–were criticized by members but not well recognized by professionals. Yet earlier interviews and surveys of professionals working with mutual aid self-help groups and of self-help group members reveal a prevalent perception of a professional knowledge gap, with the vast majority of professionals reporting little or no coverage in their educational programs, rating their current knowledge and self-help group as either fair or poor, and desiring further information about such groups (e.g., Black & Drachman, 1985; Meissen, Mason & Gleason, 1991; Toseland & Hacker, 1985). Professionals' lack of information concerning self-help groups and lack of preparation for appropriate roles and skills are commonly perceived barriers (Fridinger, Goodwin & Chang, 1992; Stewart, 1990a). The development of positive attitudes can be enabled by professional education (Farquharson & Cardinal, 1990).

Clearly professional preparation for partnership is paramount to self-help groups.

Health professionals need to acknowledge and accommodate lay help movements which press for professional role change. The self-help movement could be expected to affect the provider/consumer relationship and the preparation and education of health professionals. Given that mutual aid is an important vehicle of primary health care and of health promotion, the WHO (1984) recommended changes in professional educational programs to enable health professionals to develop knowledge and understanding of self-help groups. Hence, it is not surprising that the strategy ranked highest by both professionals and members in this study was education. Other strategies, such as role and goal clarification, trust building, credibility enhancement, and communication can conceivably be transmitted and pertinent skills developed through educational mechanisms. Development of trust was considered a priority by workshop participants. Trust, which was particularly valued as a characteristic of partnership by members, evolves over time. Trust entails respect for the unique knowledge of the partner and willingness to give up control. Kowaz, Roesch and Friesen (1990) identify distrust as a key barrier to professional involvement with self-help groups, while Thorne and Robinson (1988) underscore the importance of reciprocal trust in client-professional relationships. Strategies to build trust and develop effective partnerships will need to address the dynamic tensions created by struggles for control and the resulting conflicts between self-help groups and professionals. This in turn necessitates communication. Furthermore, clearinghouses are designed to provide pertinent information to the public and to professionals (Meissen, Gleason & Embree, 1991). Self-help group members could inform professionals of their roles and communication mechanisms through correspondence, the media, and clearinghouse newsletters; could participate in professional education by acting as guest speakers in classes or workshops; and could strive to build links by inviting professional consultation or leadership, as desired by the group, and by convening meetings to discuss complementary and unique roles and shared goals. Thus members of self-help groups can work to build partnerships and enable education of members and of health professionals. The need for public and professional education was stressed by workshop participants.

Accordingly, we plan a follow-up intervention study which will be conducted by an interdisciplinary team of faculty members from medicine, occupational therapy, social work, nursing, nutrition and pharmacy, along with representatives of self-help groups. Participatory action research principles of shared control (Chesler, 1991b) will guide the design. This prospective research will focus on the preparation of health professionals for partnership with consumers and their lay supporters, and will be based on the characteristics and mechanisms of partnership identified in the initial project. The joint professional-consumer team will design and implement teaching/learning strategies enabling early professional socialization through appropriate knowledge, attitude and skill development. Involving self-help groups as partners in professional education is considered empowering (Meissen, Mason & Gleason, 1991). The International Conference on Self-Help Mutual Aid held in September, 1992 in Ottawa recognized that curricula of professional schools should include content on working with self-help groups. Educational strategies can bridge the gaps identified in this study and prepare health professionals for partnership with mutual aid self-help groups.

REFERENCES

Auslander, G. & Litwin, H. (1990). Social support networks and formal help seeking: Differences between applicants to social services and a non-applicant sample. *Journal of Gerontology, 45*(3), 5112-5119.

Barbarin, O. & Chesler, M. (1986). The medical context of parental coping with childhood cancer. *American Journal of Community Psychology, 14*(2), 221-235.

Berg, B. (1989). An introduction to content analysis. *Qualitative Research Methods*. (pp. 105-127). Needham Heights, MA: Allyn & Bacon.

Black, R.B., & Drachman, D. (1985). Hospital social workers and self-help groups. *Health and Social Work, 10*, 95-112.

Borkman, T. (1976). Experiential knowledge: A new concept for the analysis of self-help groups. *Social Services Review, 50*, 445-456.

Borkman, T. (1990). Self help groups at the turning point: Emerging egalitarian alliances with the formal health care system. *American Journal of Community Psychology, 18*(2), 321-332.

Bryant, N. (1990). Self-help groups and professionals: Cooperation or conflict. In A.H. Katz & I.E. Bender (eds.), *Helping one another: Self-help groups in a changing world*. Oakland, CA: Third Party.

Cherniss, C., & Cherniss, D.S. (1987). Professional involvement in self-help groups for parents of high-risk newborns. *American Journal of Community Psychology, 15*(4), 435-444.

Chesler, M.A. (1991a). Mobilizing consumer activism in health care: The role of self-help groups. *Research in Social Movements, Conflicts and Change, 13*, 275-305.

Chesler, M.A. (1991b). Participatory action research with self-help groups: An alternative paradigm for inquiry and action. *American Journal of Community Psychology, 19*(5), 757-768.

Coyne, J.C., Ellard, J.H., & Smith, D.A.F. (1990). Social support, interdependence, and the dilemmas of helping. In B. R. Sarason, I. G. Sarason, & G.R. Pierce (eds.), *Social support: An interactional view* (pp. 129-149). New York: John Wiley & Sons.

Dakof, G., & Taylor, S. (1990). Victims' perceptions of social support: What is helpful from whom? *Journal of Personality and Social Psychology, 58*(1), 80-89.

Emerick, R. (1990). Self-help groups for former patients: Relations with mental health professionals. *Hospital and Community Psychology, 41*(4), 401-407.

Farquharson, A., & Cardinal, J. (1990). *A guide to competency profile of human service professionals working with self-help mutual aid groups*. Victoria: University of Victoria.

Fridinger, F., Goodwin, G., & Chang, C. (1992). Physician and consumer attitudes and behaviours regarding self-help support groups as an adjunct to traditional medical care. *Journal of Health and Social Policy, 3*(3), 19-36.

Galanter, M. (1988). Zealous self-help groups as adjuncts to psychiatry treatment: A study of Recovery, Inc. *American Journal of Psychiatry, 145*(10), 1248-1253.

Goldman, A. E., & McDonald, S.S. (1987). *The group depth interview: Principles and practice*. Englewood Cliffs, NJ: Prentice-Hall, Inc.

Gottlieb, B., & Farquharson, A. (1985). Blueprint for a curriculum on social support. *Social Policy, 15*(3), 31-34.

Gottlieb, B.H., & Peters, L. (1990). *A national demographic portrait of mutual aid group participants in Canada*. Report to NHRDP.

Green, L.W., & Lewis, F.M. (1986). *Measurement and evaluation in health education and health promotion*. Mountain View, California: Mayfield Publishing Company.

Greenbaum, T.L. (1988). *The practical handbook and guide to focus group research*. Toronto: D.C. Heath and Company.

Jacobs, M. & Goodman, G. (1989). Psychology and self-help groups. Predictions on a partnership. *American Psychology, 44*, 536-545.

Katz, A. (1981). Self-help and mutual aid: An emerging social movement. *Annual Review of Sociology, 7*, 129-155.

Katz, A.H. (1985). Where are self-help studies going? *Journal of Primary Prevention, 6*(2), 128-136.

Katz, A.H. (1993). *Self-help in America: A social movement perspective*. New York: Twayne Publishers.

Kowaz, A.M., Roesch, R. & Friesen, W.J. (1990). Personal needs and social goals: Issues in professional involvement in victim's self help groups. *Canadian Journal of Community Mental Health, 9*(1), 63-73.

Krueger. R. A. (1988). *Focus groups: A practical guide for applied research.* Beverly Hills, CA: Sage Publications.

LaGaipa, J.J. (1990). The negative effects of informal support systems. In S. Duck (ed.), *Personal relationships and social support* (pp. 122-139). London: Sage Publications.

Lavoie, F. (1990). Evaluating self-help groups. In J-M. Romeder, *The self-help way: Mutual aid and health.* Ottawa: Canadian Council on Social Development.

Levy, L. (1983). Mutual support groups in Great Britain: A survey. *Social Science & Medicine, 17*, 1265-1275.

Lotery, J.L. (1987). *The role of mental health and medical professionals with self-help groups*. University of California, Los Angeles: Unpublished doctoral dissertation.

Marmar, C.R., Horowitz, M.J., Weiss, D.S., Wilner, N.R., & Kaltreider, N.B. (1988). A controlled trial of brief psychotherapy and mutual-help group treatment of conjugal bereavement. *American Journal of Psychiatry, 145*(2), 203-209.

Maton, K.I., Leventhal, G.S., Madara, E.J. & Julien, M. (1989). Factors affecting the birth and death of mutual help groups: The role of national affiliation, professional involvement, and member focal problem. *American Journal of Community Psychology, 17*(5), 643-671.

Meissen, G.J., Gleason, D., & Embree, M. (1991). An assessment of the needs of mutual help groups. *American Journal of Community Psychology, 19*(3), 427-442.

Meissen, G.J., Mason, W., & Gleason, D. (1991). Understanding the attitudes and intentions of future professionals toward self-help. *American Journal of Community Psychology, 19*(5), 699-714.

Miller, G.P. (1983). Professionals' knowledge of, referrals to, utilization of, linkages with, and attitudes toward self-help groups. The University of Michigan: Ann Arbor University Microfilms International.

Morse, J.M. (1989). *Qualitative nursing research: A contemporary dialogue.* Rockville, MD: Aspen.

Popkewitz, T.S. (1984). *Paradigm and ideology in educational research.* London: The Falmer Press.

Revenson, T., & Cassel, J. (1991). An exploration of leadership in a medical mutual help organization. *American Journal of Community Psychology, 19*(5), 683-693.

Riessman, F. (1990). Restructuring help: A human services paradigm for the 1990's. *American Journal of Community Psychology, 18*(2), 221-230.

Rogers, J. (1987). *Mutual aid as a mechanism for health promotion and disease prevention.* Ottawa: Health and Welfare Canada.

Romeder, J.M. (1990). *The self-help way: Mutual aid and health.* Ottawa: Canadian Council on Social Development.

Schon, D. (1987). *Educating the reflective practitioner.* San Francisco, CA: Jossey-Bass Publishers.

Stewart, M. (1989). Nurses' preparedness for health promotion through linkage with mutual aid/self-help groups. *Canadian Journal of Public Health, 80*(2), 110-114.

Stewart, M. (1990a). Professional interface with self-help mutual aid groups. *Social Science & Medicine, 31*(10), 1143-1158.

Stewart, M. (1990b). From provider to partner: A conceptual framework based on primary health care premises. *Advances in Nursing Science, 12*(2), 9-27.

Stewart, M. (1991). Preparation for partnership: Reform of professional education. *The Canadian Journal for the Study of Adult Education, 5*(2), 1-16.

Tebes, J., & Kraemer, D. (1991). Quantitative and qualitative knowing in mutual support research: Some lessons from recent history of scientific psychology. *American Journal of Community Psychology, 19*(5), 739-756.

Thorne, S.E., & Robinson, C.A. (1988). Reciprocal trust in health care relationships. *Journal of Advanced Nursing, 13*, 782-789.

Todres, R. (1982). Professional attitudes: Awareness and use of self-help groups. *Prevention in Human Services, 1*, 91-98.

Toro, P.A. (1986). A comparison of natural and professional help. *American Journal of Community Psychology, 14*(2), 147-159.

Toro, P.A., Zimmerman, M.S., Seidman, L., Reischl, T.M., Rappaport, J., Luke, D.A., Roberts, L.J. (1988). Professionals in mutual help groups: Impact on social climate and members' behaviour. *Journal of Consulting and Clinical Psychology, 56*(4), 631-632.

Toseland, R. W. (1990). Long-term effectiveness of peer-led and professionally led support groups for caregivers. *Social Service Review, 64*(2), 301-327.

Toseland, R. W., Rossiter, C. M., Peak, T., & Hill, P. (1990). Therapeutic processes in peer led and professionally led support groups for caregivers. *International Journal of Group Psychotherapy, 40*(3), 279-303.

Toseland, R.W., & Hacker, L. (1985). Social workers: Use of self-help groups as a resource for clients. *Social Work, 30*(3), 232-237.

Toseland, R.W., Rossiter, C.T., & Labrecque, M. (1989). The effectiveness of three group intervention strategies to support family caregivers. *American Journal of Orthopsychiatry, 59*(3), 420-429.

Tracey, T.J. & Toro, P.A. (1989). Natural and professional help: A process analysis. *American Journal of Community Psychology, 17*(4), 443-458.

Warner, A. (1992). *Participants' views on the impact of self-help on health.* Halifax, Nova Scotia: Self Help Connection (unpublished).

World Health Organization. (1984). *Progress in implementation of the global strategy for health for all.* Geneva: WHO.

Yoak, M., & Chesler, C. (1985). Alternative professional roles in health care delivery: Leadership patterns in self-help groups. *Journal of Applied Behavioural Science, 21*(4), 427-444.

Chapter 10

Predictors of Burnout Among Self-Help Group Leaders

Gregory J. Meissen
Fred Volk
Wichita State University

SUMMARY. This research focused on role related variables and problems of self-help groups that were predictive of burnout in self-help group leaders. A random sample of 132 peer leaders of self-help groups were drawn from the database of the Self-Help Network of Kansas, a statewide self-help clearinghouse in Wichita, Kansas, which is located in the center of the United States. Peer leaders were administered the Maslach Burnout Inventory as well as measures related to their role in the group. Results indicated that role satisfaction, role conflict and role ambiguity were significant predictors of burnout along with the self-help group problems of overworked leaders and recruiting new members. It was also found that role satisfaction, role conflict and the problems of recruiting and keeping new members, and attendance at meetings significantly differentiated those in shared versus sole leadership roles. This information was disseminated to self-help groups in our database with a focus on the development of shared leadership and ways to prevent leader burnout.

Issues related to leadership in self-help groups have been widely discussed but little research has actually been conducted regarding

---

Address correspondence to Gregory J. Meissen, Self-Help Network, Department of Psychology, Wichita State University, KS USA 67208.

[Haworth co-indexing entry note]: "Predictors of Burnout Among Self-Help Group Leaders." Meissen, Gregory J., and Fred Volk. Co-published simultaneously in *Prevention in Human Services* (The Haworth Press, Inc.) Vol. 11, No. 2, 1994, pp. 241-262; and *Self-Help and Mutual Aid Groups: International and Multicultural Perspectives* (ed: Francine Lavoie, Thomasina Borkman, and Benjamin Gidron) The Haworth Press, Inc., 1994, pp. 241-262. Multiple copies of this article/chapter may be purchased from The Haworth Document Delivery Center [1-800-3-HAWORTH; 9:00 a.m. - 5:00 p.m. (EST)].

the roles, activities, or functioning of persons in these positions. Research to understand self-help group leadership is important because a group is influenced by those in leadership positions, and it is believed that the likelihood the group will disband is higher when leader burnout and turnover occurs. The purpose of this research was to determine what role related variables and characteristic problems of self-help groups were predictive of higher levels of burnout in peer leaders of self-help groups, and to determine what role related and group problem variables distinguish those in a sole leadership role from those peer leaders who share leadership with other members in the group.

LEADERSHIP ISSUES IN SELF-HELP GROUPS

Little is actually known about peer leadership in self-help groups, the roles leaders play, the structure of leadership, the range of activities of leaders or even how long a typical leader remains in their position. Some self-help groups do not recognize formal leaders, most notably those groups who follow a traditional Twelve-Step model (e.g., Alcoholics Anonymous, Overeaters Anonymous). Nonetheless, there is still one member, or more typically a small core of experienced members in these Twelve-Step groups who conduct the activities that maintain the viability of the group (Kurtz, 1990). Even though "leader" is not the accepted term in some self-help groups, it is used in this study in order to describe persons who conduct the activities that maintain the viability of the group.

In terms of leader activities, Revenson and Cassel (1991) collected data on peer leaders of scoliosis self-help groups and identified 364 different leadership activities. They developed five categories of leader activity including (a) Help Provision, (b) Advocacy, (c) System Maintenance, (d) Organizational Growth, and (e) Building Membership. The scoliosis self-help group leaders rated the activities of Help Provision and Advocacy as significantly more enjoyable and challenging than the more administratively based categories of System Maintenance, Organizational Growth, and Building Membership (Revenson & Cassel, 1991). At the same time, the leaders spent nearly 80% of their time on administrative tasks in these categories (Revenson & Cassel, 1991). If peer leaders are spending so much time on the less preferred administrative duties, there is a possibility they could encounter some of the issues professionals face when they find their work unrewarding.

One such problem that often is a catalyst for ineffective performance, dissatisfaction, and turnover in professional helpers is burnout (Cherniss, 1980; Maslach & Jackson, 1986; Pines & Aronson, 1988). The results of a needs assessment of self-help group leaders and members supported this point as participants reported that one of the significant problems facing their groups was "overworked and tired leaders" (Meissen, Gleason & Embree, 1991). From our experience of working with many peer leaders through a self-help clearinghouse, many of the concerns expressed on a day to day basis by leaders sound much like the "burnout" described in the literature on professionals. Though unlike professionals, the stress resulting from the work of the group is often exacerbated by having to also maintain a job, and dealing with their own personal situation that defines their membership in the self-help group. Unfortunately, when peer leaders of self-help groups experience burnout and turnover, the group is believed to be at higher risk of being disrupted or even disbanding (Maton, Leventhal, Madara, & Julien, 1989). At the same time, peer leaders of self-help groups could be considerably less susceptible to burnout because of the support of other members. One of the most common techniques recommended to prevent burnout among professionals is the development of support groups (Spicuzza & DeVoe, 1982; Pines & Aronson, 1988). Even though the concept of burnout was devised to describe professional roles, it provides a conceptual model to attempt to understand issues related to self-help group leader stress and turnover. It could be advantageous to determine predictors of peer leader burnout as that information could be shared with self-help groups, national self-help organizations and self-help clearinghouses to be used to prevent potential group disruption due to leader turnover.

BURNOUT

"Burnout" has been defined as ". . . a syndrome of emotional exhaustion, depersonalization, and reduced personal accomplishment that can occur among individuals who do 'people work' of some kind" (Maslach & Jackson, p. 1, 1986). Burnout is characterized most notably by exhaustion, both psychological and physical, and is often accompanied by cynicism and negativism (Zastrow, 1984). Burnout is not a dichotomous condition, but rather a continuum which ranges from low levels to high levels. Based on extensive research, Maslach and Jackson (1986) have identified three factors as making up the burnout construct which include "Emotional Exhaustion," "Personal Accomplishment," and "Depersonalization." Emotional Exhaustion (EE) is defined as the feeling of being overextended and exhausted. Personal Accomplishment (PA) can be described as having feelings of competence and successful achievement in one's work with people. Lack of Personal Accomplishment contributes to burnout. Depersonalization (DP) is defined as an unfeeling and impersonal response towards recipients of one's service, care, treatment, or instruction.

Stress and burnout. The vast majority of burnout research has been on human service workers such as teachers, mental health providers, nurses, and social service workers (e.g., Maslach & Jackson, 1984b; Epstein & Silvern, 1990; Vanyperen, Buunk, & Schaufeli, 1992). Much research has been conducted attempting to understand the relationship between stressors and burnout (e.g., Belcastro, Gold & Grant, 1982; Caputo, 1991; Maslach, 1982; Pines & Aronson, 1988). Stressors are often separated into two distinct categories which include environmental or role related factors which produce external stressors, and individual or personality factors which effect how a person mediates a potentially stressful event (Maslach, 1982, Sutherland & Cooper, 1990; Vanyperen, Buunk & Schaufeli, 1992). The present research focused on the factors which produced external stressors that past research has found to have negative effects on human service professionals, and that are conceptually related to the activities of peer self-help group leaders. Research indicates that role ambiguity, role conflict, consistently heavy workloads, low job satisfaction and organizational problems that are perceived to be intractable are often accompanied by higher levels of burnout (Cherniss & Egnatios, 1978; Golembiewski & Munzenrider, 1984; Maslach & Jackson, 1984a; Pines & Aronson, 1988; Rosenthal, Teague, Retish, West & Vessell, 1983; Zastrow, 1984). The purpose of this research was to examine similar variables to determine if they were predictors of burnout in peer leaders of self-help groups.

ROLE ISSUES AND BURNOUT

Role Conflict. Role conflict occurs when an individual's personal values, expectations, or abilities are incongruent with their prescribed role or with the expectations of significant others (Kahn, Wolfe, Quinn, Snoek & Rosenthal, 1964; Rizzo, House & Lirtzman, 1970). Role theory hypothesizes that when role conflict occurs it will be accompanied by dissatisfaction with the role and decreased performance of activities (Kahn et al., 1964). This hypothesis has been substantially supported in a number of studies (e.g., Jackson, Schwab & Schuler, 1986; Rizzo, House & Litzman, 1970; Schwab & Iwanicki, 1982). Peer leaders of self-help groups could be at risk for role conflict based on non-congruent or inconsistent expectations with group members, their national or local organizational affiliate or local service providers that have a relationship with the group (Powell, 1990).

Role Ambiguity. Role ambiguity occurs when there is vagueness concerning expectations or responsibilities related to one's role or position, when it is unclear what tasks need to be accomplished, or how to accomplish those tasks (Kahn et al., 1964; Rizzo, House & Lirtzman, 1970). Role theory states that when role ambiguity occurs it will be accompanied by anxiety, dissatisfaction with the role and impaired performance (Kahn et al., 1964). A number of studies have substantiated the negative impact of role ambiguity (e.g., Jackson, Schwab & Schuler, 1986; Rizzo, House & Litzman, 1970; Schwab & Iwanicki, 1982). Role ambiguity could occur if the leader of a self-help group lacks the information necessary for satisfactory performance of tasks, the role is poorly defined or understood, or leaders are confused about what they are to perform or accomplish (Cherniss, 1980). Peer leaders of self-help groups could be particularly susceptible to role ambiguity as many groups do not have clearly defined, formal roles for leaders (Block & Llewelyn, 1987; Revenson & Cassel, 1991).

There have been a number of studies that have specifically found burnout, as measured by the Maslach Burnout Inventory (MBI), to be significantly related to role ambiguity and role conflict in human service workers (Ursprung, 1986a). Cherniss (1980) found that role ambiguity defined as the lack of clarity of goals was related to burnout of newly trained human service professionals. Research has found that the reduction of role ambiguity through increased organizational structure and clarity in day care settings also produced less burnout (Maslach & Pines, 1977; Pines & Maslach, 1980). Role clarity measured by the Work Environment Scale, was found to be one of the three most important variables related to burnout in a group of recreation professionals (Rosenthal et al., 1983). Role ambiguity combined with role conflict was the most important predictor of burnout of teachers in one study (Schwab & Iwanicki, 1982), and had similar negative impacts on social workers (Harrison, 1980) and paraprofessional residential service workers (Ursprung, 1986b).

Role Satisfaction. Role and job satisfaction have been found to be negatively correlated with burnout consistently (Cherniss & Egnatios, 1978; Maslach & Jackson, 1984a; 1984b; Wolpin, Burke & Greenglass, 1991). While some have argued that role satisfaction and burnout are simply measuring the same phenomena, Maslach has consistently claimed they measure different constructs (Maslach & Jackson, 1984a; 1986). Cherniss (1980) considers burnout a primary reason for job dissatisfaction among human service workers, resulting in increased cynicism, apathy, intention to quit and ultimately higher turnover rates (Caputo, 1991; Cherniss & Egnatios, 1978; Maslach & Jackson, 1984a; Rosenthal et al., 1983; Wolpin, Burke & Greenglass, 1991). Although being a peer leader of a self-help group is not a job in a formal sense, low levels of satisfaction with their role are likely to be significantly related to higher levels of burnout.

Shared vs. Sole Leadership Role. Revenson and Cassel (1991) found that scoliosis group leaders engaged in a broad range of activities. Many self-help groups have more than one person performing these tasks. More specifically, groups who follow a Twelve-Step model do not acknowledge formal leaders but instead encourage many different roles with different members sharing the work of the group (Kurtz, 1990). There are other self-help groups that do not follow a Twelve-Step model but have developed shared leadership structures or complementary leadership roles. It is possible that shared leadership could mitigate burnout through reduction of time spent in leadership activities while also proving a more supportive structure. At the same time, the research on role ambiguity and role conflict would suggest that unless these different tasks for different members were well differentiated and clearly defined that burnout could actually be increased.

PROBLEMS OF THE GROUP AND BURNOUT

Organizational or work setting conditions such as uncertainty regarding the flow of clients, unpredictability of funding, heavy workload, and bureaucratization often have been found to produce higher levels of burnout especially if problems are viewed as intractable (Arches, 1991; Cherniss, 1980; Wolpin, Burke & Greenglass, 1991). Problems associated with the functioning of a self-help group could be considered analogous to the problems that have influenced burnout in professional organizational settings. Based on a needs assessment of a representative sample of self-help group leaders and members, it was found that recruiting new members, keeping new members, getting members to regularly attend meetings, getting members to share the work, and lack of public awareness were considered the most important problems facing the group (Meissen, Gleason & Embree, 1991). Related to these concerns was the attendant problem of overworked and tired group leaders which also was considered a significant problem. These primary problems are interconnected and possibly of the nature Sarason (1978) described as intractable for many self-help groups. Consequently, these problems could also contribute to burnout among self-help group leaders.

The primary purpose of this study was to determine what role related variables and what common problems of self-help groups were predictors of burnout in peer leaders of self-help groups. Using a multiple regression approach, the role related variables of role ambiguity, role conflict, role satisfaction, time spent on leader activities, duration of time in leader role and shared vs. sole leadership were included in a regression using burnout as the dependent variable. The variables reflecting the problems of recruiting new members, keeping new members, getting members to regularly attend meetings, getting members to share the work, lack of public awareness, and overworked and tired leaders were also entered into the regression. It was also hypothesized that peer leaders of self-help groups in shared leadership roles would show lower levels of burn-out than peer leaders of self-help groups in sole leadership roles. Further, a discriminant analyses was conducted to determine which role variables and group problem variables best differentiated those in shared leadership roles and those in sole leadership roles.

METHOD

Procedure

A random sample of 150 active peer led self-help groups was drawn for phone interview from the data base of 1600 groups of the Self-Help Network of Kansas, a statewide self-help clearinghouse. The Self-Help Network in an action research unit of the Department of Psychology at Wichita State University which is located in Wichita, Kansas, USA. Wichita is a city of almost a half-million in a primarily rural state with a population of 2.5 million located in the center of the United States.

A self-help group had to meet the following criteria to be listed in the Network database: (1) composition of members who share a common situation or problem; (2) a mutual assistance orientation–members helping members as the primary form of assistance; and (3) no user fees or fees for service. Of the 150 active self-help groups in the sample, nine could not be reached after repeated attempts. Of the 141 groups successfully contacted, nine declined participation, producing only a 6% refusal rate. Of the total 150 peer led self-help groups in the sample, 132 completed interviews were obtained representing an 88% overall response rate.

Interviewers were recruited from undergraduate and graduate psychology classes at Wichita State University. They were trained in telephone interview techniques and received information about self-help groups during the training sessions. A mock interview was conducted with all the interviewers as a part of training. Peer leaders were telephoned, and asked permission to conduct the interview. It was made clear that participation was voluntary, that they could end the interview at any time, and that all information was completely confidential. The survey took about 20 minutes.

Group Leaders

The sample consisted of 132 peer leaders of self-help groups. Leaders had been in their role for an average of 5.5 years, ranging from less than one year to 33 years. About 65% had been in their leadership role for three years or less. Fifty-eight percent of the leaders surveyed were involved in the founding of their group. Leaders spent an average of 5.1 hours per week on group activities, ranging from 1 to 30 hours per week. Of the 132 groups in the sample, 60% had others serving in leadership roles and 40% had a sole leader. Almost half (47%) of the leaders had full-time jobs, 13% worked part-time, 27% were not working and 13% were retired. The greatest portion of group leaders were female (84%) and married (82%). The mean age of the leaders was 47.

Almost half (46%) of the self-help groups met monthly, 28% met weekly, and 9% met twice a month. Of the 132 groups in the sample, 55% were affiliated with a national organization (e.g., Compassionate Friends), and 29% reported no formal affiliation with any organization or agency. The remaining 16% of the groups were affiliated with a local organization (e.g., Sexual Assault Center). Of the 132 groups in the sample, 18% of the participants considered their self-help group to be a Twelve-Step group.

Instrument

The survey focused on aspects of the respondents leadership role, the Maslach Burnout Inventory (MBI), and on perceived group needs.

Leadership Role. Each leader was asked to rate their satisfaction with their leader role on a 4-point scale from (1) very satisfied, (2) satisfied, (3) unsatisfied, to (4) very unsatisfied. Role ambiguity was assessed by three items that focused on the (a) clarity and understanding of their leader role, (b) having the necessary information for adequate performance of their leadership role, and (c) confusion about what to do in their leadership role. A role ambiguity construct was formed by summing these three questions which had a Cronbach's alpha of .60. Role conflict was also assessed by three items that focused on (a) if members and leaders have congruent expectations regarding leadership activities, (b) if members have inconsistent expectations of leaders, and (c) if members expectations are congruent with the leader's personal values. A role conflict construct was formed by summing these three items which had a Cronbach's alpha of .68. Leaders were asked to rate each of the role items on a 4-point scale that ranged from (1) never, (2) often, (3) sometimes and (4) always.

Other peer leader data was also collected including how long leaders had been in their current role, how much time was spent on group related activities, and how they first got involved in their leadership role. Leaders were asked to describe their roles as well as roles of other members engaged in leadership activities in the group. Individual leader demographics (e.g., gender, age) and group demographics (e.g., affiliation, frequency of meeting) were also obtained.

Burnout. Burnout was assessed using the 22-item Maslach Burnout Inventory (MBI) which is comprised of the three sub-scales of Emotional Exhaustion (EE), Personal Accomplishment (PA), and Depersonalization (DP). Emotional Exhaustion is a 9-item subscale which assesess feelings of being emotionally overextended and exhausted by one's work (e.g., I feel emotionally drained from my work with the group). The Depersonalization sub-scale is a 5-item scale which measures an unfeeling and impersonal response towards recipients of one's service, care, treatment or instruction (e.g., I feel I treat some members as if they were impersonal objects). The Personal Accomplishment sub-scale is an 8-item scale which measures feelings of competence and successful achievement in one's work with people (e.g., I feel I'm positively influencing other people's lives through my work with the group). Extensive research on the MBI has been conducted that has consistently supported the three factor solution of Emotional Exhaustion, Depersonalization and Personal Accomplishment, and has supported the discriminant and convergent validity of the burnout inventory and the three sub-scales (Maslach & Jackson, 1986). Internal consistency measured by Cronbach's alpha and test-retest reliability for the three sub-scales are reported by Maslach and Jackson (1986) respectively: Emotional Exhaustion (.90; .60), Depersonalization

(.79; .54), and Personal Accomplishment (.71; .57). All the individual items on each sub-scale were measured in this study by a 4-point scale ranging from (1) never, (2) sometimes, (3) often, and (4) always. A total burnout score for use as a dependent variable was derived by summing the composite scores for the Emotional Exhaustion, Depersonalization and "Lack of Personal Accomplishment" sub-scales. The "Lack of Personal Accomplishment" score which was obtained by subtracting the Personal Accomplishment composite from the total possible for Personal Accomplishment as recommended by Maslach & Jackson (1986).

Group Problems. Data was collected on the occurrence of the six most frequent needs or problems of self-help groups that were identified from an earlier study (Meissen, Gleason & Embree, 1991). Leaders were asked to rate the frequency of the problems of recruiting new members, keeping new members in the group, getting members to share the work of the group, getting the members to attend the group meetings/activities regularly, overworked and tired leaders, and lack of public awareness concerning the group on a 4-point scale ranging from (1) never, (2) sometimes, (3) often, and (4) always.

RESULTS

Using a multiple regression approach, the role related variables of role ambiguity, role conflict, role satisfaction, time spent on leader activities, duration of time in leader role, and shared vs. sole leadership were included in a stepwise regression using burnout as the dependent variable. The variables reflecting common problems of self-help groups of recruiting new members, keeping new members, getting members to regularly attend meetings, getting members to share the work, lack of public awareness, and overworked and tired leaders were also entered into the regression as independent variables. The regression achieved a multiple R of .6212, with five of the independent variables entering the equation including: role satisfaction, the problem of overworked and tired leaders, role ambiguity, role conflict, and the problem of recruiting of new members (see Table 1). More specifically, lower levels of role satisfaction and higher levels of role ambiguity and role conflict were

TABLE 1. Regression Summary: Role and Group Variables Predicting Burnout (n = 132)

Variables	R^2	R^2 Change	F^a
Current Satisfaction	.1602	.1602	24.79
Overwork/Tired Leader	.2458	.0856	21.02
Role Ambiguity	.3169	.0711	19.78
Role Conflict	.3511	.0342	17.18
Recruiting New Members	.3859	.0348	15.83

$^a p < .05$

indicative of higher levels of burnout (see correlation matrix in Table 2). The higher reported frequency of the group problems of recruiting new members, and overworked and tired leaders were also predictors of the higher levels of burnout.

Distinguishing Between Shared and Sole Leadership

Of the total sample of 132, 79 (60%) were in shared leadership roles and 53 (40%) were in sole leadership roles. There were no significant differences in levels of total burnout or the sub-scales of Emotional Exhaustion, Depersonalization or Personal Accomplishment between those in shared and those in sole leadership roles as measured by t-tests (see Table 3). The hypothesis that participants in shared leadership roles would report lower levels of burnout was not supported.

A discriminant analysis was performed to determine which role related and group problem variables maximally discriminated between those in shared versus sole leadership roles. The variables included in the discriminant analysis were role ambiguity, role conflict, role satisfaction, time spent on leader activities, duration of time in leader role, the six common problems of self-help groups, the three burnout sub-scales of Emotional Exhaustion, Depersonalization and Personal Accomplishment, and total burnout. Table 3 shows the means for these variables across shared and sole leadership roles. Of these variables, five contributed to the discriminant function. The variables that made a significant contribution in dis-

TABLE 2. Correlations Between Leader Role and Group Problem Variables (n = 132)

Variable	Role Ambiguity	Role Conflict	Role Satisfct	Total Burnout	Duration in Role	Hours Per Wk	Recruit Members	Tired Leaders	Members to Work	Keep Members	Member Attend	Public Aware
Role Ambiguity	.....											
Role Conflict	.211[a]	.....										
Satisfaction	–.309[a]	–.344[a]	.....									
Burnout	.367[a]	.397[a]	–.400[a]	.....								
Duration in Role	.178[a]	.143	–.128	–.127	.....							
Hours/Week	.060	.000	.068	–.099	.053	.....						
Recruiting New Members	.060	.095	–.314[a]	.338[a]	.091	–.003	.....					
Overwork Tired leaders	.033	.273[a]	–.215[a]	.372[a]	–.027	.079	.263[a]	.....				
Members Share Work	.065	.317[a]	–.191[a]	.275[a]	–.114	–.093	.170	.514[a]	.....			
Keep New Members	.124	.123	–.298[a]	.338[a]	–.029	–.039	.509[a]	.251[a]	.357[a]	.....		
Get Member to Attend	.151	.294[a]	–.402[a]	.286[a]	.057	–.050	.439[a]	.223[a]	.316[a]	.545[a]	.....	
Lack Public Awareness	–.023	.153	–.019	–.042	–.192[a]	.074	.213[a]	–.092	.116	.062	.126	

[a]$p < .05$

TABLE 3. Mean Comparisons: Shared vs. Sole Leadership Roles

Variable	Shared	Sole
Emotional Exhaustion	6.5	7.7
Lack Personal Accomplishment	15.7	16.8
Depersonalization	1.4	1.6
Total Burnout	23.7	26.2
Role Satisfaction	3.3	2.8[a]
Role Conflict	10.4	9.8[a]
Role Ambiguity	10.0	9.8
Hours Spent/Week	5.6	4.4
Years in Leader Role	4.0	3.8
Recruiting New Members	2.0	2.5[a]
Keeping New Members	2.8	3.3[a]
Members Share Work	2.1	2.0
Getting Members to Attend	1.8	2.2[a]
Overwork/Tired Leaders	1.7	1.7
Lack of Public Awareness	2.3	2.4
Number of Peer Leaders	79	53

[a]$p < .05$

tinguishing shared leadership from sole leadership included role satisfaction, role conflict and the problems of getting members to attend meetings/activities, recruiting new members, and keeping new members. Those in shared leadership roles had greater levels of role satisfaction but also reported greater levels of role conflict. Those in shared leadership roles experienced significantly lower frequencies of the three discriminating group problems of getting members to attend meetings, recruiting new members, and keeping new members (see Table 3). The Wilk's Lambda for the discriminant function was .8125 resulting in 63% of the grouped cases being correctly classified (Table 4).

TABLE 4. Differential Factors Between Shared and Sole Leadership Roles

Variables	Discriminant Function Coefficients		
	Shared	Sole	Sig
Members to Attend	.353	.203	$p < .05$
Role Satisfaction	3.431	2.650	$p < .001$
Role Conflict	5.155	4.832	$p < .05$
Keeping New Members	4.798	4.058	$p < .01$
Recruiting New Members	2.018	1.803	$p < .05$

Actual Group	No. of Cases	Shared	Sole
Shared Leadership	79	55	24
(Group 1)		69.6%	30.4%
Sole Leadership	53	25	28
(Group 2)		47.2%	52.8%

Percent of Grouped Cases Correctly Classified: 62.88%
Wilk's Lambda: .8125 Chi-squared Significance: $p < .0l$

DISCUSSION

Predictors of Burnout

The role related variables of role satisfaction, role ambiguity and role conflict, and the group problem variables of overworked and tired leaders, and recruiting of new members were found to be significant predictors of burnout for peer leaders of self-help groups. This combination of variables provides some insight into why self-help groups leaders have high levels of burnout and possibly of greater importance, why some leaders show low levels of burnout. Role satisfaction was negatively related to burnout–peer leaders lower in role satisfaction were found to report higher levels of burnout as measured by the MBI. This finding is consistent with past burnout literature on professionals which has consistently found a negative relationship between job satisfaction and burnout (e.g., Maslach & Jackson, 1984a; 1984b; Pines & Aronson, 1988).

Initial research attempting to determine the directionality of the causal relationship between role satisfaction and burnout has supported Cherniss' (1980) original hypotheses that dissatisfaction with role is a consequence rather than an antecedent of burnout (Wolpin, Burke & Greenglass, 1991). Longitudinal designs that would follow new self-help group leaders through different stages of their role would provide greater information about the relationship between role satisfaction and burnout. Considering that almost 60% of the peer leaders in this sample were involved in the founding of their group, research in collaboration with a self-help clearinghouse, which would be aware of the new groups, would allow the tracking of these new leaders over time.

Higher levels of role ambiguity and role conflict were also found to be predictors of higher levels of burnout. These findings are again consistent with past burnout research which has routinely found that higher levels of role ambiguity and role conflict have been related to higher levels of burnout in professionals (Harrison, 1980; Rosenthal et al., 1983; Schwab & Iwanicki, 1982; Ursprung, 1986b). Consistent with role theory (Kahn et al., 1964), it appears that the less well defined or clear the role, the higher the level of burnout in peer leaders of self-help groups. It also appears that the higher the level of role conflict, as measured by incongruent and inconsistent expectations and values between leaders and members, the greater the likelihood of higher levels of leader burnout. We focused on non-congruent expectations and values specifically between the leader and members for this study. The impact of role conflict could even be greater if conflict existed between leaders and external entities such as local or national affiliated organizations or area professionals. The leader could also find themselves the mediator between the needs of members and external agencies making role conflict an even more powerful determinant of burnout. For example, one common complaint we hear from AA group members are that judges routinely require those on probation or parole to attend AA group meetings if they have had past difficulties with alcohol. While the intentions of the judges are positive, it produces a conflict between the values and traditions of AA groups concerning voluntary involvement based on a personal desire to quit drinking. Future research could examine role conflict using a broader measure to determine the impacts of expectations beyond members which could generate role conflict.

The amount of time spent in leader activities or number of years in leader role were not predictors of burnout. A number of studies have found that consistently heavy workloads are predictive of higher levels of burnout in professionals (Arches, 1991; Cherniss, 1980; Wolpin, Burke & Greenglass, 1991). In this sample, leaders spent an average of about 5 hours per week on the tasks that define their leader role. This is considerably less time than the professionals found to be suffering from burnout due to heavy workload as they were consistently spending well over 40 hours per week on their job (Pines, Aronson & Kafry, 1981). The time spent on group activities by self-help leaders was in addition to the time these group leaders spent in their own jobs but only 47% of the leaders were employed fulltime while 27% were not working and 13% were retired. It appears that the quantity of time spent on a weekly basis or how long one was in the leadership role was not an issue as found in studies with professionals (Epstein & Silvern, 1990) but possibly the quality of time could be an issue as the group problem of "overworked and tired leaders" was a significant predictor of burnout.

It is not surprising that participants who reported that overworked and tired leaders were more frequently a problem of the group would also report higher levels of burnout. Recruitment of new group members may have contributed to being an overworked and tired leader. It appears that the group problem of recruiting new members was a significant stressor as higher levels of this problem were also a predictor of burnout (see Table 2). The process of recruiting new members is an ongoing task and is critical to the long-term survival of the group. Many groups struggle to maintain membership as natural turnover occurs in the group. The need for new members to maintain the viability of the group is important as some veteran members naturally discontinue active membership as they work through the problem that brought them to the group. Recruitment of new members is a never ending task and is somewhat unique to self-help groups in that the long-term survival of the group is dependent on continuously and successfully conducting this activity (Meissen, Gleason & Embree, 1991).

While these findings provide some important insights into burnout among self-help group leaders, the significant variables explain only about 39% of the variance. The type and range of activities in which self-help group leaders engage could account for significant variance not explained in this study. It is quite possible that other activities operate like recruiting new members in that they contribute significantly to burnout (e.g., newsletter, advocacy, arranging meetings). The range of individual and personality factors that might have an impact on burnout were also not considered in this study. In one particularly relevant study, it was found that nurses who approached their work with patients from a social exchange orientation had significantly higher levels of burnout than nurses with a communal orientation defined as providing help when needed (Vanyperen, Buunk & Schaufeli, 1992). Incorporating personality variables, particularly communal and exchange orientation into a model of burnout of self-help group leaders would provide more comprehensive explanations.

Shared versus Sole Leadership Roles

Of this representative sample of peer leaders of self-help groups, 60% were in shared leadership roles. The hypothesis that those in shared leadership roles would report lower levels of burnout was not substantiated for total burnout or for the sub-scales of Emotional Exhaustion, Depersonalization or Personal Accomplishment. Neither total burnout nor any of the burnout sub-scales loaded significantly in the discriminant analysis that differentiated shared and sole leaders.

The discriminant analysis did find that the role related variables of role satisfaction and role conflict contributed to the maximal differentiation of those in shared vs. sole leadership roles. Those in shared leadership roles had greater levels of role satisfaction but also greater role conflict. One of the most important factors that mitigate burnout and increase role satisfaction is collegiality (Cherniss, 1980). Those leaders with other members in leadership roles have at least two important communalities. Not only do they share in the work of the group but also share the same problem that brings them to the self-help group. At the same time, having others in leadership roles appears to increase role conflict, probably in part due to tensions and communication issues regarding responsibility for different tasks (Pines, Aronson & Kafry, 1981). Having more than one person doing the work of the group also appears to have an impact on the frequency of some common problems of self-help groups.

The group problems of getting members to attend meetings and other activities, recruiting new members, and keeping new members also contributed to significantly discriminating between those in shared and sole leadership roles. Those in sole leadership roles reported significantly higher frequencies of these group problems. Being able to share the work and responsibility for these tasks appears to make them more manageable. These problems of self-help groups that discriminated between shared and sole leadership are again potentially linked to group survival (Meissen, Gleason & Embree, 1991). They are interconnected and possibly of the nature Sarason (1978) described as intractable. The dynamic nature of self-help groups naturally produces turnover, attendance and involvement problems which in turn generates the ongoing need to find new members to help sustain the groups. Members are a group's primary resource, and being unable to sustain a steady membership represents a continuing threat to the survival of groups not unlike how discontinued funding or loss of clients threatens a human service organization. Shared leadership appears to be a reasonable way to reduce the impact of these problems.

Shared leadership for this research was defined as having at least one other member serving in a leadership role. This measure of shared leadership may not be a sensitive enough indicator as it is likely that there are differing levels of help that members provide across groups possibly accounting for a lower percentage of correctly classified in the discriminant analysis than might have been expected. Assessing how many others are in leadership positions, how much time they actually contribute and what percentage of the work they perform could be more powerful predictors of burnout than simply the existence of others in a leadership role.

CONCLUSION

It is possible the concept of burnout does not perfectly fit the role of peer self-help group leader. The concept of burnout was developed to describe job related behavior of paid workers and professionals. Being a leader of a self-help group is not a job in the formal sense. The participants in this study were peers and not paid for the activities related to their role as leader. The research on burnout has been predominately used to reflect reactions to full-time employment but the peer leaders in this sample spent just over five hours per week on group activities. At the same time, the significant predictors of burnout for peer leaders of self-help groups were quite consistent with the literature on burnout in professionals. Burnout may be a viable construct to use in examining issues related to self-help group leader activities but should be used with some caution always taking into account the critical differences between self-help group leaders and employees.

One future research question that would allow a better understanding of burnout among self-help group leaders would be to compare levels of burnout across the three sub-scales of Emotional Exhaustion, Personal Accomplishment and Depersonalization with national norms for different populations (e.g., social service worker, teacher, mental health worker). In particular, peer self-help group leaders are likely to be less susceptible to depersonalization because they also share the problem that defines the group. Research in social psychology has consistently found that members of an "in-group" are much less likely to develop negative attitudes toward other members of their in-group because of high levels of empathy and self identification (Brewer, 1979; Wilder, 1981). Unfortunately, we modified the typical seven point response scale upon which national norms are computed to a four point scale in order to use a telephone survey format. Most burnout studies use a pencil and paper administration in a personal interview situation, typically at the participants' place of employment. Personal interviews were also not possible as leaders were spread throughout the state, and a mail questionnaire would probably have resulted in a considerably lower return rate (35% +/− 10%). One important goal in attempting to discover predictors of burnout was to provide useful information to self-help groups to prevent leader burnout and disruptive leader turnover in groups. Consciously taking into account the costs and benefits of self-help groups helped focus this research on the acquisition of practical and theoretical knowledge. This information was disseminated to self-help groups in our database with a focus on the development of shared leadership and ways to prevent leader burnout.

REFERENCES

Arches, J. (1991). Social structure, burnout, and job satisfaction. *Social Work, 36*, 202-206.

Belcastro, P., Gold, R., & Grant, J. (1982). Stress and burnout: Physiological effects on correctional teachers. *Criminal Justice and Behavior, 9*, 387-395.

Block, E., & Llewelyn, S. (1987). Leadership skills and helpful factors in self-help groups. *British Journal of Guidance and Counseling, 15*, 257-270.

Brewer, M. B. (1979). In-group bias in the minimal intergroup situation: A cognitive-motivational analysis. *Psychological Bulletin, 86*, 307-324.

Caputo, J. (1991). *Stress and burnout in library service*. Phoenix, AZ: Onyx Press.

Cherniss, C. (1980). *Staff burnout*. Beverly Hills: Sage Publications, Inc.

Cherniss, C., & Egnatious, E. (1978). Is there job satisfaction in community mental health? *Community Mental Health Journal, 14*, 309-318.

Epstein, S. R., & Silvern, L. E. (1990). Staff burnout in shelters for battered women: A challenge for the 90's. *Response, 13*, 9-12.

Goblembiewski, R., & Munzenrider, R. (1984). Active and passive reactions to psychological burn-out: Toward a greater specificity in a phase model. *Journal of Health and Human Resources Administration*, 7, 264-289.

Harrison, W. D. (1980). Role strain and burnout in child protective service workers. *Social Service Review, 54*, 31-44.

Jackson, S. E., Schwab, R., & Schuler, R. (1986). Toward an understanding of the burnout phenomenon. *Journal of Applied Psychology, 71*, 630-640.

Kahn, R. L., Wolfe, D. M., Quinn, J., Snoek, J. D., & Rosenthal, R. A. (1964). *Organizational stress: Studies in role conflict and ambiguity*. New York: Wiley.

Kurtz, L. F. (1990). Twelve-Step Programs. In T. J. Powell (ed.), *Working with self-help*. Silver Spring, Maryland: NASW Press.

Maslach, C. (1982). *Burnout: The cost of caring*. Englewood Cliffs, NJ: Prentice-Hall.

Maslach, C. & Jackson, S. E. (1984a). Burnout in organizational settings. *Applied Social Psychology Annual, 5*, 133-153.

Maslach, C. & Jackson, S. E. (1984b). Patterns of burnout among a national sample of public contact workers. *Journal of Health and Human Resources Administration*, 7, 189-212.

Maslach, C., & Jackson, S. E. (1986). *Maslach burnout inventory* (2nd ed.). Palo Alto, CA: Consulting Psychologist Press.

Maslach, C., & Pines, A. (1977). The burnout syndrome in the day care setting. *Child Care Quarterly, 6*, 100-113.

Maton, K. I., Leventhal, G. S., Madara, E. J., & Julien, M. (1989). Factors affecting the birth and death of mutual-help groups: The role of national affiliation, professional involvement, and member focal problem. *American Journal of Community Psychology, 17*, 643-671.

Meissen, G. J., Gleason, D. F., & Embree, M. G. (1991). An assessment of the needs of mutual-help groups. *American Journal of Community Psychology, 19*, 427-442.

Pines, A., & Aronson, E. (1988). *Career burnout: Causes and cures.* New York: Macmillian, Free Press.

Pines, A., Aronson, E., & Kafry, D. (1981). *Burnout: From tedium to personal growth.* New York: Macmillian.

Pines, A., & Maslach, C. (1980). Combatting staff burnout in a day care center: A case study. *Child Care Quarterly, 9,* 5-16.

Powell, T. J. (1990). Differences between national self-help organizations and local self-help groups: Implications for members and professionals. In T. J. Powell (ed.), *Working with self-help.* Silver Springs, Maryland: NASW Press.

Revenson, T. A., & Cassel, J. B. (1991). An exploration of leadership in a medical mutual help organization. *American Journal of Community Psychology, 19,* 683-698.

Rizzo, J. R., House, R. J., Lirtzman, S. I. (1970). Role conflict and ambiguity in complex organizations. *Administrative Science Quarterly, 15,* 150-163.

Rosenthal, D., Teague, M., Retish, P., West, J., & Vessell, R. (1983). The relationship between work environment and attributes of burnout. *Journal of Leisure Research, 15,* 151-160.

Sarason, S. B. (1978). The nature of problem solving in social action. *American Psychologist, 33,* 370-380.

Schwab, R. L., & Iwanicki, E. F. (1982). Perceived role conflict, role ambiguity, and teacher burnout. *Educational Administration Quarterly, 18,* 60-74.

Spicuzza, F. J., & DeVoe, M. W. (1982). Burnout in the helping professions: Mutual aid groups as self-help. *Personnel and Guidance Journal, 61,* 95-99.

Sutherland, V., & Cooper, C. (1990). *Understanding stress: A psychological perspective for health professionals.* New York: Chapman and Hall.

Ursprung, A. W. (1986a). Burnout in the human services: A review of the literature. *Rehabilitation Counseling Bulletin, 27,* 191-197.

Ursprung, A. W. (1986b). Incidence and correlates of burnout in residential service settings. *Rehabilitation Counseling Bulletin, 27,* 225-238.

Vanyperen, N., Buunk, B., & Schaufeli, W. (1992). Communal orientation and the burnout syndrome among nurses. *Journal of Applied Social Psychology, 22,* 173-189.

Wilder, D. A. (1981). Perceiving persons as a group: Categorization and intergroup relations. In D. L. Hamilton (ed.), *Cognitive processes in stereotyping and intergroup behavior.* Hillsdale, NJ: Lawrence Erlbaum.

Wolpin, J., Burke, R. J., & Greenglass, E. R. (1991). Is job satisfaction an antecedent or a consequence of psychological burnout? *Human Relations, 44,* 193-207.

Zastrow, C. (1984). Understanding and preventing burnout. *British Journal of Social Work, 14,* 141-155.

Chapter 11

Social Climate Correlates of Effectiveness in Alliance for the Mentally Ill Groups

David V. Perkins

Ball State University

Joan Esterline Lafuze

Indiana University-East
Indiana Alliance for the Mentally Ill

Carole Van Dusen

Indiana Alliance for the Mentally Ill

SUMMARY. To examine how various social climate characteristics predict group effectiveness (i.e., overall strength, and benefits and

The authors thank Ken Maton for providing the primary survey instrument used in this study, Bernard E. Whitley, Jr., for statistical consultation, and the editors for useful suggestions on a previous draft.

Presented at the International Conference on Self-Help, Mutual Aid, sponsored by the Canadian Council on Social Development in Ottawa, Canada, September 4, 1992. This research was supported by Grant #1 H87 MH47953-01 from the National Institute of Mental Health, U.S. Department of Health and Human Services.

Address correspondence to David V. Perkins, Department of Psychological Science, Ball State University, Muncie, Indiana USA 47306.

[Haworth co-indexing entry note]: "Social Climate Correlates of Effectiveness in Alliance for the Mentally Ill Groups." Perkins, David V., Joan Esterline Lafuze, and Carole Van Dusen. Co-published simultaneously in *Prevention in Human Services* (The Haworth Press, Inc.) Vol. 11, No. 2, 1994, pp. 263-277; and *Self-Help and Mutual Aid Groups: International and Multicultural Perspectives* (ed: Francine Lavoie, Thomasina Borkman, and Benjamin Gidron) The Haworth Press, Inc., 1994, pp. 263-277. Multiple copies of this article/chapter may be purchased from The Haworth Document Delivery Center [1-800-3-HAWORTH; 9:00 a.m. - 5:00 p.m. (EST)].

satisfaction members experience) in Alliance for the Mentally Ill (AMI) mutual help groups, information on the group climate and effectiveness of all 22 AMI affiliates in Indiana was gathered using two independent procedures: (1) rank-and-file members from each affiliate (N = 221) provided demographic information and completed Maton's (1988) 43-item measure of social climate (including perceived benefits and satisfaction), and (2) affiliate leaders supplied information on the human and material resources available to their groups plus an overall assessment of the group's current strength. From both member and leader perspectives, social climate experiences of members were strong predictors of AMI group effectiveness, while material resources and member demographics were not. Support Received, Leadership, and Order/organization were especially important, while extramural contact among members was consistently unrelated to group effectiveness. Efforts to initiate and/or increase the effectiveness of AMI groups should focus on the leadership, internal structure, support activities, and role opportunities provided to members.

Families of persons with long term mental illness provide the primary supports for many consumers (Lefley, 1987; Torrey, 1988), and the substantial burdens families bear include stigma, shame, financial pressures, and strained relationships with mental health professionals (Francell, Conn, & Gray, 1988; Hanson & Rapp, 1992; Lefley, 1989; Schene, 1990). Specific needs and interests of family members do not always coincide with those of professionals or consumers, suggesting a beneficial role for organized support systems to assist and advocate on behalf of families. Strengthening families so that they can participate in and support the recovery of their ill members is also associated with a more independent living situation for the ill family member, even when controlling for severity of illness (Goldstein, Dziobek, Clark, & Bassuk, 1990).

Alliance for the Mentally Ill (AMI) mutual help groups have been organized at local, state, and national levels in the United States to provide information and support to family members of persons with severe mental illness, to advocate for policies which enhance the well being of the mentally ill, and to improve public understanding of the problems faced by persons with mental illness (Hatfield, 1991). AMI group activities involve member education and support (including sharing common experiences as well as practical advice), and in some cases grass-roots advocacy efforts (e.g., public education via newsletters and brochures). Involvement in an AMI group and acceptance of its message has been associated with reduced feelings of stigma, guilt and personal responsibility in family members, and more comfortable interactions with a mentally ill child (Medvene & Krauss, 1989). Although effects like these may reduce feelings of hopelessness and frustration in families, and to that extent *prevent* some of the serious emotional consequences associated with having a mentally ill family member, it is important not to confuse these "preventive" benefits with the prevention of schizophrenia or other serious mental disorder in the ill family member. AMI groups do not consider serious mental illnesses preventable at this time.

Quantitative research on AMI groups has been relatively limited to date. An early survey of members of the California Alliance for the Mentally Ill (CAMI; Williams, Williams, Sommer, & Sommer, 1986) identified several kinds of resources that members perceived had helped the ill person in their family (e.g., neuroleptic medication, locked facilities) but provided little information about CAMI itself. Data from Israel reported by Gidron, Chesler, and Chesney (1991) indicated that greater amounts of education, support, and social and public activism were all associated with participation in self-help groups for parents of persons with mental illness. Norton, Wandersman, and Goldman (1993) found that AMI members perceive greater benefits (e.g., coping solutions, knowledge about mental illness) and fewer costs (e.g., interpersonal conflict, giving up other opportunities) as consequences of belonging to this organization than do nonmembers.

Research to date thus suggests that AMI groups are beneficial to their members, although it tells us little about possible reasons for their effectiveness. Further research might usefully be directed at identifying specific factors associated with AMI group effectiveness (i.e., overall strength, and benefits and satisfactions members experience). Conceptually AMI groups are an important and increasingly visible example of a locally-controlled "significant-other" mutual help group (Schubert & Borkman, 1991). The high degree of local control suggests that differences may evolve more rapidly among individual AMI groups than in self-help organizations where strong centralized controls exist. Luke, Rappaport, and

Seidman (1991) demonstrated the usefulness of attending to variations among individual groups within a single self-help organization in understanding how and why groups might differ in effectiveness.

What kinds of variations might be relevant here? One issue for mutual help groups in general is that of optimal size. Larger groups may be relatively rich in human and other resources but less sensitive to individual members' needs for meaningful participation and support. Small groups may be more responsive to individual needs but also more likely to fail if the means needed for survival outstrip their human or material resources (Zimmerman et al., 1991). With respect to other sources of variability, how well do such objective features as member demographic characteristics and the adequacy of material resources predict group effectiveness? How are various "process" or social climate characteristics within individual AMI groups related to effectiveness?

The present research investigated these possible correlates of effectiveness in a survey study of the entire population of AMI groups in Indiana. In Indiana the AMI movement developed in response to the outreach efforts of family support groups in Indianapolis and Ft. Wayne. Eight AMI affiliates organized themselves into the Indiana Alliance for the Mentally Ill (IAMI) in 1985, and by 1991 there were 22 affiliates statewide with a total membership of approximately 900. As a population these AMI groups varied widely on several key dimensions, including size, member demographic characteristics, geographic locale (i.e., rural as well as urban), material resources, and overall strength.

METHOD

Participants

Participants were 221 members drawn from all 22 AMI affiliates in Indiana and the leaders of 18 of these groups. Rank-and-file participants approximated the state-wide and national AMI membership in gender (70% female), race (96% Caucasian), and median age (62 years), education (13 years), and annual household income ($32,000 per year). Twenty-nine percent of those in the sample had a mentally ill relative living at home with them, while 58% did not (13% did not answer this question). Thirty-nine percent of the sample described themselves as "very active" in their AMI affiliate, 29% as "moderately active," and 20% as "inactive" (12% did not answer).

Measures

Member perceptions of the AMI groups were based on responses to Maton's (1988) 43-item survey, which includes eight scales. Six of these scales (Support Received, Support Provided, extramural Friendship patterns, Role Differentiation, Leadership, and Order/organization) were used as indices of social climate, while the remaining two (Satisfaction with the group, Benefits of group membership) were used to measure group effectiveness. Scale reliability analyses indicated that for the present sample each of the eight scales measured a unidimensional construct, as did the 33 items measuring overall climate and the 10 items measuring outcome. Cronbach *alpha* coefficients for these scales are presented in Table 1.

Affiliate leaders completed a two-page survey designed to assess the extent of certain human and material resources available to the group and a summary rating of the group's overall strength on a 1 to 7 scale. Sixteen of the items were organized into one of four scales assessing Communications (e.g., newsletter and other activities), Facilities (space and equipment), Leadership resources (adequacy of local, state and national AMI leadership), and group process (e.g., support, organization, "caring and sharing"). Overall these 16 items also comprised a unidimensional scale, which we labeled "Assets" (see Table 1). This leader survey is included in the Appendix.

Procedure

Surveys were mailed from IAMI's central office with a cover letter from the IAMI president requesting cooperation. Rank-and-file AMI members provided demographic information and completed Maton's (1988) 43-item measure of social climate at approximately the same time that affiliate leaders independently rated the

TABLE 1. Scale Statistics for AMI Samples

Scale	Alpha	Mean	(SD)
	Scales from Maton (1988)		
Support Received	.76	16.1	(3.1)
Support Provided	.69	17.1	(3.8)
Friendship	.74	15.7	(4.7)
Role Differentiation	.77	18.2	(4.4)
Leadership	.79	21.5	(3.7)
Order/Organization	.89	35.8	(7.3)
SUM ("Climate")	.91	124.4	(12.7)
Benefits	.86	20.1	(4.5)
Satisfaction	.87	18.5	(4.9)
SUM ("Outcome")	.91	38.7	(8.7)
	16-Item Leader Survey		
SUM ("Assets")	.84	46.6	(11.0)

human and material resources available to groups and their current strength. Member and leader surveys were returned to the state office individually by mail.

RESULTS

Completed surveys were returned from 221 rank-and-file members. Based on IMAI records regarding total statewide membership, the overall response rate was 31%, with response rates among the affiliates ranging from 11% to 56%. Although return rates varied across the population of groups, rate of return was not correlated with mean social climate of the group, material assets, or leader-rated strength. Thus there is no reason to think that differences in return rate biased the sample of respondents on any variable of importance to this study.

Although the maximum range in scores (i.e., from lowest possible to highest possible) was reported for nearly every scale across the sample as a whole, in general participants were positive about the climate of their affiliates (i.e., the obtained means for all scales were well above the theoretical midpoints of the scales). Participants had especially positive perceptions of affiliate Leadership (median score = 23 of a possible 25), Order/Organization, and the Support and other Benefits they had received as AMI members. However, among the 22 affiliates there was considerable variation in mean climate, with one or more affiliates scoring below the theoretical midpoint for each of the scales other than Leadership.

According to the leaders' reports, the number of *active* members ranged from 3 to 205 (mean = 26.7, SD = 45.7). Six of the 22 affiliates distributed their own newsletters. The physical facilities available to groups ranged from "inadequate" to "completely adequate," while process features of meetings (e.g., "caring and sharing") and AMI leadership (local, state, and national) were generally seen as "mostly adequate." Overall affiliate strengths as rated by the leaders ranged from 1-7 (mean = 3.9). Interestingly, since the data for this study were collected, two of the three affiliates given "1" ratings by their leaders have in fact ceased to function.

Because all data were self-report, we proceeded cautiously in first examining the global dimensions tapped by each survey (leader and member). Six scales from Maton (1988) were combined to summarize AMI group "Climate," while the other two scales (Benefits and Satisfaction), which correlated strongly (r = .72), were combined into a single scale called "Outcome."

Using data aggregated at the affiliate level (N = 22), we predicted mean Outcome (as perceived by members) and overall Strength (as rated by the leader) based on three characteristics: number of active members and total material assets (both provided by the leaders), and mean perceived Climate (as reported by the members). In terms of zero-order correlations, Outcome was correlated only with Climate (r = .86), while Strength was correlated with number of active Members (.51), material Assets (.50), and Climate (.79). [Outcome and Strength were also correlated, r = .71.] In a multiple regression analysis of these same data, however, only mean Climate made a unique contribution to predicting Outcome and Strength, and in each case the correlation was substantial (*betas* = .85 for Outcome and .79 for Strength).

Separate hierarchical regression analyses were then performed at the participant level (N = 221) to identify specific demographic and social climate predictors of Benefits and Satisfaction, as reported by rank-and-file members, and overall affiliate Strength as rated by leaders. For each equation, member demographic characteristics (gender, age, income, education) were entered on step 1, while individual climate scales (Support Received and Provided, extramural Friendship patterns, Role Differentiation, Leadership, and Order/organization) were entered on step 2 (cf. Maton, 1988). All multiple *R*s and individual predictors identified below were significant at $p < .05$.

Benefits were positively related (multiple R = .76) to Support Received (*beta* = .41) and Order (*beta* = .27). Satisfaction was positively related (multiple R = .90) to male gender (*beta* = .13), Order (*beta* = .35), Support Received (*beta* = .28), Leadership (*beta* = .21) and Role Differentiation (*beta* = .24). Overall affiliate Strength was positively related (multiple R = .67) to Leadership (*beta* = .56), and negatively related to the amount of Support Provided by members (*beta* = -.21). These results are summarized in Table 2.

We did one final regression to identify predictors of one additional index of group strength, the total Assets reported by the leader of each group. Member demographic characteristics (e.g., income) and most individual climate variables were not significant predictors, and instead only member perceptions of affiliate Leadership (*beta* = .36) made a unique contribution to predicting total Assets (multiple R = .52).

DISCUSSION

It is clear that the perceived effectiveness of individual AMI groups in this study was not uniquely associated with their size or the demographic background of their members, nor was it predicted by the overall level of material resources enjoyed by these groups. Rather, effectiveness as judged both by rank and file members and by leaders was strongly and consistently associated with specific social climate features reported by members. Support Received, Leadership, and Order/organization were especially important to group effectiveness, while the degree of extramural contact among

TABLE 2. Hierarchical Multiple Regression Analyses of Benefits, Satisfaction, and Strength on Member Demographics and Perceived Social Climate

Predictor Variable	Benefits	Satisfaction	Strength
Demographics:			
Gender	.05	.13**	.14
Age	–.00	.01	–.01
Education	–.02	–.08	–.05
Income	–.10	.09	.13
Social Climate:			
Support Received	.41***	.28***	.10
Support Provided	.04	–.04	–.21*
Friendship	.12	–.05	.05
Role Differentiation	.04	.24**	.13
Leadership	.05	.21**	.56***
Order/Organization	.27*	.35***	–.11

*$p < .05$
**$p < .01$
***$p < .001$

Overall equation, Benefits:
$R = .76$, $R^2 = .57$, $F(10, 117) = 15.7$, $p < .001$.
Overall equation, Satisfaction:
$R = .90$, $R^2 = .80$, $F(10, 118) = 49.0$, $p < .001$.
Overall equation, Strength:
$R = .67$, $R^2 = .44$, $F(10, 101) = 8.1$, $p < .001$.

members was consistently unrelated to outcome and overall strength. These findings are consistent with those of Biegel and Yamatani (1987), who found that nondirective activities providing social support occurred frequently in support groups for families of the mentally ill and that the occurrence of these activities predicted member satisfaction. Our results supplement those of Gidron et al. (1991) and Norton et al. (1993) in suggesting which specific features of AMI groups are perceived by their members to be most beneficial.

The lack of a relationship between contact outside of meetings and perceived effectiveness is useful in suggesting that efforts to initiate and/or increase the effectiveness of individual AMI groups should focus primarily on the group meetings, and especially the leadership, internal structure, role opportunities, and support activities they provide to members. For example, although it is traditional in many self-help groups to rotate leadership responsibilities among the members, our results indicate that the presence of specific leader competencies (e.g., obtaining and managing resources) is still very important. Interestingly, member perception of leader effectiveness was the only predictor of the adequacy of material assets enjoyed by the group.

In this study fully 80% of the variance in reported Satisfaction was accounted for by the various predictors, a larger proportion than for reported Benefits or leader-rated Strength. Benefits largely concerned personal changes in the respondent attributable to his or her participation in the group, while Satisfaction was based on the perceived effectiveness of the group in meeting the needs of members in general. Thus, while they successfully predicted all indices of group effectiveness in this study, the various dimensions of social climate appear to be more closely related to global perceptions of AMI's effectiveness than to its direct impact on the personal lives of individual members.

Self-help groups vary widely in structural and process features (Schubert & Borkman, 1991), and the findings reported here may or may not apply to other kinds of groups. In contrast to Maton's (1988) earlier results using the same survey of social climate variables, support provided was unrelated to benefits and satisfaction and *negatively* associated with leader-rated strength. One explanation for these differences is certainly differences between AMI groups and the specific organizations Maton studied (Overeaters Anonymous, a support group for Multiple Sclerosis, and Compassionate Friends, a group for bereaved parents). Furthermore, with respect to the negative correlation between support provided and affiliate strength in our data, it is worth noting that an entire state population of AMI groups participated in this study, and that some of these groups were very small and of doubtful viability (as subsequent history showed). Having to provide a great deal of support (e.g., information, continued leadership, liaison to the state organization and to other advocacy/provider groups) may occur more often in weak groups than in strong groups. On the other hand, regular changes in leadership, confidence in the other members, and intermittent involvement by oneself may characterize strong groups more than weak ones. Of course, had only stable, healthy groups been surveyed in this study, the findings might well have been different.

We should also note that the correlational relationships identified in this study do not necessarily indicate direct cause-and-effect links between social climate variables and outcome. For example, higher satisfaction with the group may elicit greater effort to perform contributing roles and more positive perceptions of the leadership, rather than vice-versa. Furthermore, our use of regression assumes strictly linear relationships among variables, e.g., demographics and effectiveness. That is, if variables such as member income are related to group effectiveness in a curvilinear way (e.g., groups are more effective for middle-income persons than for either high- or low-income individuals) no relationship would be apparent in the regression results.

The most significant limitation of these data is probably the modest 31% rate of participation by rank-and-file members. For example, the generally positive perceptions of AMI groups reported by study participants may serve to confirm AMI's reputed success as a mutual help organization, but may also reflect a biased sample in which strong supporters of AMI were over-represented. Moreover, given our partial reliance on group leaders to distribute the surveys, and the generally very positive perceptions of leaders which we obtained, the sample of participants may have been more positive about affiliate leadership than is the statewide membership as a whole.

On the other hand, study participants were accurately representative of AMI members in terms of demographic characteristics and geographic location, and the fact that 100% of affiliates from an entire state participated provided a relatively comprehensive sample of AMI groups. Although the data were entirely self-reported, significant variability was present among the groups in size, material resources, and social climate, and none of this variability was related to differences in return rate among the groups. It is also important to note that member perceptions predicted not only other responses by these same members but also ratings made independently by affiliate leaders.

With respect to the international dimensions of self-help, several points are worth noting. First, schizophrenia and other serious mental illnesses are prevalent world-wide (albeit to varying degrees in different countries; Torrey, 1988), suggesting a cross-cultural need for organized efforts in support of families (Schene, 1990). Second, the fact that participants in this study approximated AMI members in the United States in demographic background (e.g., 96% Caucasian), while important for our purposes, seriously limits the immediate generalizability of these results to other countries and cultural contexts. Third, given that AMI groups also exist in Canada, Uruguay, and South Africa (NAMI, 1993), comparative international research would be useful in identifying commonalities and differences among groups in light of differences in national service delivery systems and cultural traditions regarding voluntary associations, grass-roots activism, and so on (Gidron et al., 1991). For example, it is possible that the indigenous leadership and local control favored by AMI groups in the U.S. reflect American preferences and would not be as prevalent (nor as important to group effectiveness) in cultures with a tradition of stronger, more centralized state controls over organized helping efforts.

Given these caveats, our central finding that structural and process features are much better predictors of AMI group effectiveness than are member demographics or material resources has suggested a useful focus for ongoing efforts to promote the spread of AMI groups in the U.S. Indeed, results of the survey were published in the IAMI newsletter a few months after it was completed and have been used since then in consultation efforts with ongoing groups and in the creation of new AMI affiliates in Indiana.

REFERENCES

Biegel, D. W., & Yamatani, H. (1987). Help-giving in self-help groups. *Hospital and Community Psychiatry, 38*, 1195-1197.

Francell, C. G., Conn, V. S., & Gray, D. P. (1988). Families' perceptions of burden of care for chronic mentally ill relatives. *Hospital and Community Psychiatry, 39*, 1296-1300.

Gidron, B., Chesler, M. A., & Chesney, B. K. (1991). Cross-cultural perspectives on self-help groups: Comparison between participants and nonparticipants in Israel and the United States. *American Journal of Community Psychology, 19*, 667-681.

Goldstein, J. M., Dziobek, J. F., Clark, R., & Bassuk, E. L. (1990). Supportive housing for the chronically mentally ill: Matching clients with community environments. *Journal of Nervous and Mental Disease, 178*, 415-422.

Hanson, J. G., & Rapp, C. A. (1992). Families' perceptions of community mental health programs for their relatives with a severe mental illness. *Community Mental Health Journal, 28*, 181-197.

Hatfield, A. B. (1991). The National Alliance for the Mentally Ill: A decade later. *Community Mental Health Journal, 27*, 95-103.

Lefley, H. P. (1987). The family's response to mental illness in a relative. In A. Hatfield (ed.), *Families of the mentally ill: Meeting the challenges* (New Directions in Mental Health Services No. 34, pp. 3-22). San Francisco: Jossey-Bass.

Lefley, H. P. (1989). Family burden and family stigma in major mental illness. *American Psychologist, 44*, 556-560.

Luke, D. A., Rappaport, J., & Seidman, E. (1991). Setting phenotypes in a mutual help organization: Expanding behavior setting theory. *American Journal of Community Psychology, 19*, 147-167.

Maton, K. I. (1988). Social support, organizational characteristics, psychological well-being, and group appraisal in three self-help group populations. *American Journal of Community Psychology, 16*, 53-77.

Medvene, L. J., & Krauss, D. H. (1989). Causal attributions and parent-child relationships in a self-help group for families of the mentally ill. *Journal of Applied Social Psychology, 19*, 1413-1430.

National Alliance for the Mentally Ill. (1993). *NAMI affiliate directory*. Arlington, VA: Author.

Norton, S., Wandersman, A., & Goldman, C. R. (1993). Perceived costs and benefits of membership in a self-help group: Comparisons of members and nonmembers of the Alliance for the Mentally Ill. *Community Mental Health Journal, 29*, 43-160.

Schene, A. H. (1990). Objective and subjective dimensions of family burden: Towards an integrative framework for research. *Social Psychiatry and Psychiatric Epidemiology, 25*, 289-297.

Schubert, M. A., & Borkman, T. J. (1991). An organizational typology for self-help groups. *American Journal of Community Psychology, 19*, 769-788.

Torrey, E. F. (1988). *Surviving schizophrenia: A family manual*. Revised edition. New York: Harper & Row.

Williams, P., Williams, W. A., Sommer, R., & Sommer, B. (1986). A survey of the California Alliance for the Mentally Ill. *Hospital and Community Psychiatry, 37*, 253-256.

Zimmerman, M. A., Reischl, T. M., Seidman, E., Rappaport, J., Toro, P. A., & Salem, D. A. (1991). Expansion strategies of a mutual help organization. *American Journal of Community Psychology, 19*, 251-278.

APPENDIX. Leader Survey

Affiliate ______________________________ Date ________________________

IAMI AFFILIATE RESOURCES SURVEY

For A and B below, please provide the most accurate information you have. For C through F, please *circle* the most appropriate alternative. It is very important that you complete *all* items as best you can.

A. HUMAN RESOURCES

1. How many active members does your affiliate have? ________________

2. How many of these active members are members of *racial* or *ethnic minority* (i.e., culturally diverse) groups? ____________ Which specific culturally diverse groups are represented? ______________________________

3. How many active members are *single* parents? ________________

4. Approximately how many other people *not* active in your affiliate are affected by your affiliate's activities? ______________________________

B. COMMUNICATIONS

1. Does your affiliate distribute its own newsletter? ________________

2. How does your affiliate announce meetings? ________________________

3. How do you try to reach prospective new members? ______________

4. How do you communicate with the general public? ________________

Please respond to the remaining items by *circling* the most appropriate alternative. Use the scale below:

1 = completely inadequate	3 = minimally adequate	4 = mostly adequate
2 = somewhat inadequate		5 = entirely adequate

C. FACILITIES (based on ease of access as well as suitability)

1. Space in which to hold meetings	1	2	3	4	5

	completely inadequate				entirely adequate
2. Space for storing materials	1	2	3	4	5
3. Equipment (VCR, TV, etc.)	1	2	3	4	5
4. Library (books, tapes, journals)	1	2	3	4	5
D. LEADERSHIP RESOURCES					
1. Leadership within your affiliate	1	2	3	4	5
2. Leadership from the State AMI	1	2	3	4	5
3. Leadership from the National AMI	1	2	3	4	5
E. GROUP PROCESSES					
1. Accessibility of contact person(s)	1	2	3	4	5
2. Member contacts outside meetings	1	2	3	4	5
3. "Sharing and caring" in meetings	1	2	3	4	5
4. Support members provide each other	1	2	3	4	5
5. Degree of order and organization	1	2	3	4	5

F. OVERALL STRENGTH

On the scale below, please *circle* the number which most accurately represents your affiliate's current overall strength:

1	2	3	4	5	6	7
serious difficulties		some problems		reasonably good shape		extremely strong

G. COMMENTS

Finally, what resources have we missed? Please identify any additional characteristics or issues which either support or interfere with your affiliate's success. You may also use this space to add further information clarifying or elaborating upon any of your earlier responses.

____

____

____

Chapter 12

The Involvement of Self-Help Groups with Mental Health and Medical Professionals: The Self-Helpers' Perspective

Jennifer L. Lotery
Marion K. Jacobs
University of California

SUMMARY. Controversy continues about whether mental health and medical professionals and self-help groups can productively collaborate or are inherently antagonistic. This survey of 426 groups, from the state of California in the United States, the largest and broadest ever conducted, indicates that over 80% of groups already have professionals working with them in a wide variety of roles and that members generally believe that as long as the professionals do not attempt to co-opt or dominate the group, professional expertise adds to the effectiveness of the group. The least positive views regarding the involvement of mental health and medical professionals were expressed by those 12-step "Anonymous" groups that address substance abuse problems. Distinctions between medical versus non-medical groups, 12-step versus all other groups, and 12-step groups for substance abuse versus all other problems have

---

Address correspondence to Dr. Jennifer Lotery, 5055 Cedar Ravine Court, Placerville, CA 95667.

[Haworth co-indexing entry note]: "The Involvement of Self-Help Groups With Mental Health and Medical Professionals: The Self-Helpers' Perspective." Lotery, Jennifer L., and Marion K. Jacobs. Co-published simultaneously in *Prevention in Human Services* (The Haworth Press, Inc.) Vol. 11, No. 2, 1994, pp. 279-302; and *Self-Help and Mutual Aid Groups: International and Multicultural Perspectives* (ed: Francine Lavoie, Thomasina Borkman, and Benjamin Gidron) The Haworth Press, Inc., 1994, pp. 279-302. Multiple copies of this article/chapter may be purchased from The Haworth Document Delivery Center [1-800-3-HAWORTH; 9:00 a.m. - 5:00 p.m. (EST)].

proven useful in analyzing the data. Some broad issues regarding the definition and nature of the self-help group phenomenon are raised.

Self-help groups, by definition, are collectives of people sharing a common serious life-disrupting predicament, not charging for participation in the group, and retaining ownership and control over the workings of the group (see Katz, & Bender, 1976; Levy, 1976; Jacobs & Goodman, 1989). Many believe the empowerment inherent in the self-help ethos of (1) giving as well as getting help, and (2) retaining control over the functioning, goals and ultimate destiny of the group, is central to the successful functioning of these groups (e.g., Riessman, 1990, Maton, 1988).

Such self-led consumer independence leaves considerable room for tension between self-helpers and mental health and medical professionals. Indeed, some groups spring up precisely in reaction to intense consumer dissatisfaction with professional services ("Unite and Conquer," 1990). Others, such as the huge and growing 12-step recovery movement, do not share the mental health values and goals of some professionals (Peele, 1989). Some professionals, for their part, distrust the self-help format, which to them appears to amount to the "blind leading the blind "("Unite and Conquer," 1990).

Within the self-help group field, which includes self-helpers, paraprofessionals, those who run regional, state and national self-help clearinghouses, and those professionals who work with or do research on self-help groups, one often hears the belief that self-helpers are antagonistic toward professional involvement ("Professional" in this article refers to mental health and medical professionals.). But supporting evidence turns out to be more anecdotal than empirical, probably in part reflecting the difficulty of doing research in the self-help community. Lieberman (1986) offers an excellent summary of the problems facing researchers. These include gaining entry to groups, developing research designs collaboratively with group members to keep studies syntonic with member values, and non-intrusive data collection. In addition, myriad other problems arise when dealing in naturalistic settings with these organizations that typically keep no records, have fluctuating membership, and highly value their privacy.

Yet the limited data that do exist suggest something other than self-helper/professional antagonism. Professionals, both in agencies and privately, do refer to groups and sometimes involve themselves as consultants, group facilitators, and lecturers. Lotery (1987) offers a detailed review of this evidence, and Powell (1987) explicates many of the issues involved in professional/self-helper relationships. Of course, demonstrating the relationships that do exist does not account for those that do not, leaving the very real possibility that a small number of professionals account for most of the contacts. For example, a recent survey of 1,550 university-based physicians (Jacobs, Goodman, & Shoptaw, 1990) about their knowledge, attitudes, and referrals to self-help groups produced 260 uniformly positive responses. The unanswered question is who are the other 1,290? Are they antagonistic towards self-help groups, indifferent, non-responding but positive, or simply not knowledgeable about them?

Even less is known from the perspective of the self-help groups, but the sparse available data are suggestive. A survey of 300 groups by the California Self-Help Center (Burstein, 1985) about their needs for technical assistance found a full 84 percent of groups having some type of involvement with professionals and desiring more. Toseland and Hacker (1982), in a three-county (district) survey of 43 groups, found 72 percent had involvement with one or more professionals. Knight, Wollert, Levy, Frame, & Padgett (1980), with data from 80 respondents from seven groups, also found groups wanting more involvement. The 18 Canadian self-help organizations studied by Gottlieb (1982) specified a preference for indirect involvement such as referral and consultation over direct participation by professionals in meetings. Stewart (1990, p.1143) in a review of seven studies examining self-help group members' perceptions concludes that ". . . professional interaction with self-help groups is desirable but that professional lack of information concerning self-help groups and lack of preparation for appropriate roles are perceived as barriers to such interaction. These studies clearly show that the indirect, non-authoritarian role of the professional as consultant receives the most support."

Powell (1987) notes that while existing contact seems generally positive, studies to date have not adequately explored the question of the quality and quantity of these connections. Lotery (1987) adds that most studies have samples that are limited geographically, are limited by the type of professionals or groups surveyed, are weighted towards obtaining the views of professionals, and are small, regardless of who is surveyed.

The present study was designed to obtain information concerning mental health and medical professionals' involvement with self-help groups from a broad, statewide sample of self-help group members. The study taps self-helper beliefs regarding, and experiences with these professionals, including an analysis of the roles professionals have assumed, the members' views of the desirability of such roles, and the amount of time spent in contact with professionals.

METHOD

Subjects

A random sample, taken in 1987, of 764 of the approximately 3,000 self-help groups listed by the state-funded, California Self-Help Center located at the University of California, Los Angeles in the United States was surveyed. Although the universe of self-help groups is not and cannot be known, this statewide data base, which is the largest, most comprehensive known to be available, includes information about each group's history, goals, structure and format.

Three-hundred and ninety groups responded to the survey. This represents 51 percent of surveys actually delivered to an active self-help group. Groups were evenly distributed in terms of size of self-help organization and addressed a wide range of issues. Forty-one percent of the groups were for non-psychiatric medical problems (meaning physical conditions such as cancer or heart disease). Using the Self-Help Center's categories (descriptive categories not used for data analysis) between 10% and 11% of responding groups addressed bereavement, emotional/developmental problems, or transition/lifestyle issues. Seven to eight percent of groups addressed substance abuse, parenting, or violence related problems and four percent addressed other compulsive behavior. Ten percent of responding groups used the 12-step model originally developed in Alcoholics Anonymous.

Respondents were generally long-term members, the majority having attended their group for over one year, and one-third for over five years. Ninety-three percent reported continuing, regular attendance. Eighty-five percent reported leadership or organizational roles, usually shared with other members (for example, co-leading or acting as one of the group coordinators).

All non-respondents were encouraged to respond, first with a postcard, then with a phone call. At the close of data collection, phone contact was made with a random sample of 10 percent of the non-responding groups. A request was made to speak to someone who attends group meetings on a regular basis and information was gathered for comparison with respondents.

In terms of representativeness of the sample, there were no differences between respondents and non-respondents regarding size or type of group, use of the 12-step model, or percentage addressing medical problems. The only significant difference was that respondents had a greater number of professionals involved with their groups, although these professionals did not devote more time than did the professionals involved with the non-respondents.

A supplementary mailing to 101 groups, all using the Alcoholics Anonymous "12-step" model was also conducted. This was done because this type of group was underrepresented in the original sample due to the fact that the large "anonymous" groups only provide the Center with regional contact points, not individual listings of groups. A mailing was sent to all available contact points of Overeaters Anonymous (N = 14), Families Anonymous (N = 7), Narcotics Anonymous (N = 6), Gamblers Anonymous (N = 11), Emotional Health Anonymous (N = 3), Cocaine Anonymous (N = 4), and Spenders Anonymous (N = 1), as well as to most regional contact points of Alcoholics Anonymous. In addition, a non-systematic sample of individual chapters of Alcoholics Anonymous (N = 20) and Overeaters Anonymous (N = 20) located by phone was surveyed because these are the largest of such organizations. (Because of differences in the way the sample from the supplementary mailing was collected compared to the initial mailing and due to its non-random nature, it was not treated as part of the larger sample in the Tables or the data analyses except as indicated.)

Thirty-six of the 101 anonymous groups contacted in the supplementary mailing responded. Those dealing with substance abuse had a markedly lower response rate than the other Anonymous groups as follows: Gamblers-55%; Families-50%; Overeaters-45%; Emotional Health-33%; Narcotics-20%; Cocaine-25%; Alcoholics-8%. All respondents had attended meetings regularly for at least one year and half had attended for over five years.

Materials

The survey was developed for this study after extensive review of the literature and in consultation with the California Self-Help Center and the Institute for Social Science Research, both at UCLA. It was designed to be read easily, take about 15 minutes to complete, and was piloted on 50 non-randomly selected groups from the Center's data base. The final version contained four sections. The first section of 17 items with a 5 point Likert scale (from strongly disagree to strongly agree) assessed beliefs about the involvement of mental health and medical professionals with self-help groups. Sample questions follow: "Self-help groups can be even more effective when they have the assistance of professionals than without it" and "Self-help group members lose control if professionals are involved." (See Appendix A for complete survey.)

The second section listed 13 roles professionals might have assumed. Respondents indicated the frequency of actual involvement and their assessment of the most desirable level. Sample statements follow: "A professional has acted as a consultant or advisor regarding our group's common problem or concern" and "A professional has been the only group leader for our group meetings." The third section of 10 items explored the types of professionals the group had contact with and the frequency of their involvement. The Fourth section listed eight types of experiences groups might have had with professionals such as "Professional has actively done things which helped the functioning of our group," and "Professional has tried to dominate or take over the group." The final section assessed the importance of various group functions such as "providing and receiving emotional support" and "educating the public."

Design and Procedure

An attempt was made in the present study to avoid having only group leaders and coordinators complete the survey, yet not exclude them completely. There was concern that their views might not be representative of those of the group as a whole since they might have more information about the group's historical and present involvement with mental health and medical professionals than the average member. Half of the groups were sent a cover letter requesting that the survey be completed by someone who attends group meetings regularly but is not a mental or medical health professional, group leader, or coordinator. Half received an identical cover letter except that it excluded only mental health and medical professionals.

Despite the instructions, 12 percent of the respondents were professionals. A decision was made to retain these respondents in the sample since many indicated that they do not act in a professional capacity within their groups and because they differed from non-professionals on only three of the 13 dependent variables. The differences were as follows: professionals reported a greater number of professionals involved with the group ($M = 6.4$ versus $M = 4.9$), t $(379) = 2.12$, $p < .04$; they less frequently expressed the view that only those who share the problem can be helpful t $(354) = 3.61$; $p < .01$, and they reported more integral professional involvement (e.g., co-leading or coordinating) t $(376) = 4.13$, $p < .001$. There was no significant difference found between professional and non-professional respondents regarding reported time mental health and medical professionals devote to groups.

RESULTS

Professional Involvement. Eighty-three percent of groups reported that one or more professionals had been involved in ways other than as a regular group member. Sixty-four percent reported the involvement of three or more professionals. The average number was 5.1. Medical groups reported the most involvement with an average of 6.4 professionals, 12-step groups (including the supplementary mailing) the least with an average of 2.9. Table 1 shows the involvement by profession for medical and non-medical groups. Medical

TABLE 1. Percentage of Groups Reporting Involvement of Mental Health and Medical Professionals by Discipline

	Percent Reporting One or More	
	Medical Groups (N = 160)	Non-Medical Groups (N = 230)
Social Worker	58%	39%
Psychologist	44%	39%
Psychiatrist	24%	18%
Counselor	41%	44%
MFCC	17%	29%
Nurse	61%	31%
Medical Doctor	68%	23%

groups were most frequently involved with doctors, nurses, and social workers, non-medical groups with "counselors," social workers and psychologists.

Although the number of professionals involved in groups suggests considerable involvement, the mean total time per group was 0.8 (where 0 = no time and 1 = less than two hours per month). Seven percent of respondents indicated that professionals devote "more than 10 hours per month" to their group, 20% endorsed "between 2 and 10 hours per month," 37% endorsed "less than 2 hours per month" and 11.5% indicated that no mental health or medical professionals are involved with their group in a professional capacity. Among 24.5% of groups, information regarding time devoted was not available.

Professionals' Roles. Thirteen roles were listed in the survey. A wide range of roles was endorsed as "sometimes" or "often" assumed by professionals. Sixty-eight percent of respondents endorsed at least seven roles, and 38 percent endorsed 10 or more roles. Only 6 percent endorsed two or fewer roles. The most frequently endorsed roles were that of referral source (96%), speaker (80%), and consultant or advisor (78%). Table 2 gives the total listing. Of particular interest is the frequency of professional involvement in a group co-leader role; 31 percent reported often

TABLE 2. Mental Health and Medical Professionals' Roles as Reported by Self-Help Group Members in Rank Order of Frequency Reported

	Present Involvement		Desired Involvement		
Role	Often	Sometimes	More	Same	Less
Referral source	57%	39%	73%	26%	2%
Group has sent people to professional	39%	54%	29%	68%	3%
Speaker	35%	45%	46%	53%	1%
Consultant or Advisor	35%	43%	33%	66%	2%
Observer	17%	60%	43%	52%	4%
Equal, regular group member	38%	37%	32%	66%	2%
Co-Leader	31%	35%	25%	70%	4%
Teacher (e.g., problem-solving techniques or communication skills)	18%	46%	44%	55%	2%
Resource Person (e.g., locate financial assistance, meeting place, office space)	29%	31%	38%	59%	3%
Group has taught professionals (e.g., lectures, workshops)	14%	35%	48%	50%	2%
Evaluator	12%	32%	33%	64%	3%
Coordinator or Organizer	25%	17%	13%	82%	5%
Leader	14%	23%	13%	76%	11%

and 35 percent sometimes. That would suggest 66 percent have professionals as one of the leaders at least some of the time.

Respondents were also asked whether they would like mental health and medical professionals to participate more, less, or the same amount. At least 95% of respondents desired the "same" or "more" involvement in every role except having a professional single-handedly lead the group.

Beliefs and Attitudes. Table 3 gives a complete listing of beliefs and attitudes toward professional involvement. An overview was obtained by computing the average percent agreement with pro-in-

TABLE 3. Beliefs Regarding Professional Involvement

Item	Percent agreeing with statement
Professionals can be useful to self-help groups by providing information.	93%
It is a good idea for professionals to learn about self-help groups by sitting in on meetings.	92%
Professionals can be useful in helping start new self-help groups.	80%
Professionals usually see self-help groups as useful.	63%
Self-help groups are more helpful for coping with *my group's* concern (problem, issue, or focus) than professional mental health services are.	62%
Self-help groups can be even more effective when they have the assistance of professionals than without it.	58%
Our self-help group began because professional services weren't helpful enough.	58%
In general, professionals do not know enough about self-help groups.	45%
The only way to get useful help is to talk with others who have the same problem or concern.	40%
Self-help groups are more helpful for coping with *most* concerns than professional mental health services are.	37%
Self-help group members lose control of the group if professionals are involved.	23%
Professionals are of no use to a self-help group unless they have the same problem or concern as the rest of the group.	19%
The ways professionals and self-help group members think about and do things are too different for them to work well together.	11%

Note. The percentages represent the total of those who endorsed "agree" and those who endorsed "strongly agree."

volvement items combined with percent disagreement with anti-involvement items. Seventy-three percent of responses indicated pro-involvement sentiment. The pro-involvement item most frequently endorsed (93%) was "Professionals can be useful to self-help groups by providing information." The most frequently endorsed anti-involvement item (23%) was "Self-help group members lose control of the group if professionals are involved." Sixty-one percent wanted to continue with the same amount of involvement, 36 percent wished for more, and 3 percent desired less.

The survey items concerning beliefs end attitudes regarding professional involvement were factor analyzed. Principle components factor analysis with varimax rotation was used. Three factors with eigenvalues greater than 1.00 were extracted. Items with loadings greater than .50 are listed in Table 4 as are the factor-based scales which were created by summing these items. Inspection of these items suggests that Factor 1 reflects a dimension of perceived benefit and non-destructiveness regarding the involvement of mental health and medical professionals with self-help groups. Factor 2 appears to reflect the view that only people who share a problem can be useful to one another. Factor 3 appears to reflect a dimension of perceived awareness among professionals of the usefulness of self-help groups. There was no overlap in terms of which items loaded on which factors.[1]

Experiences with Professionals. Ninety-one percent of respondents reported more positive than negative experiences with professional involvement. The most frequently reported positive experiences were, "Professional has said positive and/or helpful things about our group or about self-help groups in general" (91%) and "Professional has actively done things which helped the functioning of our group" (85%). The most frequently reported negative experiences were, "Professional has said critical, unhelpful things about our group or about self-help groups in general" (20%) and "Professional has actively done things which hurt or interfered with the functioning of our group" (14%).

Members vs. Leaders. T-tests showed there were significant differences in average responses between the two groups. Leaders identified significantly more professionals involved with their groups than non-leaders, $t(108) = 3.62$, $p < .001$; members more frequently

TABLE 4. Factors: Beliefs Regarding Professional Involvement

Summary of Factor	Items	Loading
Helpfulness, non-destructiveness of professional involvement	Professionals can be useful in helping start new self-help groups.	.74
	Professionals can be useful to self-help groups by providing information.	.74
	Self-help groups can be even more effective when they have the assistance of professionals than without it.	.68
	Self-help group members lose control of the group if professionals are involved.	−.59
	The ways professionals and self-help group members think about and do things are too different for them to work well together.	−.64
Level of belief that only fellow sufferers can be helpful	The only way to get useful help is to talk with others who have the same problem or concern.	.74
	Self-help groups are more helpful for coping with *my group's* concern (problem, issue, or focus) than professional mental health services are.	.68
	Self-help groups are more helpful for coping with *most* concerns than professional mental health services are.	.69
Perceived professional usefulness, awareness regarding self-help groups	In general, professionals do not know enough about self-help groups.	.73
	Our self-help group began because professional services weren't useful enough.	.58
	Professionals usually see self-help groups as useful.	.63

expressed the view than leaders that professionals are helpful and non-destructive, $t(357) = 2.11$, $p < .04$; members reported more positive experiences with professional involvement, $t(309) = 1.95$, $p < .05$; members described more integral involvement of professionals (e.g., co-leading, advising), $t(379) = 6.94$, $p < .001$; group leaders described more peripheral involvement (e.g., observers, learners, referral sources), $t(379) = 1.96$, $p < .05$; leaders more often believed professionals were aware of self-help groups, $t(357) =$

3.49, $p < .0005$ and leaders more often emphasized the importance of education and social change, $t(380) = 2.03$, $p < .05$.

Medical vs. Non-Medical Groups. Medical group respondents (n = 160) reported significantly more professional involvement on every measure of involvement except regular group membership of professionals. They reported a greater number of both medical professionals, (M = 1.7 and .7), $t(384) = 2.02$, $p < .05$, and mental health professionals, (M = 2.3 and 1.95), $t(384) = 2.02$, $p < .05$; higher amounts of total time professionals devoted to their groups, (M = 1.4 and 1.1), $t(291) = 2.99$, $p < .01$; and higher levels of both integral $t(382) = 2.83$, $p < .01$; and peripheral involvement, $t\ (382) = 2.00$, $p < .05$. They also more frequently expressed the view that professionals are helpful and non-destructive, while non-medical groups more frequently reported negative experiences with professionals.

Twelve-Step Groups (n = 75). From anecdotal information, it was expected that groups using AA's 12-step model would report less professional involvement and less favorable attitudes toward such involvement than other types of groups. The following comparisons were performed in two ways, including and excluding the supplementary (12-step only) mailing. Data are presented for the combined samples since, except for one comparison (noted), the pattern of significant differences was identical either way. As expected, 12-step group respondents identified fewer professionals as involved with their groups in a professional capacity (M = 3.1 and 5.3), $t(423) = 3.81$, $p < .001$ and indicated that professionals devote less time to their groups, (M = .64 and 1.34 with 1 representing less than two hours per month), $t(320) = 6.09$, $p < .001$, but said that more professionals are involved as regular group members with no special role, (M = 2.1 and 1.3), $t(331) = 3.22$, $p < .01$. They also reported less frequently that professional involvement is helpful and non-destructive, $t(93) = 4.69$, $p < .001$, and more frequently endorsed the view that only those who share the problem can be helpful, $t(396) = 2.35$, $p < .02$ (this comparison was not significant when the supplementary mailing was excluded). They also reported fewer positive $t(327) = 4.27$, $p < .001$, and more negative experiences with professionals, $t(327) = 4.27$, $p < .001$. Finally, they saw education and social change as less important, $t(418) = 4.36$, $p <$

.001, and meeting personal needs of members as more important, $t(418) = 5.05, p < .001$.

Substance Abuse 12-Step Groups (n = 35). When compared with other 12-step groups, two significant differences emerged. Substance abuse groups were more likely to feel that only those with the problem could be helpful, $t(344) = 2.65, p < .03$, and to report negative experiences with professional involvement, $t(344) = 3.76$, $p < .002$.

Mental Health Groups (n = 34). These respondents, consumers or ex-consumers of psychiatric services, were less likely to perceive professional involvement as helpful and non-destructive $t(363) = 2.41, p < .02$ than were members of other groups. Not surprisingly, they had more involvement with psychiatrists than did respondents from other types of groups (M = .65 and M = .26) and less with other medical doctors overall, than did other types of groups (M = .71 and M = .21), $t(51) = 4.89, p < .001$.

Size of Self-Help Organization. One-way ANOVA's were performed for medical vs. non-medical groups over four levels of group size: single self-help groups, 2-10 chapters, 11-50 chapters and over 50 chapters. There were no significant differences regarding the number of professionals involved. Self-help groups with 2-10 chapters reported more total time from professionals than did organizations with over 50 chapters $F(3, 164) = 4.41$, $p < .006$. Mean time for the smaller organizations was 1.45, and .84 for the larger ones (1 represented less than two hours per month and 2 represented 2-10 hours per month). No significant differences were found by size of organization in the general areas of beliefs regarding professional involvement and experiences with professional involvement.

DISCUSSION

The topic of mental health and medical professionals and their relationship to self-help groups has generated more debate than data in the literature. This study, utilizing the largest, broadest, and geographically most widely distributed sample of self-help groups to date, provides us with an in-depth look at group member perceptions of relationships with mental health and medical professionals.

Overall, the results support the limited previous research findings and those who argue in favor of collaborative relationships, as opposed to those who feel that tension between self-helpers and professionals is inherent in the nature of the relationship and that antagonism is inevitable. However, the support is not unqualified and varies with the type of group. Particularly sharp distinctions emerged for medical versus non-medical groups, groups using the 12-step model originated by Alcoholics Anonymous versus all other types of groups, and those 12-step "Anonymous" groups for substance abuse versus all other 12-step groups.

A key finding is that 83 percent of the respondents report involvement with professionals in a wide variety of roles, the average number of professionals being just over five. This is in line with two smaller studies. Toseland and Hacker (1982) found 77 percent of groups had professional involvement and Burstein (1985) found 84 percent. However, this study also examined the extent of involvement. The average is less than two hours a month, which immediately suggests that much collaboration is of a limited nature.

Also, the types of professionals varied, with physicians, nurses and social workers predominating in medically related groups, and "counselors," social workers, and psychologists predominating in all other types of groups. An unexpectedly high degree of mutuality was found, with groups and professionals making cross referrals, serving as educators to each other, and working as co-leaders of groups.

With regard to attitudes and beliefs about professionals, most respondents in the present study felt that professional involvement adds to the group's effectiveness. Ninety-seven percent desire the same amount or more involvement in the future, and 91 percent report more positive than negative experiences with professional involvement. These findings are similar to the limited data available in the literature. Toseland and Hacker (1982), in a three-county (district) survey of forty-three groups, reported that most (no figures given) self-help groups sampled were satisfied with the current level of professional involvement (a substantial majority had professionals involved with their groups). With qualifications, 62 percent favored the involvement of "social workers and other professionals," 17 percent were unsure, and 21 percent did not favor professional involvement. Knight et al. (1980), in their investigation of seven major self-help groups, rated the potential involvement of mental health professionals higher than present involvement (but did not report data regarding present involvement).

Respondents in the present study were not wholeheartedly positive regarding professional involvement. Fourteen percent reported negative experiences, particularly in the area of professionals trying to co-opt or dominate the group.

Experiences with, and attitudes toward, professional involvement varied somewhat by type of group. Medical groups' respondents reported more mental health and medical professional involvement than those from non-medical groups and more frequently expressed the view that professionals are helpful and non-destructive. Respondents from 12-step groups, particularly those which address substance abuse, were less favorable regarding professional involvement than respondents from other groups. They had less involvement with professionals, a less favorable opinion about such involvement, and a more strongly held belief that only those with the same problem can be effective helpers. In addition, consistent with one of the 12 traditions banning opinions on issues outside the group, they returned the survey much less frequently than did other types of groups. That the 12-step substance abuse groups such as Alcoholics Anonymous represent such a well-known subset of self-help organizations may help explain why self-help groups in general appear to be perceived as more antagonistic towards professional involvement than the present study suggests they actually are. Interestingly, it was the 12-step substance abuse groups that reported the highest percentage of professionals as regular group members, suggesting that while professionals may have other resources for most problems, when it comes to substance abuse, a self-help group is sometimes the treatment they choose.

Another distinction emerged when the respondents were leaders in their own groups as opposed to simply being regular group members. Leaders tended to be less positive in their views of professional involvement. These leaders were long-term members; thus they are likely to have added knowledge about the group (but on the other hand, their views may not be representative of the views of the average member). This underlines the importance of researchers being careful to specify exactly who is responding to a self-help group survey.

Limitations of the study, beyond the general limitations of all survey research, must be noted, along with some interesting questions these limitations raise. The universe of self-help groups is not and cannot be known. Although our follow-up with non-respondents suggests that the sample was representative of the data base of the California Self-Help Center from which it was drawn, that data base itself is statewide only and is probably biased toward groups with professional involvement. That is so partly because groups with professional involvement are more likely to be organizationally or institutionally affiliated and therefore easier to locate, and partly because small, unaffiliated groups are not only hard to locate, they may have no interest in being listed or in recruiting new members. So, involvement with professionals may look stronger and more widespread than it is. Nonetheless, it exists in substantial amounts. Should such involvement then alter the picture many hold of self-help groups as independent, self-regulating, self-empowered entities? Is there in fact a somewhat blurred boundary between self-help/mutual aid in its "purist" form (Jacobs & Goodman, 1989; Goodman & Jacobs, in press), and either (1) professionally sponsored/controlled support groups or (2) psychotherapy groups for members with a common problem? Future research might profitably address these questions.

Another intriguing question is about the professionals who are not involved with self-help groups at any level, not even to refer clients/patients to them. Are these professionals not knowledgeable, not interested, or actively antagonistic? And what proportion of professional opinion do such people represent? Another important area for future research concerns the negative experiences self-helpers have had with professionals. These need to be more closely documented and studied. In addition, future research on all aspects of professional involvement would benefit from the development of a standardized survey which would be very helpful in allowing for comparisons across researchers. Such an instrument should go beyond the present one in distinguishing between past and present professional involvement, in exploring fees received, and in rating the intensity of the professional involvement. The results of the factor analyses performed in the present study suggest that several factors concerning beliefs regarding and attitudes toward professional involvement can be readily identified and could be useful in the development of future surveys.

The shared group leader model, which is not often mentioned in the literature, emerged as quite prevalent in this study, where a professional and a group member serve as co-leaders. Sixty-six percent of the sample had experienced a professional co-leading "sometimes" or "often," and 95 percent wanted "the same" level of participation or "more." Research in this area is difficult to locate but one study (Yoak & Chesler, 1985) explored the effects of self-help group members and mental health professionals sharing the group leadership. It was found that, compared with professionally-led and member-led groups for parents of children with cancer, shared leadership groups had the most longevity, were best able to retain parents of deceased children, and were most likely to work for change in medical and social care. The benefits and limitations of the shared group facilitation model seem worthy of further exploration.

In conclusion, the overall picture for professional involvement with self-help groups seems positive. Education of professionals and self-help groups might enlighten both groups about successful collaborative efforts thus far and encourage their participation in future efforts.

NOTE

1. Factor analyses were also performed on the sections of the questionnaire concerning professionals' roles in groups, experiences with professional involvement, and group functions. See Lotery (1987) for further information.

REFERENCES

Burstein, B. (1985). California Self-Help Center of UCLA. *Survey of self-help groups involvement with professionals.*

Goodman, G. & Jacobs, M.K. (in press). Self-help mutual support groups. In A. Fuhriman & G. Burlingame (eds.) *Handbook of group psychotherapy.* New York: Wiley & Sons

Gottlieb, B. (1982). Mutual-help groups: Members' views of their benefits and of roles for professionals. *Prevention in Human Services, 1*, 55-67.

Jacobs, M.K., Goodman, G. & Shoptaw, S. (1990). California Self-Help Center of UCLA. (Unpublished) *Survey of Physician Beliefs About and Use of Self-Help Groups.*

Jacobs, M.K., & Goodman, G. (1989). Psychology and Self-Help Groups Predictions on a Partnership. *American Psychologist, 44*,3, 536-545.

Katz, A.H., & Bender, E. (1976). *The strength in us: Self-help groups in the modern world.* New York: Franklin Watts.

Knight, B., Wollert, R.W., Levy, L.H., Frame, C.L., & Padgett, V.P. (1980). Self-help groups: The members' perspectives. *American Journal of Community Psychology, 8*, 53-65.

Levy, L.H. (1976). Self-help groups: Types and psychological processes. *Journal of Applied Behavioral Science, 12*, 310-322.

Lieberman, M. (1986). Self-help groups and psychiatry. *American Psychiatric Association Annuals Review, 5*, 744-760.

Lotery, J.L. (1987). *The role of mental health and medical professionals with self-help groups.* Unpublished doctoral dissertation, University of California, Los Angeles, CA.

Maton, K.I. (1988). Social support, organizational characteristics, self-help group population. *American Journal of Community Psychology, 16*, 53-88.

Peele, S. (1989). *Diseasing of America: Addiction treatment out of control.* Lexington, Mass: Lexington Books.

Powell, T.J. (1987). *Self-help organizations and professional practice.* Silver Spring, MD: National Association of Social Workers, Inc.

Riessman, F. (1990). Restructuring help: A human services paradigm. *American Journal of Community Psychology, 18*, 221-230.

Stewart, M. (1990). Professional interface with mutual-aid self-help groups: A review. *Social Science and Medicine, 31*, 1143-1158.

Toseland, R.W., & Hacker, L. (1982). Self-Help groups and professional involvement. *Social Work, 27*, 341-347.

Unite and Conquer. (1990, February). *Newsweek*, pp. 50-55.

Yoak, M. & Chesler, M. (1985). Alternative professional roles in health care delivery; Leadership patterns in self-help groups. *The Journal of Applied Behavioral Science, 21*(4), 427-444.

SELF-HELP GROUPS AND PROFESSIONALS: A SURVEY

Please tell us what you think about the involvement of medical and mental health professionals with self-help groups so that we can let professionals know how they can be of the greatest help to groups.

Using the scale below, please circle the number which best represents how much you agree or disagree with each statement. The word "professionals" means people in the mental health professions (such as psychologists, psychiatrists, and social workers) or people in the medical professions (such as doctors and nurses).

	strongly disagree	disagree	neither agree nor disagree	agree	strongly agree	(office use) ___ ___ ___ ___ 1 2 3 4
Professionals can be useful in helping start new self-help groups.	1	2	3	4	5	(5)
In general, professionals do not know enough about self-help groups.	1	2	3	4	5	(6)
Professionals can be useful to self-help groups by providing information.	1	2	3	4	5	(7)
The only way to get useful help is to talk with others who have the same problem or concern	1	2	3	4	5	(8)
Self-help groups are more helpful for coping with *my group's* concern (problem, issue, or focus) than professional mental health services are.	1	2	3	4	5	(9)
Self-help groups are more helpful for coping with *most* concerns than professional mental health services are.	1	2	3	4	5	(10)
Self-help groups can be even more effective when they have the assistance of professionals than without it.	1	2	3	4	5	(11)
Self-help group members lose control of the group if professionals are involved.	1	2	3	4	5	(12)
It is a good idea for professionals to learn about self-help groups by sitting in on meetings.	1	2	3	4	5	(13)
The ways professionals and self-help group members think about and do things are too different for them to work well together.	1	2	2	2	2	(14)
Our self-help group began because professional services weren't helpful enough.	1	2	3	4	5	(15)
Professionals usually see self-help groups as useful.	1	2	3	4	5	(16)
Professionals are of no use to a self-help group unless they have the same problem or concern as the rest of the group.	1	2	3	4	5	(17)

Please circle the number under OFTEN, SOMETIMES, or NEVER to indicate how much *any* mental health or medical professionals have been involved with your group in that particular way.

Then, regardless of that answer, please circle the number under MORE if you'd like professionals *in general* to be more involved with your group in that way than they are. Circle the number under LESS if you'd like them to be less involved, and the number under SAME if you're satisfied with the amount of involvement.

	often	sometimes	never	don't know		more	same	less	
A professional has been an equal, regular group member.	1	2	3	4	(18)	1	2	3	(19)
A professional has sat in on group meetings as an observer.	1	2	3	4	(20)	1	2	3	(21)
A professional has referred (sent) clients or other people to our group.	1	2	3	4	(22)	1	2	3	(23)
Our group has sent people who want or need other help to a professional.	1	2	3	4	(24)	1	2	3	(25)
A professional has helped lead our group along with another group member or members.	1	2	3	4	(26)	1	2	3	(27)
A professional has been the only group leader for our group meetings.	1	2	3	4	(28)	1	2	3	(29)
A professional has come to our group as a speaker to provide information about our group's common problem or concern.	1	2	3	4	(30)	1	2	3	(31)
A professional has acted as a consultant or advisor regarding our group's common problem or concern.	1	2	3	4	(32)	1	2	3	(33)
A professional has taught our group's members or leader specific skills (for example, problem-solving techniques or communication skills).	1	2	3	4	(34)	1	2	3	(35)
Our group has taught professionals formally (for example, giving lectures or putting on workshops).	1	2	3	4	(36)	1	2	3	(37)
A professional has been the group's main coordinator or organizer.	1	2	3	4	(38)	1	2	3	(39)
A professional has helped our group get resources (for example, helped us get money, a place to meet or office space).	1	2	3	4	(40)	1	2	3	(41)
A professional has evaluated our group to see how it's doing and/or help it work better.	1	2	3	4	(42)	1	2	3	(43)

Please indicate whether one, more than one, or zero professionals of the types listed have been involved with your group *other than* as regular group participants. (It's o.k. if they've been regular participants in addition to their other involvement.)

	one	more than one	none
(44) Social Worker	1	2	3
(45) Psychologist	1	2	3
(46) Psychiatrist	1	2	3
(47) Counselor	1	2	3
(48) M.F.C.C.	1	2	3
(49) Nurse	1	2	3
(50) Medical Doctor	1	2	3
(51) Therapist (title not known)	1	2	3
(52) Medical person (title not known)	1	2	3

(53) Other————————————

(54) How many mental health and/or medical professionals have been regular participants in your group (*with no special role*) that you're aware of? (Please circle the number next to your answer.)

One .... 1 Four or more .. 4
Two .... 2 None 5
Three ... 3 Don't know ... 6

(55) How many mental health and/or medical professionals have been involved with your group in any way *besides* as regular members or participants that you're aware of? (They could have been regular members also.)

One ... 1 Four or more .. 4
Two ... 2 None 5
Three .. 3 Don't know ... 6

(56) If you were to add up the time these people *usually* spend on the group in any way (other than participating as regular group members), roughly how much time *per month* would that be?

Less than 2 hours 1
Between 2 and 10 hours .. 2
Over 10 hours 3
Don't know 4

Please circle the number under the appropriate answer to indicate how much your group has had the experience with mental health *or* medical professionals. If your group has had no involvement with these professionals, check here___and skip this section.

	often	sometimes	never	don't know	(office use)
Professional has said positive and/or helpful things about our group or about self-help groups in general.	1	2	3	4	(57)
Professional has said critical, unhelpful things about our group or about self-help groups in general	1	2	3	4	(58)
Professional has actively done things which hurt or interfered with the functioning of our group.	1	2	3	4	(59)
Professional has actively done things which helped the functioning of our group.	1	2	3	4	(60)
Professional has tried to dominate or take over the group.	1	2	3	4	(61)

Professional has involved himself or herself but did not try to dominate the group.	1	2	3	4	(62)
Our group has asked professionals for assistance or help	1	2	3	4	(63)
If yes, they have generally been willing to assist us for free.	1	2	3	4	(64)
If yes, they have generally been willing to assist us for payment.	1	2	3	4	(65)
Professional(s) have offered some kind of help to our group without being asked.	1	2	3	4	(66)

It would be helpful to have some background information about you and your group. Please circle the number next to or below the correct answer to each question.

Do you:	YES	NO
(67) Attend group meetings on a regular basis?	1	2
(68) Lead group meetings by yourself every meeting?	1	2
(69) Lead group meetings by yourself sometimes	1	2
(70) Lead group meetings with someone else every meeting?	1	2
(71) Lead group meetings with someone else sometimes? ...	1	2
(72) Act as the *only* group coordinator or organizer?	1	2
(73) Act as one of the group coordinators or organizers?	1	2

Other______________________

(74) People participate in your group because:

They themselves have a concern, problem, or condition 1

Someone they care about has a concern, problem, or condition 2

Both of the above 3

(75) How many, if any, other groups (other chapters or meetings) are part of your group's organization?

None 1
1 to 10 2
11 to 50 3
Over 50 4
Don't know 5

(76) How long have you been coming to meetings of this group or another branch of it?

Less than 3 months 1
Between 3 months and 1 year 2
Between 1 and 5 years .. 3
More than 5 years 4

(77) Are you a mental health or medical professional?

No 1
Yes 2

If yes, what is your profession and type of degree?

____

What is the name of your group (or your group's organization)?

____

Any additional comments would be welcomed and appreciated.

How important are the following to your group?

	very important	somewhat important	Not very important
(1) Helping members change a behavior or habit	1	2	3
(2) Dealing with and/or adjusting to a situation or problem	1	2	3
(3) Providing and receiving emotional support	1	2	3
(4) Education of group members	1	2	3
(5) Educating the public	1	2	3
(6) Political action/Social change	1	2	3

Other————————————————

If you have any questions, please call or write:

Jennifer Lotery
California Self-Help Center
U.C.L.A.
405 Hilgard Avenue
Los Angeles, CA 90024
(213) 825-1799

Thank you very much for your help!

Chapter 13

Workshop on "Good Practice" in the Collaboration Between Professionals and Mutual Aid Groups

Francine Lavoie

Université Laval

Andy Farquharson

University of Victoria

Mellen Kennedy

University of Illinois

SUMMARY. The workshop's purpose was to initiate a dialogue concerning "good practice" issues in research and collaboration with mutual aid groups with the long range goal of developing ethical guidelines for professionals and for mutual aid organizations. Participants represented mutual aid groups, professionals and self-help clearinghouses. Three of the topic areas addressed during the workshop were analysed from the perspectives of the professionals:

Address correspondence to Francine Lavoie, École de psychologie Université Laval, Cité universitaire, Québec, Canada.

[Haworth co-indexing entry note]: "Workshop on "Good Practice" in the Collaboration Between Professionals and Mutual Aid Groups." Lavoie, Francine, Andy Farquharson, and Mellen Kennedy. Co-published simultaneously in *Prevention in Human Services* (The Haworth Press, Inc.) Vol. 11, No. 2, 1994, pp. 303-313; and *Self-Help and Mutual Aid Groups: International and Multicultural Perspectives* (ed: Francine Lavoie, Thomasina Borkman, and Benjamin Gidron) The Haworth Press, Inc., 1994, pp. 303-313. Multiple copies of this article/chapter may be purchased from The Haworth Document Delivery Center [1-800-3-HAWORTH; 9:00 a.m. - 5:00 p.m. (EST)].

respecting the autonomy, integrity and unique culture of each group, ensuring that guidelines for confidentiality are adhered to, and respecting experiential knowledge. From the perspectives of mutual aid organizations, preserving autonomy and self-determination, incorporating new information and maintaining confidentiality were also discussed.

A one-day workshop on problems of collaboration between mutual aid groups and professionals was held in September 1992 in Ottawa, preceding the first International Conference on Self-help and Mutual Aid. The workshop's purpose was to initiate a dialogue concerning "good practice" issues in research and collaboration with mutual aid groups with the long range goal of developing ethical guidelines for both parties.

Workshop organizers sought to include representation of a variety of perspectives among the participants. The 18 people who participated represented mutual aid groups, professionals and self-help clearinghouses. Mutual aid organizations represented were the Compassionate Friends, groups for widows, groups for ex-psychiatric patients and some regional clearinghouses from Canada and United States. The professionals came from Canada, United States, Israel, Scotland and United Kingdom. The disciplines represented were psychology, sociology, nursing, social work and public health administration.

Writings on collaboration between professionals and mutual aid groups have considered the variety of roles that professionals could play and their satisfaction with such roles but have not taken care of naming the difficulties they could face or provoke in such roles as consultant, co-facilitator or researcher. Only when reporting some case studies or when writing educational materials were such difficulties described by a researcher (Fry, 1977) and by consultants (Cardinal & Farquharson, 1991; Kleiman, Mantell, & Alexander 1976; Lusky & Ingman, 1979). Generally, the problems experienced by self help organizations, groups or clearinghouses, in handling such issues, were even less frequently mentioned (Stewart, 1990). This workshop is thus the first attempt to solicit ideas from representatives of the two perspectives, professionals and mutual aid members, on controversial behaviors that they have identified in their encounters with each other and on principles of good practice that they would like to see implemented in such encounters.

Prior to the workshop, the organizers solicited vignettes describing real life experiences of conflicts between mutual aid groups and professionals. The vignettes were gathered from the workshop participants and from other self-helpers and professionals through notices in appropriate journals and newsletters. The work of Cardinal and Farquharson (1991) was also a source of inspiration. The vignettes were compiled for use in the workshop. Examples of the vignettes are included in Appendix A and the complete list of vignettes is available from the first author. The structure of the workshop consisted of discussions among the entire group and in small groups. After an orientation concerning definitional issues, the participants discussed what was called for the purpose of this workshop "ethical issues" using some of the vignettes as a stimulus. Specific questions addressed responsibilities and rights of both self-helpers and of professionals, the possible courses of action and key issues.

Principles for good practice were suggested during the workshop; some of these principles are discussed below addressing first the responsibilities of the professionals and second the responsibilities of mutual aid organizations. A few of those principles could be presented as ethical considerations as they are generally included in ethics code of many professions but they are mentioned here as principles of good practice. In future work, it would be appropriate to distinguish more what is effective practice and what is an ethical or moral consideration. It is important to emphasize here that this report on the workshop is a very preliminary start on the elaboration of principles for responsible collaboration between professionals and members of self-help groups and has no intent of proposing ethical guidelines as such.

PRINCIPLES FOR PROFESSIONALS

Principles for professional practice that were suggested by the participants were grouped by the authors in ten perceived categories. These are outlined in Appendix B and for the purposes of this discussion we have chosen to focus on just five practice guidelines that have been further blended into three topic areas: (a) respecting the autonomy, integrity and unique culture of each group, [items 2,3, and 6 from Appendix B], (b) ensuring that guidelines for confidentiality are adhered to [item 5], and (c) respecting experiential knowledge [item 7].

Autonomy, Integrity and Group Culture

Participants suggested that there are three areas in which professionals should recognize the autonomy and integrity of self-help groups, they should respect the way in which a given group makes decisions, they should be scrupulous in not violating the boundaries of the group and they should respect the right of a self-help group to be self-determining. Respect for the way in which a particular group chooses to make decisions is important for this recognizes that each group is to some extent unique and will develop patterns of decision-making that are accepted by the majority of group members. Viewed from a professional perspective some of these practices may seem time-consuming or awkward but for many self-helpers time is not a scarce commodity, and we need to be humble about the effectiveness of some of our own professional decision-making behaviours. In those situations where a professional has been invited to a self-help group meeting it is important that they resist any temptation to intervene to 'improve' any group processes unless they have specifically been asked for this advice. It can be helpful to think of each group as having it's own culture and thus the responsible professional will observe all of the guidelines for sensitive cross-cultural practice.

Respect for the boundaries of a group suggests that professionals likewise need to constantly question the need for on-going involvement with a particular self-help group if this is the pattern that has emerged. Even if there does seem to be a role for a professional to play, for example, in playing the role of convener at the initiation of a new group, that person should have a clear plan for the way in which they will conduct a phased withdrawal of the group at the earliest possible moment.

Underpinning respect for the autonomy and integrity of these groups is the fundamental principle of respect for the right to self-determination of both self-helpers and the groups to which they belong. Professionals should be alert to the limitations of their own constructed practice paradigms and value the capacity of group members to be capable of self-direction.

Confidentiality

In most of the health and human service professions guidelines with respect to confidentiality are built in to the Code of Ethics where these exist. The issue of confidentiality is of particular importance to many people who are members of those self-help groups in which anonymity is a central belief and right. It is important for professionals to recognize that even where they themselves may attach no stigma to a particular condition or circumstance the person with the benefit of an insider's perspective may indeed have experienced humiliation or reproach. Professionals also need to clarify the extent to which they can assure confidentiality given the mandate of their professional role and/or their employer.

Participants in the consultation also noted that confidentiality is also an issue when carrying out research on mutual aid groups and self-help processes. It is important that members really are giving informed consent when they agree to participate in a research project, and it is important that all who will be touched by this decision have a chance to make an independent choice. There is a danger that several unrepresentative members might commit the group to a research project that would be unacceptable to the majority of membership.

Experiential Knowledge

The other major consideration for responsible professional practice in relation to self-help/mutual aid groups hinges on the nature and value of experiential knowledge; that is specialized information on a problem based on personal experience (Borkman, 1989). The effective professional is increasingly one who listens to a person's [patient or client] own Health Belief Model. That is the individual's own perception of their difficulty, their own conception of 'wellness' and their own conception of the way in which such well-being can be achieved. This is particularly true in relationships with self-help groups in which the conception of the nature of the difficulty and the path to resolution may be quite different from the conceptualizations of the professional. An appreciation for the value of experiential wisdom is hard to accomplish without an accompanying humility about the limitations of professional knowledge and ways of knowing. The responsible professional is seen as one who can accept that there is frequently a complimentarity between experiential and professional know-how and can deal with the tensions when the two types of knowledge appear to contradict one another.

PRINCIPLES FOR SELF-HELPERS

The workshop participants identified a number of guidelines for the ways in which self-help groups should manage their relationships with professionals in the health and human services and these were grouped into four perceived categories. These categories have been blended in the following discussion of: (a) autonomy and self-determination, (b) incorporating new information and (c) confidentiality.

Autonomy and Self-Determination

Several participants expressed the view that it was the responsibility of self-help groups to safeguard their own autonomy in their relationships with professionals. The groups should recognize that ultimately they are answerable to their own membership and that responsibilities should be shared in order to achieve this kind of accountability.

In their contacts with professionals, group members need to be vigilant in keeping their own interests at the forefront and be constantly asking themselves what benefits will flow from professional contact. This is not meant to suggest that all professionals have malevolent intent but rather to remind self-helpers that some professionals may be unwittingly blinded by their own paradigms and their power to impose these on others. In agreeing to collaborate with professionals on research projects, members need to ensure that they are fully informed about the nature, procedures and use of the research, any potential adverse effects on group members, and what opportunities they may have to be involved in interpreting the research findings. Self-helpers were encouraged to commit themselves to a continuing process of assessment in monitoring any evolution of mutual roles and responsibilities in relationships with professionals.

Incorporating New Information

Participants felt that one aspect of responsible self-help group membership was the desire to remain open to new information whether derived from personal experiences or from professional practice. This new information should be carefully assessed and integrated with existing know-how to the extent that this is possible. The challenge for groups will be to embrace new information about their shared concerns that may contradict some of their foundation beliefs about their mutual difficulties. This kind of disconfirming information is never easy to accept.

Confidentiality

The results of the consultation suggest that self-helpers need to consider the issue of confidentiality in two different ways: what are group members needs for confidentiality and what boundaries with regard to confidentiality should apply to observers, researchers and other outsiders?

In deciding internal guidelines to protect privacy, members should be guided by the standard of confidentiality required to ensure 'perceived safety' for group members. Among the factors to be considered are whether the meetings will be open to people who do not directly share the concern that unites members and ways to deal with those who attend only sporadically. Participants felt that it was important to clarify the expectations of each member with regard to confidentiality.

CONCLUSION

We have to take into consideration some limits of the present workshop. Results were limited by time constraints and by the scope of the vignettes discussed as those vignettes were not obtained from a representative sample of self-helpers or professionals working with self-help groups. For example, if we consider the roles identified as appropriate for professionals in surveys of self-help groups members by Wollert et al. (1980), by Todres (1982) and by Bryant (1983;1990) we find that the role of guest speaker was not included in the vignettes. The authors had tried to avoid suggesting that these findings in any way represent a code of ethics to guide professional and mutual aid group relationships. Rather, this is a beginning propositional statement in what will hopefully be a continuing dialogue about a principled and mutually respectful collaboration between self-helpers and professionals. The emergence of new and creative blends of formal and informal helping make it imperative to continue this dialogue if we are to avoid mutual estrangement on the one hand or a colonial takeover on the other.

AUTHOR NOTES

Thanks to a grant from the Social Science and Humanities Research Council of Canada, researchers from University of Victoria and Université Laval and the Canadian Council on Social Development and its action-research team on self-help groups held a workshop on mutual aid groups and problems of collaboration with professionals.

The authors gratefully acknowledge the support of Ann Chudleigh and Hector Balthazar of the late action research group on self-help at the CCSD. The organization that has taken over is now called Self-Help Canada-Entraide du Canada (address: P.O. Box 64094, 1620, Scott Street, Ottawa, Ontario, Canada, K1Y 4V1).

The authors also express thanks to the participants at the Institute: Dyane Adam, Linda Bayers, Jean-Paul Blais, Françoise Beauregard, Thomasina Borkman, Judi Chamberlin, Nancy Edmonds, Molly Hill Folken, Benjamin Gidron, Michëal Hough, Thomas Powell, Gail Rows, Phyliss Silverman, Miriam Stewart, John Trainor, Marie-Josée Vaillancourt and Judy Wilson, and to the two students assistants: Isabel Simard and Annick Simard.

REFERENCES

Borkman, T. (1989). Experiential, professional and lay frames of reference. In T. Powell (ed.), *Working with self help* (pp. 3-29). Silver Spring, MD: National Association of Social Workers.

Bryant, N. (1990). Self-help groups and professionals: Cooperation or conflict? In A. H. Katz & E. I. Bender, *Helping one another; self-help groups in a changing world*. Oakland, CA: Third Party Publishing Co.

Cardinal, J., & Farquharson, A. (1991). *Self-help resource kit*. Victoria, B.C.: University of Victoria.

Fry, L. J. (1977). Research grants and self-help programs: What price knowledge? *Journal of Health and Social Behavior, 18(4)*, 405-417.

Kleiman, M. A., Mantell, J. E., & Alexander, E.S. (1976). Collaboration and its discontents: The perils of partnership. *Journal of Applied Behavioral Science, 12*, 403-410.

Lusky, R. A., & Ingman, S. R. (1979). The pros, cons and pitfalls of self-help rehabilitation programs. *Social Science and Medicine, 13A*, 113-121.

Stewart, M. J. (1990). Professional interface with mutual-aid self-help groups: A review. *Social Science and Medicine, 31(10)*, 1143-1158.

Todres, R. (1982). Professional attitudes, awareness and use of self-help groups. *Prevention in Human Services, 1*, 91-98.

Wollert, R., & Barron, N. (1983). Avenues of collaboration. In D.L. Pancoast, P. Parker, C. Froland (eds.), *Rediscovering self-help* (pp. 105-123). Beverly Hills: Sage.

APPENDIX A

Vignettes Depicting Collaboration Incidents Between Mutual Aid Groups and Professionals and Questions on "Good Practice."

You are asked to attend the meeting of a self-help group in order to explain the function of your human service agency to the members. It is clear to you that one person dominates the discussion and blocks others from participating.

Do you feel any responsibility to intervene in some way in this situation?

A professional colleague has been involved in starting up a self-help group for people wishing to lose weight. From what you understand she did an excellent job of bringing the potential members together for an initial meeting and allowing them to begin the development of their own group processes. However, two months later this colleague is still attending the meetings and she mentions her enthusiasm about the group and her plan to teach them methods of behaviour modification.

What do you think about this?

How would you respond?

You learn at the coffee break during your weekly self-help group meeting that a young woman attending your meeting is in fact a student observing the group as a school assignment. She is reluctant to share this with the members and she explains that their college teacher asked them not to reveal their identity to the group.

What types of ethical principles might be violated in this kind of situation?

What type of action, if any, should you take?

APPENDIX B

Good practice principles for professionals collaborating with mutual aid groups as suggested by workshop participants:

1. Educate self about the groups
2. Respect unique culture and contributions of SHG
3. Respect autonomy and integrity
4. Think before intervening
5. Respect confidentiality
6. Work with groups whose values are consistent with your own
7. Respect experiential knowledge
8. Share know-how sensitively
9. Offer a role model for dealing with difficulties
10. Implement collaborative research

Chapter 14

Self-Help Group Participation Among People with Severe Mental Illness

Caroline L. Kaufmann
Herbert C. Schulberg
Nina R. Schooler

University of Pittsburgh

SUMMARY. An experimental design was attempted to test the effectiveness of self-help group participation among people with severe and long-standing mental illnesses. A sample of 90 individuals was randomized to either experimental or control groups with experimentals invited to join self-help groups and given outreach to encourage participation. Control subjects were not invited to join self-help groups. Results showed low rates of 17% participation in the self-help groups for both experimental and control subjects. The small number of experimental subjects participating and the presence of cross-overs from the control group yielded a sample too small for statistical analyses and the experiment was ended. Post hoc

---

A first draft of this paper was presented at the International Conference on Self-Help and Mutual Aid held in Ottawa, Canada, September 2-4, 1992. Research for this paper was supported by a grant from the National Institute of Mental Health, Clinical Services Research Branch (MH45218).

Address correspondence to Dr. Caroline L. Kaufmann, Western Psychiatric Institute and Clinic, University of Pittsburgh Medical Center, Suite 301 Iroquois Building, 3811 O'Hara Street, Pittsburgh, PA 15213.

[Haworth co-indexing entry note]: "Self Help Group Participation Among People with Severe Mental Illness." Kaufmann, Caroline L., Herbert C. Schulberg, and Nina R. Schooler. Co-published simultaneously in *Prevention in Human Services* (The Haworth Press, Inc.) Vol. 11, No. 2, 1994, pp. 315-331; and *Self-Help and Mutual Aid Groups: International and Multicultural Perspectives* (ed: Francine Lavoie, Thomasina Borkman, and Benjamin Gidron) The Haworth Press, Inc., 1994, pp. 315- 331. Multiple copies of this article/chapter may be purchased from The Haworth Document Delivery Center [1-800-3-HAWORTH; 9:00 a.m. - 5:00 p.m. (EST)].

analyses comparing subjects who participated in self-help (15), non-participating subjects (75) and a comparison group of existing self-help group members (90) showed participants to have more severe psychiatric symptoms than either non-participants or members. Participating subjects were more likely to be female, though the self-help groups had more male members. Results indicate the need for multi-site studies in self-help group research.

INTRODUCTION

In community mental health services, self-help has been promoted as part of a broader effort to reform psychiatry through patient self-advocacy (Chamberlin, 1977). Consumer involvement in mental health services has been mandated by federal law (Public Law 99-660, 1986) and actively promoted by projects at the federal and state levels (Parrish, 1989; National Institute of Mental Health, 1991). The mental health consumers movement has made strong claims for the relevance of self-help groups and peer supports as an important and heretofore missing component in the system of community mental health services (Chamberlin and Rogers, 1990; Zinman, Harp and Budd, 1987).

This paper describes our experience in attempting a randomized clinical trial of the effects of self-help group participation among people with mental illness. Essentially, we found very few people in the study sample actually participated in self-help group activities, and statistical comparison between experimental and control subjects was not possible in the time frame of the study. Because of this, we conducted post hoc analyses to determine possible causes for low participation. Preliminary results on psychiatric treatment and symptoms are reported in this note because these results were readily interpreted from a standpoint of self-help group effectiveness in a *clinical* context where symptom reduction is an important goal. Analysis of all five outcome areas is underway and will be presented in future publications. We discuss the applicability of an experimental design in self-help group research and suggest avenues for improving the design and implementation of research on outcomes of self-help group participation.

STUDY DESIGN AND METHODS

In 1989, we were funded by the National Institute of Mental Health to conduct an experimental test of the effects of self-help group participation among people with severe mental illness (Kaufmann, Schulberg, & Schooler, 1989). We designed an outcome study analogous to a clinical trial with randomized assignments to experimental and control conditions and independent assessment of outcomes (Spilker, 1991). People who met preestablished criteria for severe mental illness were identified and randomly assigned to either self-help or non-self-help conditions while they continued with their customary care in the community mental health system. Baseline and follow up measures were obtained on enrollment and at regular six month intervals. We hypothesized that persons who participated in self-help would show better outcomes. Five areas of outcome were assessed, including psychiatric symptoms, self-esteem, employment, social support, and use of professional services.

The sample of subjects recruited from a roster of people currently receiving treatment at a community mental health center (CMHC) were randomly assigned to either the experimental or control conditions. Subjects in the experimental group were invited to join one of three self-help groups operating in their neighborhoods. Each group operated under the sponsorship of the CMHC from which subjects received mental health care. Subjects in the control group were told nothing about the self-help groups and were encouraged to continue with their usual care at the mental health center. We assumed that the majority of people in the experimental group would take advantage of the opportunity to join a self-help group and the majority of those in the control condition would not, thus permitting us to compare outcomes between experimental and control groups over time.

Instruments. Data were gathered through a review of psychiatric records and face-to-face interviews. All diagnoses were confirmed through the person's psychiatrist or regular therapist. The medical records were reviewed to determine treatment history and previous hospitalizations. Psychiatric symptoms were assessed using the Brief Psychiatric Rating Scale (BPRS; Overall, 1974) and the Symptom Check List-90 (SCL-90; Derogardis, 1977). The BPRS, a clinical rating instrument administered by a trained mental health professional, was used in face-to-face interviews with the subjects. Eighteen psychiatric symptoms reported or observed within a two-week period were rated on a scale of one (1 = not reported) to seven (7 = extremely severe). Administration time varied from 20 to 45 minutes, and average inter-rater reliability was .85. Individual items on the BPRS were grouped into four factors indicating major areas of psychiatric symptoms, as suggested by Overall (1974). Confirmatory factor analysis on the BPRS reproduced four subscales of thought disturbance, depression-anxiety, withdrawal, and hostility. A measure of Global Functional Impairment assessed the professional raters' judgments of the subject's ability to function in the community on a scale of one to seven (1 = Normal, not impaired; 7 = Among the most impaired clients).

The SCL-90, a self administered check list consisting of 90 items rated on a five-point scale (0 = not at all; 4 = extremely), measured the degree to which each subject felt distress from symptoms in the past week. Eight sub-scale scores were computed from the item scores. In addition, three global indices were computed (Global Severity Index, Positive Symptoms Distress Index, and Positive Symptom Total) as described by Derogatis (1977). All subjects completing questionnaires were assigned code numbers, and identifying information was coded separately in a database system so that responses to the questionnaires could not be easily linked to individual subjects' names.

Setting for the Study. People in the experimental group were referred to self-help groups run by current and former psychiatric patients. Group meetings occurred once a week at three "drop-in centers" operated, under the sponsorship of the CMHC, as a program in psychosocial rehabilitation similar to the clubhouse approach originally described by Fairweather (1974). These centers were not run solely by mental health consumers, and they differed from fully consumer-run drop-in centers recently described (Kaufmann, Ward-Colasante, & Farmer, 1993). Administration and budget allocations were controlled by the CMHC. The centers utilized a model of collaboration between consumers and providers that stressed self-help and peer supports as the core component of the program (Kaufmann, Freund, & Wilson, 1989). The drop-in centers had member councils that set and enforced rules for behavior and decided on local activities. Each center had a minimum of one self-help group member in a paid staff position, and the presence of a paid staff was required during operating hours.

The study required a collaboration among self-help group members, staff at the CMHC and the investigators. All research contacts with self-help group members were made only with the agreement of the membership, and individual members could exercise a veto over their participation in the project. Specific instances of membership vetoes included the decisions to bar all forms of tape recording from any activity at the drop-in centers and to limit access by investigators to prearranged times. Also, the research team provided a cash honorarium to those members who collected data for the research project. A community Advisory Board comprised of current and former clients of the CMHC, family members of people in psychiatric treatment, and local community mental health professionals held public meetings at the drop-in centers twice annually during the three years of the research project. At these meetings, the research team updated the Board on progress in the research project and members presented demonstrations and personal accounts of activities at self-help group meetings.

Sample Selection and Randomization. We generated a roster of 1185 clients at an urban CMHC who received treatment during a period of 27 months. From this roster, we recruited a sample of individuals with severe mental illness based on a criteria established by the investigators. The study was limited to people with a psychiatric diagnosis of either schizophrenia, schizoaffective disorder or major mood disorder (DSM-III-R, 1987) normal intelligence, and recent psychiatric treatment as either an inpatient or outpatient. We intentionally excluded people diagnosed with personality disorders because, in the opinion of the CMHC staff, such individuals were infrequent participants in self-help group activities. None of the subjects had participated in self-help group activities before the study began, all were living in the community at the time of their initial recruitment, and all gave their written informed consent. Subjects were told that they were volunteers in a study of self-help and were paid for completing research interviews. They were also told that they could withdraw from the study at any time. Subjects were not paid to participate in either their customary mental health treatment or the self-help group meetings.

From the roster of 1185 people, 823 met eligibility criteria. Of these, 582 were excluded from the potential list of subjects because they were either in a psychiatric in-patient unit, were enrolled in a partial hospital program that met at the same time as the self-help groups, or were already members of the self-help groups. Of the remaining 241, 93 individuals (39% of those available) agreed to participate and completed baseline assessments. Two subjects withdrew after initial consent, and one had incomplete data, leaving a final sample of 90 individuals.

These 90 individuals were randomly assigned to either the experimental (n = 54) or control (n = 36) groups. Experimental subjects were invited to attend one of three self-help group meetings in their neighborhoods. They were mailed a printed card inviting them to join the self-help group. A member of the research staff also phoned each experimental subject or met with him/her face-to-face to extend the invitation. The research staff offered assistance to all experimental subjects to facilitate their attending an initial self-help group meeting. Such assistance included paid cab or bus fare to the meeting and a map describing its location with instructions on how to reach the center by public transportation or by car. Consumer outreach workers from the self-help groups also attempted to contact experimental subjects and invite them to join their group. Where possible, outreach workers visited prospective new members in their homes and offered to accompany them to their first self-help group meeting. The self-help groups held a New Members Party and similarly mailed invitations to subjects randomized to the experimental group. Subjects in the control group were not contacted by either the research staff or the consumer outreach workers and were not told about the self-help group activities. Both control and experimental subjects continued to receive their customary professional care at the community mental health center.

Monitoring Self-Help Group Participation. Participation in self-help groups for the entire sample of subjects was monitored for a period of at least 6 months post study recruitment through daily logs that recorded exact hours of attendance at self-help meetings. Both groups were monitored for self-help group attendance in order to detect crossovers between experimental and control conditions (Spilker, 1991). An outreach worker reviewed daily sign-in sheets and completed an attendance record on each study subject. The sign-in sheets also provided a record of total daily attendance at the self-help meetings. As the study progressed, we discovered that a large proportion of experimental subjects, i.e., those invited to join the neighborhood self-help groups, did not attend any meetings. At the end of the first year of recruitment, only three people in the experimental group attended one or more self-help group meeting, making statistical comparisons of experimental and control groups unfeasible.

We speculated that people already participating in the self-help group may have differed in some way from those newly randomized to it and that a comparison of the study sample and self-help group members characteristics would be useful. We assumed the sampling frame from which the subjects were recruited reflected characteristics of the existing membership of the self-help group, and that there would be some affinity between the existing self-help group membership and the research subjects invited to join the groups. This assumption was central to the experimental test in the following way. The existing membership of the self-help groups claimed that the groups were effective in many ways, including symptom reduction. Hence, if we recruited a sample of subjects with no prior exposure to the self-help group but essentially like the existing members in other respects, we should be able to demonstrate similar results in the study sample to those reported by members. Essentially, we were attempting to produce experimental results that would substantiate the claims to effectiveness made through anecdotal reports.

We took low participation to indicate a limited appeal of these self-help groups to these study subjects, and looked for reasons why this was so. One possible reason was that we were wrong to assume that the study sample was similar to the members of the self-help groups. Therefore, we recruited a sample of 93 long-standing members of the self-help groups to which the study sample were to be referred and assessed them using identical measures. Data collection from the self-help group membership was completed after the recruitment of subjects to the study sample.

RESULTS

Nine of the 54 experimental subjects (17%) participated in the self-help group activities compared to six of the 36 control subjects (17%). Therefore, it is self-evident that there was no significant difference in rate of self-help group participation between experimental and control subjects. Analysis of baseline assessment data showed no statistically significant differences between experimental and control subjects on any of the assessed characteristics, an expected result given randomized group assignments.

Of the 15 subjects who participated in self-help group meetings, seven attended the drop-in center for informal discussions with members but did not join a scheduled meeting of the self-help groups. Three people attended only one meeting, and five attended two meetings or more. Only three people from the study sample attended three or more self-help group meetings and were regarded as regular participants by the self-help group members. Both the overall low rates of participation and the number of subjects who were cross-overs (i.e., assigned to the control group but choosing to participate in self-help activities) made it impossible to complete the study within the period allotted for the experiment. Therefore, we stopped collecting follow up outcome data and searched for factors in the sample's composition and the self-help group membership which might account for low participation. This constitutes a *post hoc* design aimed at uncovering reasons for low participation in self-help activities among subjects in the study sample.

For this analysis, the study sample was divided into two groups, participants (n = 15) and non-participants (n = 75) in self-help activities, regardless of whether the person was initially assigned to the experimental or control condition. Subsequent analyses compared the group of participants and non-participants in self-help group activities to a sample of current self-help group members (n = 93). For interval level data, differences among groups were tested using one-way analysis of variance. For ordinal and nominal measures, the non-parametric Kruskal-Wallis test was employed with a probability distribution approximating the chi-square distribution (Hollander & Wolfe, 1973). Results for which statistically significant differences were found are reported in Table 1.

The typical person recruited to this study was white (64%), never married (51%) and unemployed (87%), and had a mean age of 42 years. Non-participants showed a slightly higher level of formal education than either participants or self-help group members, and the difference was statistically significant (p = .03). Significantly more women (67%) were in the group of participants than either the non-participants (60%) or self-help group members (41%) (p = .02). The three groups differed significantly with respect to number of life-time psychiatric admissions and life-time number of months spent in a psychiatric hospital, with self-help group members experiencing fewer total admissions than either the participants or non-participants. A significantly larger proportion of both participants and non-participants were diagnosed with schizophrenia than were self-help group members. Among self-help group members, the majority (40%) carried other diagnoses such as personality disorders, atypical psychoses, or phobias. No statistically significant differences were found among the three groups on age, ethnicity, marital status, employment, and age at first psychiatric admission. Results from the Brief Psychiatric Rating Scale (BPRS) indicate statistically significant differences among the three groups in the Thought Disturbance factor (p = .01). No significant differences were noted with respect to the Depression-Anxiety, Withdrawal, or Hostility factors. Clinical ratings of individual symptoms on the BPRS demonstrated statistically significant differences among the three groups on symptoms of Suspiciousness (p = .01) and Unusual Thought Content (p = .004). Among self-help group participants, non-participants, and members, there was a statistically significant difference in ratings of Global Functional Impairment (p = .04), with new participants rated as more functionally impaired than either non-participants or self-help group members. Factor analysis (not shown here) on the BPRS indicated that the Unusual Thought Content symptom was strongly associated with other symptoms in the Thought Disturbance factor (r = .77) while the Suspiciousness symptom was moderately associated with both Depression-Anxiety (r = .41) and Thought Disturbance (r = .39) factors. This may account for the lack of statistical significance in group comparisons on the Hostility factor despite a significant difference in ratings of the individual Suspiciousness symptom on the BPRS. Self ratings

TABLE 1. Characteristics and Reported Symptoms of Self-Help Group Non-Participants, Participants and Members

	Non-Participants (n = 75)		Participants (n = 15)		Members (n = 93)			
Gender	%	#	%	#	%	#	X^2	p
% Female	60	(45)	67	(10)	41	(38)	3.97	.02*
Psychiatric Diagnoses							13.22	.00*
Schizophrenia	53	(40)	60	(9)	35	(31)		
Schizoaffective	15	(11)	7	(1)	6	(5)		
Major Affective	32	(24)	33	(5)	19	(17)		
Other	– 0 –		– 0 –		40	(36)		
	Mean	SD	Mean	SD	Mean	SD	F	p
Education	12.9	1.8	12.4	1.7	12.2	1.5	3.67	.03*
Lifetime Admissions	3.0	1.1	3.1	1.3	2.3	1.4	7.53	.001*
Lifetime Months in Hospital	18.1	8.0	16.4	8.0	14.1	7.1	5.26	.01*

Brief Psychiatric Rating Scale – Factor:								
Thought Disturbance	1.7	(1.2)	2.6	(1.3)	1.6	(0.8)	5.26	.01*
Selected Symptoms:								
Suspiciousness	2.3	(1.2)	3.3	(2.0)	2.1	(1.2)	4.96	.01*
Unusual Thought Content	1.9	(1.6)	3.5	(2.0)	1.5	(1.1)	12.62	.00*
Global Functional Impairment	3.7	(1.6)	4.3	(1.7)	3.3	(1.4)	3.40	.04*
Symptom Check List-90 Subscales								
Somatization	0.6	(0.6)	0.9	(0.8)	0.7	(0.7)	3.27	.04*
Hostility	0.4	(0.6)	0.4	(0.6)	0.8	(0.8)	5.41	.01*

*Probability of a significant difference between groups is greater than .05. Actual probability values are reported.

of symptoms on the SCL-90 were compared using mean raw scores for each of the three groups. Analysis of variance indicates statistically significant differences between the groups on the Somatization and Hostility subscales. For self ratings on the Somatization sub-scale, participants rated themselves higher than either self-help group members or non-participants. On the Hostility sub-scale, self-help group members rated themselves higher than both non-participants and participants. No significant differences were noted among non-participants, participants, and self-help group members on global measures from the SCL-90, including the Global Severity Index.

DISCUSSION

There is growing evidence that self-help and mutual aid have a selective rather than universal appeal. Among individuals with mental illness, average participation in self-help groups varies with treatment status and diagnosis. Based on the Epidemiological Catchment Area (ECA) Studies, participation in self-help group activities by all persons in treatment for a psychiatric disorder is 5.2%. Participation rates are higher for people in treatment for personality disorders (16.1%) than for affective disorders (6.0%) and schizophrenia (3.4%) (Narrow et al., 1993). However, the ECA results were not published at the time we designed and implemented this study. Our decision to exclude people diagnosed with personality disorders may have artificially reduced rates of participation.

Outreach efforts did not appear to affect participation. Repeated calls, personal visits, and invitations to social gatherings had only a marginal effect on participation, and many of the experimental subjects complained that they were being called repeatedly after they had made their decision not to attend. This finding suggests that one's decision to participate or not participate in a self-help group is not easily changed through routine outreach efforts. One outreach worker was successful in recruiting two new members by establishing a personal relationship and making repeated visits and offers of assistance which the subject accepted. Some experimental subjects noted that they just did not like certain people whom they knew in the self-help groups. Others stated that they knew all about the groups and did not want to associate with mental patients. All the self-help groups had existed for a number of years before this study began and had established reputations among clients at the CMHC. Forming new groups that do not have established histories may be one way of attracting new members. If use of self-help groups is limited among people with mental illness, then an experimental study of outcomes will require recruitment from more than one geographic site. This indicates the need for a multi-site study of self-help to produce a sufficiently large sample to allow for meaningful comparisons among groups.

It is important to note that all the self-help groups involved in this study operated under the auspices of a mental health provider agency. In that they were not independent of the provider system, they do not represent the type of free-standing consumer-run alternative service advocated by some critics of the mental health system. These groups defined their mission in terms of general social support. They did not follow a structured format in their meetings, and concentrated on social and recreational activities. Several of the self-help group leaders were very active in the mental health consumers' movement at the state and national levels. Otherwise, the group members engaged in little political advocacy. The nature of the self-help activities may have influenced the subjects' decisions to participate. Perhaps different types of self-help would attract more or different people. However, this has yet to be demonstrated empirically.

The relatively small group of subjects who chose to participate in self-help group activities included more females than males in comparison with both the non-participant and self-help member groups. This finding is consistent with prior studies indicating greater self-help participation among females. However, the existing self-help groups included more males than females. It may be that self-help has a greater initial appeal to women, independently of the composition of the group they join. The results do not support the view that self-help groups preferentially appeal to people with more formal education. Both the existing members and the newer participants reported less formal education than did non-participants.

Both participants and non-participants had more admissions to a psychiatric hospital and experienced more total months of psychiatric hospitalization than did the self-help group members. Lifetime psychiatric admissions may be interpreted as a marker for severity of illness. While not a precise measure of degree of disability, psychiatric admission is an identifiable event that is likely associated with problems relevant to mental illness. Variations in patterns of hospitalization may indicate the frequency with which an individual experiences more severe symptoms of illness. Our results suggest that existing self-help group members may have a less severe course of illness than those in the study sample. Clearly, the new participants demonstrated more lifetime psychiatric hospitalizations than did the self-help group members. However, this may also reflect an artifact of the experimental design. We recruited the sample from a roster of active clients at the mental health center who were, therefore, more likely to be recently discharged from a psychiatric in-patient facility. Thus, while psychiatric hospitalization is a discrete event that identifies a person who is likely to be regarded as seriously mentally ill, it biases the study sample in favor of people with more frequent psychiatric hospitalizations. It may be that people more frequently hospitalized or more recently discharged from a psychiatric hospital are less attracted to self-help activities. Further study is needed to determine whether there is an optimal period following psychiatric hospitalization when people are more likely to be drawn to self-help activities.

The findings on diagnostic composition of the three groups suggests that individuals with a diagnosis of schizophrenia do participate in self-help group meetings, although the existing self-help group members include a larger proportion of people with other types of psychiatric diagnoses. This finding indicates that the self-help groups do attract individuals with psychotic disorders, including schizophrenia, though they do not constitute the majority of self-help group members in this study. Results from clinical rating of symptoms suggest that individuals with thought disturbance may try out a self-help group, however, self-help group members are less likely to demonstrate symptoms commonly associated with psychosis. The finding reported from the ECA studies noted earlier suggest that the inclusion of a group of individuals with diagnoses of personality disorders may have resulted in higher overall rates of self-help group participation among subjects in the study sample.

Differences in psychiatric symptoms based on independent clinical ratings indicate that the existing self-help group members have a lower level of functional impairment and less severe symptoms than do either the new participants or non-participants. The self-help groups are composed of individuals who may be less severely ill than either the new participants or non-participants in the study. Whether differences in clinical status are a result of self-help group membership or further evidence of self selection cannot be determined from these data. In terms of self ratings of symptoms using the SCL-90, self-help group members and participants tended to rate themselves higher on selected dimensions of illness than did non-participants. Individuals in the self-help groups share a common subjective experience of emotional distress that is not reflected in the structured assessments of a trained mental health professional.

From our experience, self-help groups are not easily extended to include people not immediately attracted to them. The self-help phenomenon does not behave like a treatment modality or function as an alternative to professional services. However, our failure to demonstrate effectiveness in the context of a clinical trial paradigm does not imply that self-help groups have no meaningful role in mental health services. Rather, the groups function as social cliques within the larger system of professional services. They provide ongoing and very personalized support for their members but do not easily attract new individuals to their ranks. Those that do join the groups as new members have more severe symptoms and greater functional impairments than the existing membership. Further work is underway to determine whether these new members improve over time with increasing exposure to the self-help groups.

In future studies, we suggest that researchers employ more quasi-experimental designs that are sensitive to processes of self selection. Self-help groups should be viewed as a type of voluntary association which recruits members slowly. The experimental design of this study was neither broad enough nor long enough to allow for sufficient numbers of new recruits to be obtained.

CONCLUSION

Self-help group participation appears to be a self-selective phenomenon. It appeals to a select number of people in treatment for serious mental illness, though it does not necessarily exclude people with particular types of psychiatric diagnoses. People who joined an existing self-help group were judged to be more functionally impaired than those who were established members of the group. Self-help groups are able to attract people in more acute phases of illness.

The findings from this study pertain to people with serious mental illnesses who receive treatment in the community mental health system. The findings do not readily generalize to people with less severe forms of psychiatric ailments or those who have never experienced psychiatric hospitalization. Further studies are needed to test these findings in the larger population of people with mental illnesses. Until such studies are conducted, the results from this study offer some understanding of the characteristics of self-help group participation among people with serious and persistent mental illness. Self-help activities appear to serve a subset of people in the community mental health system and recruit new members slowly. Any test of their effectiveness requires a commitment of time and resources that are beyond the current study.

Our decision to employ an experimental design to test the effects of self-help group participation was intentional. We felt that the literature on self-help and peer mutual supports contained sufficient anecdotal, and non-experimental evidence of effectiveness, and that an experimental test was warranted. The main finding is that self-selection is a central feature of self-help group membership. While we had planned that not all subjects invited to join would actually take part in the groups, we were surprised at the number who refused to attend a self-help group meeting, even though they completed research interviews and received professional mental health services on a regular basis.

Self-selection has a tremendous impact on sample size in self-help group research, such that it is unlikely that an investigator will be able to recruit an adequate randomized sample of subjects with no prior exposure to self-help groups from a single geographic area. Researchers may want to consider multi-site collaborative studies.

REFERENCES

Chamberlin, J. (1977). *On our own: Patient-controlled alternatives to the mental health system.* New York: Hawthorn.

Chamberlin, J. and Rogers J.A. (1990). Planning a community-based mental health system: Perspectives of service recipients. *American Psychologist*, 45, 1241-1244.

Derogardis, L.R. (1977). *SCL-90 manual–I R (revised) version.* Baltimore: Johns Hopkins University School of Medicine.

DSM-III-R. (1987). *Diagnostic and statistical manual of mental disorders (Third Edition–Revised).* Washington, D.C.: American Psychiatric Association.

Fairweather, G. (1974) *Creating change in mental health organizations.* New York: Pergamon.

Hollander, M. and Wolfe, D.A. (1973). *Nonparametric statistical methods.* New York: John Wiley.

Kaufmann, C.L., Freund, P.D., & Wilson, J. (1989). Self-help in the mental health system: A model for consumer-provider collaboration. *Psychosocial Rehabilitation Journal*, 13, 5-21.

Kaufmann, C.L., Schulberg, H.C., & Schooler, N.R. (1989). Self-help and severe mental illness, Grant No. MH45218, U.S. Department of Health and Human Services, National Institute of Mental Health. Rockville, Maryland: National Institute of Mental Health.

Kaufmann, C.L., Ward-Colasante, C., & Farmer, J. (1993). Development and evaluation of consumer-run drop-in centers. *Hospital and Community Psychiatry*, 33, 678-683.

Narrow, W.E., Regier, D.A., Rae, D.S., Manderscheid, R.W., & Locke, B.Z. (1993). Use of services by persons with mental and addictive disorders. Findings from the National Institute of Mental Health Epidemiological Catchment Area Program. *Archives of General Psychiatry*, 50, 95-107.

National Institute of Mental Health. (1991). *Caring for people with severe mental disorders: A national plan of research to improve services.* DHHS Pub. No. (ADM)91-1762. Washington, D.C.: Supt. of Docs., U.S. Government Printing Office, 1991.

Overall, J.E. (1974). The Brief Psychiatric Rating Scale in psychopharmacology research. In Pichot, P. (ed.), *Psychological Measurements in Psychopharmacology*, 7, 67-78. Paris: Karger-Basel.

Parrish, J. (1989). The long journey home: Accomplishing the mission of the community support movement. *Psychosocial Rehabilitation Journal*, 12, 107-124.

Pubic Law 99-660. (1986). Title V–State comprehensive mental health services plans. Drug Export Amendments Act, PL 99-660, 100 stat. 3795.

Spilker, B. (1991). *Guide to clinical trials.* New York: Raven.

Zinman, S., Harp, H.T., & Budd, S. (1987). *Reaching across: Mental health clients help each other.* Riverside, CA: California Network of Mental Health Clients.

Conclusion

Francine Lavoie
Université Laval, Canada

Thomasina Borkman
George Mason University, USA

Benjamin Gidron
Ben Gurion University of the Negev, Israel

The subject-matter of the first section of this book, international and inter-cultural perspectives of self-help, did not, as yet, receive proper attention in the research literature. The organizers of the First International Conference on Self-Help/Mutual Aid in Ottawa (1992) can take the credit for bringing the issue to the fore. This conference was also the occasion to learn about the latest developments in research on inter-organizational and intra-organizational issues. When looked at collectively, the papers that comprise our book are raising certain important questions. We would like first to briefly summarize what we see as the major contributions of this book, and then outline the research implications that follow. We identify five major areas in which we believe the book has contributed to knowledge on self-help/mutual aid:

- The definition of self-help
- The centrality of culture as a major factor explaining variability in self-help
- Devising appropriate methodological tools
- The involvement of professionals
- The differential roles of professionals in relating to self-help groups in different national or cultural contexts.

THE DEFINITION OF SELF-HELP

The focus of North American and European self-help in the past two decades, as is reflected in the literature, on health-related problems, brings with it a relatively narrow definition of self-help/mutual aid. As indicated in the introduction and shown by some articles, when dealing with international perspectives of the phenomenon, there is a need to broaden the definition of self-help/mutual aid along two dimensions. On the one hand, we need to consider broadening the issues studied under the title of self-help to include other social, material and economic problems such as immigration, housing, economic development, food, crime prevention, etc. On the other hand, we need to explore not only groups (and organizations), but other support structures such as tribes, geographical community, churches or families, and identify what functional equivalents there are to the specialized self-help groups found in urban industrialized societies. The Gidron and Chesler conceptualization of self-help as "community" facilitates this broadening process. It stresses the universal facets of self-help, as a form of human bond known to everyone, with different expressions in different contexts.

Yet broadening the definition too much will turn it useless. Specific parameters to capture the phenomenon worldwide should account for the fact that modern self-help groups in the Western World are problem-focused, are established by people who share a problem, their raison d'être (and activities) focus around the problem, and people cease to belong when they perceive their problem solved or they no longer can benefit from participation in the group. In contrast, in traditional societies, self-help is practiced within stable collective entities, such as communities, as one facet (among others) in the life of that collective, either when all need it for a limited time (as in the case of a natural disaster) or, when an individual member of the collective needs it, for as long as the need exists.

THE CENTRALITY OF CULTURE AS A MAJOR FACTOR EXPLAINING VARIABILITY IN SELF-HELP

The book clearly draws the attention to the criticality of culture as a key factor in understanding the specific type of self-help practiced in a nation, within an ethnic group, etc. In other words, how culturally embedded self-help groups are, and how superficial analyses of them can distort or misrepresent their nature. The centrality of culture is emphasized as different cultures prescribe different rules vis-à-vis (1) ways of interacting with others, differentiating between family members, community members and strangers; (2) sense of group and self; (3) revealing emotions and problems to others; and (4) ways of thinking about health and illness, and the individual's responsibility to contribute to his/her recovery. All of these are examples where cultural variability directly affects the type and form of self-help possible. In addition to those, there are quite a few other cultural traits, too numerous to list, that are less directly related but have an impact on the type and form of self-help, too. The cultural perspective on self-help groups is conceptualized by Gidron and Chesler as occurring on three levels: (a) the nation or societal level, (b) the within cultural differences in ethnic/racial/religious/gender statuses or other divisions, and (3) the definition and conceptualization of the focal problem or issue of the group.

The most striking example of the impact of the societal (as well as cultural) level on the nature of self-help practiced, is the paper by Oka on the clash between the modern practice of self-help and the underlying values of the Japanese traditional society. The apparent similarities in values–the group oriented helping–in fact hinders the development of mutual help groups because the individual focus on self-responsibility for problem solving is missing. This analysis points to the importance of maintaining the seeming paradox of mutual aid/self-help firmly in mind. A frequently heard saying "you alone can do it but you cannot do it alone" shows the two parts that need to be present–the individual responsibility and helping peers. Apparently, Japanese society has the second part, the helping in a group context, but is much weaker on the first part of individual responsibility. In contrast, the United States has been characterized as a society that is overly individualistic (Bellah, Madsen, Sullivan, Swidler, & Tipton, 1985) in which people have difficulty asking for help or mutual aid in a group context. In the attempt to develop Western-style self-help groups in Japan, this clash creates a situation whereby the frameworks of self-help are adopted, but not the content.

The cultural differences and their expressions in the self-help forms and patterns are found not only between nations but between groups and problem areas within nations, as is clearly shown in several papers. While often cited evidence shows low levels of minority participation in mainstream self-help groups in North America, this does not mean that minorities are not participating in self-help. Minorities sometimes form their own groups which incorporate their own values and norms around the issue at hand, as is very well depicted in the Medvene et al. paper.

DEVISING APPROPRIATE METHODOLOGICAL TOOLS TO CAPTURE AND MEASURE INTERNATIONAL AND INTER-CULTURAL SELF-HELP

It is logical to assume that the centrality of culture as depicted in this book is reflected not only in what to study but also in how to study self-help internationally and inter-culturally. The methodological theme of using the naturalistic paradigm of inquiry that relies especially on qualitative methods is an issue tightly associated with the need to study the cultural aspects of self-help groups and is addressed in Borkman and Schubert's paper. When one deals with cultural differences, the researcher should know, a priori, that the assumptions, language, cultural understandings and practices in one culture are likely to be different, sometimes significantly different from other cultures. The only way methodologically to uncover the content and meaning of parts of a culture is to engage in in-depth qualitative research and to use multiple methods including documents, observations, interviews with knowledgeable members of that culture, etc. In self-help groups where specialized experiential knowledge of a problem and its resolution is developed, the researcher needs to rely extensively on veteran members of the group, follow their beliefs and practices in order to obtain information about it. This suggests that participatory action research which involves bringing the participant of the group as a collaborator into the research process would be extremely valuable for in-depth understanding of the culture of the self-help group. In-depth qualitative research methods were needed to identify the content and domains of a worldview and how individual's worldview were transformed by their participation in a self-help group over time by Kennedy and Humphreys. The differences in perceptions about the role of professionals among professionals and self-helpers was also uncovered (by Stewart and colleagues) because they used qualitative methods and action research that allowed them to get richer contextualized data through interviews rather than questionnaires with fixed answer categories.

This of course does not preclude the use of quantitative approaches in the study of self-help. In fact, as can be seen in this book (in the papers of Lotery and Jacobs, Meissen and Volk, Perkins et al.) These approaches have developed considerably from the time self-help was measured by the same tools as psychotherapy. Certain, mostly aggregate, aspects of self-help can best be measured by quantitative measurements, and indeed, the quantitative research tools used by contributors of this volume are sophisticated and varied. Availability of sophisticated techniques is not the answer to everything though. The Kaufmann et al. paper illustrates some limits of an experimental design and the Lavoie et al. paper reports a few ethical constraints to be considered in research. It is a climate of mutual respect which has to be built with self-help organizations to further research (Lavoie, 1985). Research instigated under the auspices of self-help clearinghouses who can better name their own research priorities is to be encouraged and can bring interesting questions into the open, as the paper of Meissen and Volk shows.

THE INVOLVEMENT OF PROFESSIONALS

As documented in some papers of the two volumes, a greater number of self-help groups than was usually anticipated desire a strong participation from professionals even in the role of co-leader of meetings. However, others report that they prefer indirect roles as in the Stewart et al. paper on a partnership model. What remains to be accomplished, is to understand which types of groups in which cultural groups or contexts prefer a direct to an indirect role for the professional. The advantages and disadvantages of having professionals play a direct role could in the future be discussed using the framework proposed in the Lavoie et al. paper on good practice. A related issue to be clarified in the future is the differences in perception between professionals and self-helpers regarding what knowledge is useful and needed about the focal problem. From the results we now have, it would also seem necessary to investigate professions in a more specific fashion. With each profession having its own culture, norms and context of work, their particular context could impact on their relationships and priorities of intervention with self-help groups. The same could be said of self-help organizations. It is time we study a variety of self-help groups and pay more attention to differences in functioning of groups affiliated with the same self-help organizations as mentioned in the Perkins et al. paper.

THE DIFFERENTIAL ROLES OF PROFESSIONALS IN RELATING TO SELF-HELP GROUPS IN DIFFERENT NATIONAL OR CULTURAL CONTEXTS

The tendency by policymakers and professionals to view self-help as a form of human service (Borkman, 1992; Hasenfeld & Gidron, 1993) brings many professionals to become actively involved with self-help groups. The dialectic dimensions of this involvement have been discussed in addition to the present book in the literature in the North American context (see Powell, 1987; 1991). Yet, the roles of professionals in self-help in other countries, where they not only represent knowledge and expertise but authority and sanction, are different and more complex, as depicted in the Japanese example as well as the example of the paper by von Appen describing the evolution of self-help in the former East Germany. It is an issue that again relates to culture, and more specifically to civic and political culture. Can we expect the professional in such a cultural framework also to assume the role of educator for participatory democratic values?

It is obvious that the study of self-help will tremendously benefit from adding the international dimension to it. This calls for better forms of communication and dialog among researchers, worldwide, who study this phenomenon, in order first to define it, and then study, in a comparative fashion its variegated expressions. Such studies should emphasize the role of culture in defining the parameters within which self-help is practiced. Often, these comparative studies should be preceded by basic descriptive studies on the phenomenon in countries where it was not studied. When using the comparative approach, studies could begin with international groups like Alcoholics Anonymous that have the same template (guidelines for defining the problem and its resolution–12 steps and 12 traditions in the case of AA). Such comparison could begin to examine what cultural differences there are in interpretation of the same guidelines that result in different worldviews for groups in different countries.

Finally, self-help is a complex human phenomenon that at the same time affects individuals and societies. As with previous books on the subject, this volume, too, has contributors representing several disciplines, such as psychology, sociology, social work and nursing; these are the traditional disciplines interested in self-help (if the time has come yet to speak of traditions . . .). It is our conviction that the study of self-help can best be developed when conceptualized from a multi-disciplinary and even interdisciplinary perspective, as no single discipline has the conceptual tools to capture it alone. It seems to us that the field would benefit tremendously from studies by researchers from anthropology, political science and economics, adding their perspectives to our existing knowledge.

REFERENCES

Bellah, R. N., Madsen, R., Sullivan, W. M., Swidler, A., & Tipton, S. M. (1985). *Habits of the heart: Individualism and commitment in American life*. New York: Harper and Row.

Borkman, T. (1991). Introduction. Special issue on self-help groups. *American Journal of Community Psychology, 19*, 643-650.

Hasenfeld, Y., & Gidron, B. (1993). Self-help groups and human service organizations: An interorganizational perspective. *Social Service Review, 67*(2), 217-236.

Lavoie, F. (1984). Action research: A new model of interaction between the professional and self-help groups. In A. Gartner, F. Riessman (eds.). (Pp. 173-182.) *The self-help revolution*. New York: Human Sciences Press.

Powell, T. (1987). *Self-help organizations and professional practice*. Silver Spring, Maryland: NASW.

Powell, T. (1992). *Working with self-help*. Silver Spring, Maryland: NASW.

Index

Note: Page numbers followed by f indicate figures; those followed by t indicate tables.

For Product Safety Concerns and Information please contact our EU representative GPSR@taylorandfrancis.com Taylor & Francis Verlag GmbH, Kaufingerstraße 24, 80331 München, Germany

Batch number: 10725993

Printed by Printforce, the Netherlands